BUSINESS ADMINISTRATION CORE UNITS

Student Handbook

Carol Carysforth
Val Warrilow

NVQ LEVEL 2

HEINEMANN

Heinemann Educational
a division of Heinemann Educational Books Ltd,
Halley Court, Jordan Hill, Oxford OX2 8EJ

OXFORD LONDON EDINBURGH
MADRID ATHENS BOLOGNA PARIS
MELBOURNE SYDNEY AUCKLAND SINGAPORE TOKYO
IBADAN NAIROBI HARARE GABORONE
PORTSMOUTH NH (USA)

First published 1991

British Library Cataloguing in Publication Data
Carysforth, Carol
Business Administration: Core Units
1. Business Practices
I Title. II Warrilow, Valerie
650

ISBN 0 435 450 10 7

Designed by Green Door, Basingstoke
Illustrated by Gecko, Bicester, Oxon
Printed in England
by Clays Ltd, St Ives plc

ACKNOWLEDGEMENTS

The authors would like to personally acknowledge the co-operation, assistance and support of friends and colleagues, whose combined expertise proved invaluable in the writing of these books.

Especial thanks for specialist help and advice are due to David Williams AIDPM, Peter Gold LIB, Duncan Isherwood RIBA, John Haworth FCA, Mavis Williams Cert Ed, AFTComm, Alex Clark and, not least, Margaret Berriman for her encouragement and guidance throughout.

The authors and publishers would also like to thank the following organisations for permission to reproduce copyright material:

The Automobile Association
Banking Information Service
Barclays Bank plc – Retailer Services
Barclays Bank plc – Banking Services
British Airways plc
British Gas plc
British Rail
British Telecom plc
Air France Holidays and French Travel Service
Guardian Royal Exchange Assurance
GMB Apex Partnership
The Controller of Her Majesty's Stationery Office
Midland Bank plc
National Westminster Bank plc – Banking Services
National Westminster Bank plc – Retailer Card Services
The Post Office
Royal Bank of Scotland plc
French Railways SNCF
Safeguard Systems GB Ltd

CONTENTS

BUSINESS ADMINISTRATION CORE UNITS

Introduction to the office

WHAT DO OFFICES DO?

- They **initiate**, **process**, **store** and **communicate** information to anyone with an interest in their business – customers, suppliers, employees, shareholders etc.

The more efficiently they can do this, the more likely they are to be profitable.

CHECK IT YOURSELF

What is your reaction if you:

- receive a letter with spelling or typing errors?
- have to wait for ages on a telephone before being put through?
- ask someone for help in a shop or organisation and they are abrupt or unhelpful?

Ineffective, inefficient, poorly skilled or ill-mannered staff cost a company money because they upset – and lose – customers.

What do you have to do?

To work effectively in an organisation you need to know:

- the organisation and layout of the company
- who does what
- company procedures and the systems in operation.

And how to:

- communicate well both when writing and speaking
- deal with customers and clients so that you give a good impression of yourself and the organisation
- create and maintain good working relationships with your colleagues
- operate office equipment efficiently and safely
- undertake general office routines and duties competently
- carry out your work with the minimum of delay.

OFFICE ORGANISATION

The internal organisation of a company depends on:

- its size and number of employees
- whether it is in the manufacturing or service sector
- whether it is involved in exporting
- the type of work with which it is involved.

Therefore all companies are different!
Whereas a small organisation, especially in the service sector, may only have a few employees, a large organisation will be divided into separate departments each undertaking a different function. Jobs will be more *specialised* – each person will concentrate on his or her own specific job.

The layout is usually shown on an **organisation chart**.

Example of a manufacturing company

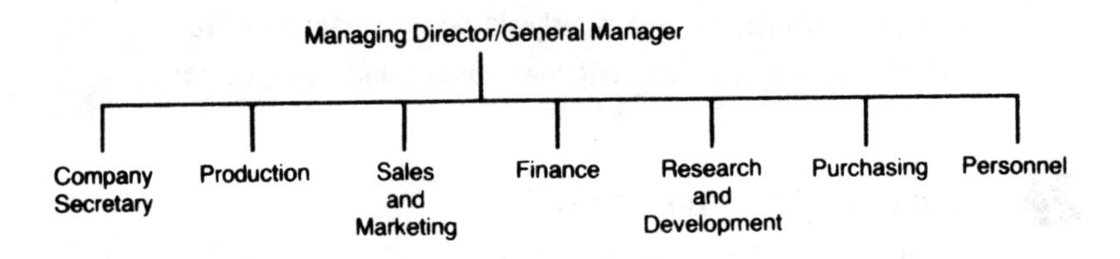

Who's who at the top

Chairman – Chairs company meetings
liaises with heads of other organisations
liaises with the media on important issues
works closely with the MD (Managing Director).

Managing Director – Co-ordinates the work of the other directors
is responsible to the Board of Directors for the effective running of the company.

Directors have a seat on the **Board of Directors** and are identified by their title, eg Sales Director. A Sales Manager would *not* have a seat on the Board.

Who does what and where

Department	Typical job titles	Departmental functions
Finance or Accounts	Chief Accountant Cost Accountant Management Accountant Chief Cashier Wages Clerks Cost Clerks Ledger Clerks Credit Control Clerks	All financial affairs of the company – Recording money inwards Issuing invoices, credit notes and statements Paying cheques and recording money outwards Wages Expense claims and petty cash Producing company accounts Costing Producing continuous financial information for management
Personnel	Personnel Manager Training Officer Welfare Officer Employment Officer Security Staff Nurses Canteen Staff	Recruitment and employment of staff Staff appraisals and promotion interviews Dismissals and redundancies Keeping staff records Industrial relations and trade union negotiations Training Staff welfare Operating suggestion schemes Salary grading schemes Induction of new staff
Purchasing	Purchasing Manager Buyers Order Clerks	Purchasing all goods and materials Keeping suppliers' records and information Researching new markets Negotiating terms and discounts
Sales and marketing	Marketing Manager Sales Manager – Home Sales Export Manager Advertising Manager Distribution Manager Shipping Clerks Sales Representatives Transport Clerks Order Clerks	Market Research* Advertising* Public Relations* Home and export sales Customer liaison Preparing sales documentation – price lists, quotations etc Attending exhibitions and trade fairs Warehousing and distribution of goods Keeping customer records

* May be contracted out to a specialist agency

Production	Works Manager Chief Engineer Factory Operatives Production Control Clerks Production Planners Draughtsmen Foremen Despatch Clerks Engineers Storemen	Production of goods Maintenance of equipment Quality control Stock control Work study Production planning and control Stores control Despatch
Management services (or Computer services)	Computer services Manager Data Processing Manager Operations Manager Technical Services Manager System Analysts Programmers Computer Operators Data Preparation Clerks	Designing computer systems for existing operations Identifying new areas and future needs for computerisation Programming computers Providing computer services to the company on a day to day basis Assisting management decision making Problem solving
Research and development (R & D)	R & D Manager Chief Designer Planning Officer Designers Engineers	Designing, developing and testing new products Keeping abreast of technological developments Improving existing products
Administration	Company Secretary Chief Administrative Officer Office Manager Typing Supervisor Caretakers Cleaners (Security Staff if not under Personnel)	All legal affairs of the company Insurance Dealing with shareholders Organising company meetings Office planning Office systems and services including telephone service, reprographic services, mail handling, telecommunications etc
NOTE **Secretarial and clerical staff are common to all departments**		

Knowing who does what, and where, enables you to

- communicate more efficiently
- deliver mail accurately
- transfer telephone calls promptly to the right person
- handle queries effectively.

COMPANY POLICIES, PROCEDURES AND SYSTEMS

In addition to companies being different in their organisational structure, they also differ in other ways, eg

policies to customers	eg	on returning/exchanging goods; credit and discount allowed; range of after sales services, etc.
policies to employees	eg	on standards of dress, appearance and behaviour; on the degree of informality allowed; on training; on whether overtime is paid to office staff, or time off given in lieu, etc.
procedures	eg	filing systems in use; layout of letters and memos; security checks; ways of dealing with emergencies, etc.
systems	eg	type and range of equipment; documentation in use; computer software, etc.

It is therefore important that

- you find out the policies, procedures and systems used in *your* organisation
- you expect to have to adjust your methods of working when you change jobs
- you *never* compare a current employer unfavourably with a past employer. Telling your new colleagues how much better things were done in your last company annoys everyone!

CHECK IT YOURSELF

- Discuss with your tutor the policies, procedures and systems in operation in your current organisation or one you have worked for in the past.
- Compare your experiences with those of your colleagues.

Certain procedures and systems may be determined by the size of the organisation, for instance:

1 *Centralisation*

Large organisations are far more likely to centralise their office services than small ones. This means that a specialist section will service the whole company in a particular area, eg reprographics, filing, incoming and outgoing mail, and typing or audio typing.

Advantages

- Systems and procedures are standardised throughout the organisation.
- Specialist staff can be employed and trained.
- More expensive machinery and equipment can be purchased.
- Less likelihood of a backlog of work during busy periods.
- Usually more economical in terms of space and cost.

Disadvantages

- The systems that suit one department may not suit another.
- There is less variety for staff – they may become bored.
- Rigid procedures may cause difficulties in coping with emergency jobs.
- There may be an increase in paperwork and form filling.

2 *Flexitime*

Another feature of larger organisations may be that their employees work **flexitime**. This means that instead of rigid starting and finishing times employees can adjust their hours, to a certain extent, to suit their own convenience.

Flexitime employees *must* be at work during their **core time**, eg 10 am–12 noon and 2 pm–4 pm. They must also work a minimum number of hours a week. They can choose when they wish to work the difference between their core hours and total hours – they may have a late start one day and an early start the next. On another day they may have an extended lunch hour.

During busy periods some employees may work longer hours than normal and build up a reserve which they can then have as time off later. However, there is a limit to the number of hours which can be held in reserve – normally about 10 or 12 a month.

Flexitime hours are usually popular with staff and can be very advantageous to companies. No hours are lost because of unpunctuality or personal appointments and overtime payments are kept to a minimum during busy periods.

CHECK IT YOURSELF

Does anyone in your group, or anyone you know, work flexitime? Find out what they like and dislike about the system and how their company checks the hours they work each week.

SECTION REVIEW

Having completed this section, you should now be able to:

1. Describe the main functions of an office.
2. List the qualities required by office staff to work effectively in an organisation.
3. Explain why organisation structure differs from company to company.
4. Differentiate between the Chairman and Managing Director.
5. Describe the functions of different departments in an organisation.
6. Identify the office staff who work in each department.
7. Give examples of how organisations differ in their policies to customers and employees, their procedures and systems.
8. List the main advantages and disadvantages of **centralisation**.
9. Explain the term **flexitime**.

REVIEW QUIZ

True or false?

1. Company policies, procedures and systems differ from one organisation to another.
2. A disadvantage of centralisation is that it is usually uneconomical in terms of space and cost.

3 Flexitime employees must be at work during core time.

4 Offices are mainly concerned with the transmission of information.

5 Chairmen of large companies can sometimes be seen discussing their company on television.

Complete the blanks . . .

6 The .... department is responsible for liaising with trade union representatives.

7 The ... . is responsible for all the legal affairs of the company.

8 Credit control clerks are usually employed in the .... department.

Work it out

9 A new employee has just started work in your office. As she will be liaising with several departments in your organisation your boss has asked you to make sure she knows the type of work which is carried out by each one. Write a brief description of the functions of the Accounts, Personnel and Sales Department for her benefit.

10 Imagine that in the future you and a friend decide to start up in business together offering a secretarial, clerical or accounts service.

a What qualities would you look for in the staff you employed and why?

b What standards of dress, appearance and behaviour do you think would be appropriate for your employees?

INTRODUCTION TO NUMERACY GUIDES

After each of the chapters in this book you will find a short numeracy guide. The aim of these guides is to:

- give you regular practice at the type of calculations you will have to do in an office
- introduce you to the type of calculations you will have to do in the next chapter of the book
- improve your ability to work both with *and* without a calculator!

If the calculation should be attempted *without* a calculator you will see this symbol in the margin

If you can use a calculator you will see this symbol

Both symbols put together means try it manually *first*, then *check* your answers on a calculator.

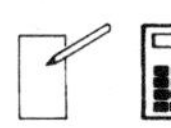

The more practice you have at trying to work things out without a calculator the easier it becomes – you eventually get quicker and quicker. This is a very useful skill – no-one carries a calculator with them *everywhere*!

To help you become good at this, every so often you will see a section marked Simple Sum Trick. These are easy shortcuts which you can learn – not only to help you to 'switch on to numbers' but also to impress your friends and colleagues!

NUMERACY GUIDE 1

Transferring numbers accurately

The easiest mistake to make when copying a list of numbers onto another sheet of paper, is to *copy one incorrectly*. It usually happens when the numbers have several digits and people try to remember too many at once. The most common mistake is for digits to be transposed, eg write 29 382 as 29 832.

TEST YOURSELF 1

How good are you? Copy the following sets of numbers on to a separate sheet of paper and then add them up. Do *not* use a calculator!

Try to copy each list more quickly than the last list and yet still be accurate. Check all your answers with your tutor.

List 1	List 2	List 3	List 4
19 827	109 382	1 309 290	391
7 092	928 382	309 291	209 385
30 003	666 391	56 001	6 004 903
4 000	17 034	4 587 398	40 509
30 487	56 091	8 875 938	247 950

SPECIAL NOTE

- With a long list use a ruler to help keep your place.
- Say the numbers to yourself in *pairs* – three digits at once is often too many.
- Always line up numbers – hundreds under hundreds, tens under tens, units under units, etc.

Reading and understanding numbers

Can you understand long numbers when someone reads them to you? Try writing the numbers below in a list and adding them up. Again check your answers with your tutor.

One thousand four hundred and ten

Fourteen thousand and seven

One hundred and fifty-seven thousand, five hundred and six

Ten thousand and four

One billion

One million, four hundred and sixty-seven thousand and three

One million, two hundred and one

CHECK IT YOURSELF

The most common error when doing this is to get confused when a number needs some noughts inserted in the middle. Remember – if a number starts with the word 'million' you have seven digits to write and some of these may be a nought, eg if no 'thousands' are mentioned.

Decimals

To list numbers correctly the decimal points *must* be aligned one under the other.

TEST YOURSELF 2

Transfer list 1, keeping it straight and remembering the numbers accurately, then add it up.

Transfer list 2, re-arranging the numbers so that all the decimals are aligned, then add it up.

Transfer list 3 from the *written* information and add it up.

List 1	List 2	List 3
45 709.3	4 389.09	One hundred and ten point four zero
6 092.92	64 092.093	Twenty thousand and five point seven two
71 509.709	402.983	Six point nine seven three five
6 008.42	6.5	Ten thousand and two point nine four
17 874.002	19 093.98	One million and three point zero four
15 758.82	14.65	One hundred and one thousand and five

SPECIAL NOTE

- If you find it easier, eg in list 1, you can fill the blank spaces on the right of the decimal point with zeros but this isn't essential.
- In list 3 above the word 'nought' for 0 has been replaced by the word zero. It is always better to use this in speech as it is clearer and results in fewer mistakes being made.

CHECK IT YOURSELF

Ask someone to read you both the *written* lists on this page and on page 10 and see if you can write them down accurately.

Check all your answers with your tutor.

Numbers in ascending and descending order

You already know that a million is greater than a thousand, a thousand greater than a hundred, etc. The more zeros before the decimal the bigger the number is, eg 10, 100, 10 000. the more zeros between the decimal point and the number on the right, the smaller it is, eg 0.1, 0.01, 0.0001.

TEST YOURSELF 3

You have written seven lists of figures so far in this section.

- Rewrite the four lists shown on page 10 in *descending* order (the *largest* number first).
- Now rewrite the three lists on page 11 in *ascending* order (the *smallest* number first).

Check all your lists with your tutor.

Health and safety at work

Health and Safety is as important in an office as in a factory. Constant absenteeism through poor working conditions or accidents is costly for any company and people do not work as productively if they are ill, tired or in an unsatisfactory environment. It is therefore in the company's interests as well as the employees' that health and safety procedures are observed.

THE LAW ON HEALTH AND SAFETY

In 1974 the Government passed the **Health and Safety at Work Act**. This places a legal responsibility on both employers *and employees* in relation to health and safety issues.

It is the employer's duty to provide:

1 Safe means of access to and egress (way out) from the place of work.
2 A safe working environment and adequate facilities and arrangements for welfare at work.
3 Safe equipment and systems of work.
4 Arrangements for ensuring the safe use, handling, storage and transport of articles and substances.
5 Information, instruction, training and supervision.
6 Investigation of accidents.

It is the employee's duty to:

1 Take reasonable care for his or her *own* health and safety.
2 Take reasonable care for the health and safety of other people who may be affected by his or her actions.
3 Co-operate with his or her employer or any other person carrying out duties under the Act.

TEST YOURSELF

Look at each of the statements below and identify under which part of the Act they would be categorised:

1 an employee ignores the usual procedure and uses the lift after the fire bell has sounded
2 inflammable liquids are stored in a busy area

3 a pile of rubbish is left near the entrance to a works
4 a boy empties the sand out of fire buckets as a joke
5 the guard on the guillotine has broken and hasn't been mended
6 the filing clerk leaves the bottom drawer of the cabinet open after use.

CHECK IT YOURSELF

Find out the correct fire procedure at your college. If you are working find out the procedure in your company. Why do you think it is important that everyone should meet at a pre-arranged assembly point? For what other reasons may a building have to be evacuated quickly?

Health and safety policy

Under the Health and Safety at Work Act organisations must produce a health and safety document for their employees giving the company rules, regulations and procedures.

It will also include:

- details of how accidents must be reported
- where the accident book and the first-aid box are situated
- details of qualified first-aiders and safety training
- the duties of the official safety representatives – and their names
- the name of the manager in charge of seeing that health and safety policy is carried out
- information on safe working practices throughout the organisation.

CHECK IT YOURSELF

Find out:

- the name and location of your nearest qualified first-aider
- where the accident book is situated and the procedure in your company (or college) for reporting accidents
- where the first-aid box in your section or department is situated.

SAFE WORKING PRACTICES

In terms of an office this can be divided into:

- **good housekeeping** – tidiness and cleanliness of working areas and safe storage of dangerous or inflammable substances, eg 'thinners', ammonia (used in some copying processes), etc.
- **equipment** – no electrical hazards through trailing leads or broken sockets. Any equipment which can give out dangerous fumes (eg a photocopier) should be kept in a well ventilated, preferably separate, room. Safety filing cabinets to be installed where only one drawer can open at a time to prevent tilting. Equipment only used in accordance with correct operating procedures.
- **new technology** – VDUs to be installed where there is plenty of light to eliminate glare, workstations large enough for equipment and papers – check with operators to ensure they are not suffering eyestrain or headaches.
- **furniture** – safety stools provided for reaching items stored on high shelves, adjustable chairs for typists to reduce backache.
- **accommodation** – no overcrowding, offices above 61°F (16°C) but not too hot, good ventilation and blinds for windows in direct sunlight. Good lighting, safe floor surfaces (not worn or slippery) and adequate toilet facilities.

- **noise** – kept to reasonable limits, eg acoustic hoods on computer printers.
- **safe work habits** – eg not running down corridors, not carrying heavy objects, not carrying so many items that vision is obscured.

- **provision of information** – all employees to know the correct procedure in case of fire, where extinguishers are situated, who are first-aiders and safety representatives, how to report an accident etc.

CHECK IT YOURSELF

- Find out the different colours of fire extinguishers in your building. What is the difference between them?
- List the other types of fire fighting equipment in your building.
- How many alarms are there and how would you activate them?
- Do you know where the nearest emergency exit is to where you are now sitting?

SPECIAL NOTE

Lifting equipment incorrectly is one of the main causes of back problems. *Always* bend your knees (so that you are sitting on your haunches) and keep your back *straight*. As you lift, take the strain in your legs, *not* in your back. *Never* try to lift too heavy objects.

First aid

Unless you are a qualified first-aider you should be careful what action you take in an emergency. You could try to move someone, for instance, who must *not* be moved without an expert being present.

Your first step in an emergency, therefore, must be to **get help**. Most organisations have a list of qualified first-aiders near every telephone and you should refer to this to get assistance.

People who are just feeling unwell or have sustained a very minor injury will be able to seek specialist medical help in a large company (where a nurse may be employed). In a small company they would be able to find the person in charge of the first-aid box so that they could get some medication. Strong drugs are *never* kept in first-aid boxes and drugs of any kind must not be given to people feeling unwell. If the person had a severe reaction to a drug, given to them by another person, they could take legal action.

ACCIDENT REPORTS

Accident records

Organisations keep a record of accidents on their premises. If you have an accident you will be asked to complete an **Accident Report Form** which will give details of:

- the injured person (name, address, age, department etc)
- the injury sustained
- details of the accident (what happened, date, time and location)
- first-aid or medical treatment received
- names of witnesses (if any).

Details are transferred to an **Accident Book** and the form is then filed.

SPECIAL NOTE

All large organisations have a **Safety Committee** which meets regularly to discuss safety issues. Each department will usually have a **Safety Representative** and any employee who notices anything which could be potentially dangerous should report it to his or her Safety Representative so that the problem can be discussed at the next meeting.

CHECK IT YOURSELF

- Find out the name and location of your departmental Safety Representative.
- Walk round your building (or department) and make a list of any potential safety hazards you see. Against each one, suggest how the hazard should be dealt with.
- If possible, submit your list to your Safety Rep.

SPECIAL NOTE

Health and safety procedures in relation to equipment and materials are given in the chapters on Reprographics, Stock Handling, Storing and Supplying Information and Information Processing.

SECTION REVIEW

Having completed this section, you should now be able to:

1. List your own and your employer's legal responsibilities under the Health and Safety at Work Act.
2. Describe your organisation's fire and emergency procedures and explain how these are related to the layout of the building.
3. List the main causes of hazards and accidents in an office.
4. Identify potential hazards and recommend corrective action.
5. Explain the term 'good housekeeping'.
6. Explain the correct procedure for reporting accidents.
7. Identify the factors which affect the health and safety of office workers.
8. Describe how you can personally contribute towards effective health and safety policies in your own organisation.

REVIEW QUIZ

True or false?

1. Buildings can be evacuated for other reasons besides fire.
2. All fire extinguishers are red.
3. An employee who wedges open a fire door is committing an offence under the Health and Safety at Work Act.
4. An employee who falls in a busy area should be moved immediately.
5. It is essential you read the instructions thoroughly before operating a new piece of equipment.

Complete the blanks ...

6. Objects placed high up should only be reached by standing on a ....

7 Keeping work areas clean and tidy and storing away dangerous substances properly is known as ....

8 You trap your finger in a swing door at work. The document you will be asked to complete is called an ....

Work it out

9 Most accidents at work are caused by:

- slipping, falling and tripping
- being struck by falling objects or colliding with objects or people
- electrical equipment
- handling materials and equipment incorrectly.

a Under *each* of the above headings see how many types of accident you can think of. Below are a few causes of accidents to give you a start – begin by putting each under the right headings.

- running along corridors and round corners
- putting broken glass in a wastepaper basket, unwrapped
- carrying a typewriter incorrectly
- balancing on a chair to reach something high (especially a swivel chair!)
- typewriter flex trailing on the floor
- plug sockets overloaded.

b In each case state how the accident could have been *prevented* in the first place.

10 From everything you have read in this chapter, identify the factors which affect the health and safety of people working in an office, in terms of:

- organisational policy and procedures
- safe working practices
- employee knowledge and responsibilities.

NUMERACY GUIDE 2

Calculators

Pocket calculators

There are two types of pocket calculator on the market – business calculators and scientific calculators. You will need the first type for this book, with the following functions:

- add, subtract, multiply and divide
- percentage and square root
- Most calculators also have a memory function (usually M+ M– MR and MC keys). You will find this extremely useful later on as it saves putting numbers in twice. Using the memory is covered on pages 160–163).

Desktop calculators

In addition to the functions on a pocket calculator, desktop calculators usually have the following additional facilities, eg:

- a print-out of all numbers and calculations. This is useful because:
  – you can check where you were if you have been interrupted
  – the list can be checked for omissions or errors
  – the list can be kept as a permanent record.
- a non-add key – used to enter the date or operator's number at the top of the print-out.
- the ability to operate to different numbers of decimal places, depending on the type of calculations being carried out.
- a constant key – so that the same number can be repeated again and again with different numeric operations.
- a sub-total key – which prints a different symbol to show that this is only the sub-total, not the total.

- the ability to repeat the same input number by pressing one key.
- double zero and treble zero keys – to save having to press zero several times when dealing in hundreds or thousands.

CHECK IT YOURSELF

If you have a calculator you should know how to use it! Pocket calculators have instruction sheets with them, desktop calculators have small instruction books.

If you are using a desktop calculator you should know the basic functions, eg how to start your listing and key in the date. Check how to do this with your tutor.

SPECIAL NOTE

- It is just as easy to go wrong with a calculator as without one – by pressing the wrong keys, or missing out an entry. Do take care when inputting numbers.
- You should also know the difference between the CE key and the C key. These stand for:
  CE = clear last entry only
  C = clear all the current calculation (to start again).
  On some pocket machines this is the same key. Pressing it *once* = CE and pressing it *twice* = C.
- Always *start* a new calculation by pressing Clear first. This ensures any previous calculations are not still stored and will not upset what you are doing.
- Always *end* a calculation printout by turning up the paper a short distance, so that you can tear off the printout without cutting off the last few lines.

TEST YOURSELF 1

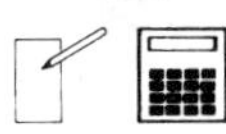

Do each of the following calculations manually and then *check* the answers on your calculator.

Addition	**Subtraction**
1 903 + 2498 + 89 + 952 =	**1** 869 584 – 435 113 =
2 9398 + 12 875 + 698 + 20 =	**2** 121 – 75 =
3 2332 + 92.8 + 15.82 + 210 =	**3** 25 827 – 17 463 =
4 647.4 + 18.6 + 403 + 37 =	**4** 298.87 – 114.35 =
5 809 + 671 + 34.28 + 3984.4 + 430.28 =	**5** 29 382.23 – 2594.3 =

CHECK IT YOURSELF

- Did you line up *all* the numbers and the decimal points accurately when writing them out?
- Look back at any you worked out incorrectly and see if you can find out why.

Necessary and unnecessary zeros

- If a number is listed as 200.00, then it is totally unnecessary to enter the zeros after the decimal point on a calculator. Therefore 48.500 = 48.5.
- However, if you are working out a sum manually then it is a good idea to *complete* any blank spaces to make the calculation easier to do, eg

$$2435.29 - 864.4 \quad = \quad \begin{array}{r} 2435.29 \\ \underline{864.40} \end{array}$$

SPECIAL NOTE

A term often used for the result of a multiplication is the word **product**. If you are asked to find the product – you multiply.

TEST YOURSELF 2

Do each of the following calculations manually and then *check* the answers on your calculator.

Multiplication	Division
1 623 × 7 =	**1** 516 ÷ 4 =
2 2983 × 18 =	**2** 2184 ÷ 26 =
3 25 × 24 =	**3** 3975 ÷ 25 =
4 5162 × 7 =	**4** 81 000 ÷ 648 =
5 5891 × 10 =	**5** 56 240 ÷ 10 =
6 74.29 × 10 =	**6** 924.89 ÷ 10 =

Multiplying and dividing by 10

You should have been able to do the last two questions in each section in two seconds flat! Did you? The short cut is to simply **move the decimal point**:

Multiplying by 10 = move decimal point one place to the *right* (with a whole number this just means adding a zero)

242 × 10 = 2 420 198.72 × 10 = 1987.2

Dividing by 10 = move decimal point one place to the *left* (if you had a whole number to start with you will now have a number to one decimal place)

242 ÷ 10 = 24.2 198.72 ÷ 10 = 19.872

SPECIAL NOTE

Multiplying and dividing by 100, 1000, 10 000 etc is just as easy. Move the decimal place the same number of places as the number of zeros you see. Therefore 100 = 2 places, 1000 = 3 places, etc. This may mean inserting extra zeros.

TEST YOURSELF 3

Do all these calculations *without* a calculator! Can you complete them within one minute?

1	4523 × 10 =	**6**	9780 ÷ 10 =
2	4787.3 × 10 =	**7**	697.38 ÷ 10 =
3	98 728 × 100 =	**8**	5570 ÷ 100 =
4	23.89 × 100 =	**9**	2342.8 ÷ 100 =
5	67.4 × 1000 =	**10**	426 281.3 ÷ 1000 =

CHECK IT YOURSELF

- Did you remember to drop the excess zero in question eight?

Money

Calculations involving money are always carried out to *two decimal places*, where the pounds are whole numbers and the pence are the same as decimals.

It is therefore important, if you are using a desktop calculator that you always check you are operating with two decimal places before you start.

If some of your entries are pence only, then on a calculator start by entering the point. However, if you are writing out the figures in a list, eg for addition, it can be useful to write one zero before the point – again so that it makes the figure easy to read.

TEST YOURSELF 4

Addition

1 £15.07 + £230 + £18.65 =
2 £1320.15 + £40.20 + £16.35 =
3 £14.50 + 53p + 79p + £10.85 =
4 £57.41 + 97p + £168.43 + 16p =
5 94p + £38.20 + £175 + £23.30 + 58p =

Subtraction

6 £19.25 – £8.10 =
7 £473.38 – £60.85 =
8 97p – 69p =
9 £1065.14 – £878.66 =
10 £3251.20 – £1768.42 =

Multiplication

11 £83 × 9 =
12 £145.20 × 12 =
13 £45.73 × 35 =
14 £16.20 × 135 =
15 £562.34 × 28 =

Division

16 £108 ÷ 9 =
17 £163.45 ÷ 7 =
18 £1011.36 ÷ 12 =
19 £2808 ÷ 18 =
20 £189.20 ÷ 215 =

Rounding

You may have to give your answer to a specified number of decimal places, even though the correct answer comes to more than this. This is always true when you are dealing with money – you can't divide 1p between two or three people!

The solution is to **round** the number to the nearest whole number as follows:

.5 and above = round *up*   below .5 = round *down*

eg £3.48 ÷ 5 = 0.696 = 0.70 = 70p   eg £2.36 ÷ 5 = 0.472 = 0.47 = 47p

If your answer contains several more decimal places than you need, then always use the place to the right of the number you need, eg 72.3471 = 72.35, 10.3417 = 10.34.

TEST YOURSELF 5

Round the following to two decimal places:

1 74.892 **2** 18.977 **3** 16.655 **4** 4.27841 **5** 6.32447 **6** 15.24442

Calculate the following and round your answers to two decimal places:

7	£142.68 ÷ 15 =	**10**	£15.24 ÷ 8 =
8	£63.70 ÷ 4 =	**11**	£182.19 ÷ 15 =
9	£27.42 ÷ 4 =	**12**	£784.38 ÷ 7 =

Storing and supplying information

Section 1 – Storing information (filing)

WHY FILE?

- **To find papers easily.**
- **To answer queries quickly.**
- **To have the most up-to-date information to hand.**

TEST YOURSELF

How quickly can you find:

- a piece of work you completed last week?
- a handout you received last month?
- your last school report?

Inefficient filing causes delays, problems, annoyance and can cost money in lost orders and lost customers.

FILING METHODS

There are five methods of filing documents which you must be able to use:

- **alphabetical** – by name
- **numerical** – by number

- **subject** – by topic
- **chronological** – by date
- **geographical** – by area

Vertical filing system

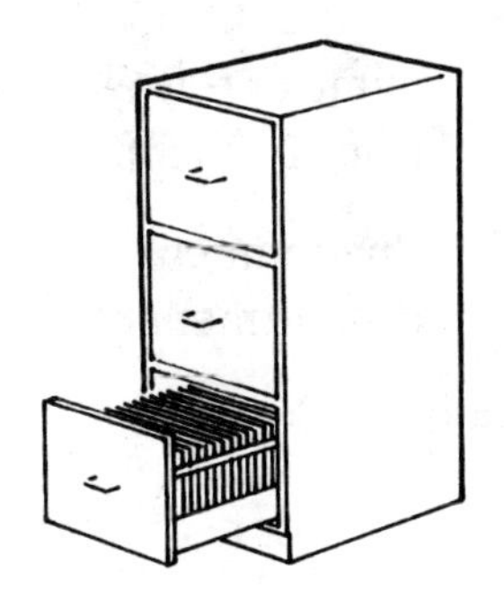

Lateral filing system

Alphabetical

Used by: small and medium-sized companies

Examples: personnel records
customer records

Because: it is quick and easy to use.

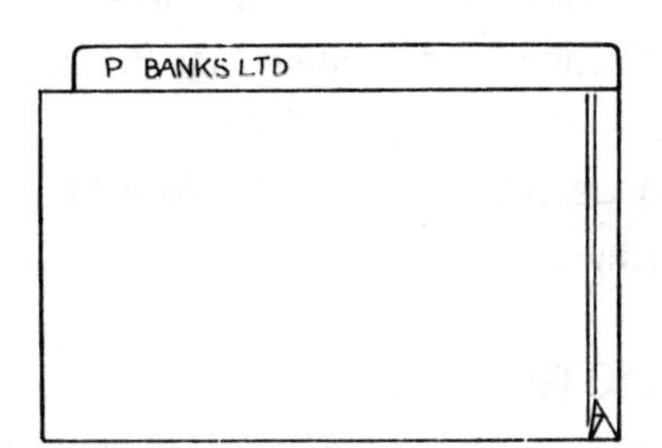

Rules to follow

Names of people

- Surname *first*
- *Short before long* – Clark before Clarke
- If identical, follow first names or initials

Names of organisations

- Ignore the word *the*
- Numbers become words – 4-Star = Four Star
- If identical name, follow street or town

- *Nothing before something* – B Lee before Barry Lee
- Mac and Mc – all become Mac – all come before 'M'
- Ignore apostrophes – O'Ryan = Oryan
- Ignore d' and de
- ABC Company comes *before* names starting with 'A'
- Saint and St – all become Saint
- File public bodies under name or town – Bath (City Council)

  Environment (Department of)

Check it out – Look in the phone book!

TEST YOURSELF

Put these names into strict alphabetical order:

Saint Thomas's Hospital
TV Sales Ltd
George Graham
Sound & Vision Ltd
Anne O'Neill
The Toy Shop
G & S Plastics Ltd
MacDonald's Health Foods
Barry Clarke
Mitchell & Cooper plc
Hotel de Gruchy
Charlotte O'Neil
St Anne's Primary School
G Graham
Department of Health
McGuire & Evans plc
Ormerod Hotel
Leonard Clark
Stevenage Borough Council
77 Gallery
SHS Mouldings Ltd

SPECIAL NOTE

- *Always* do a number check to ensure none are omitted – **Count both your list and the original list carefully!**

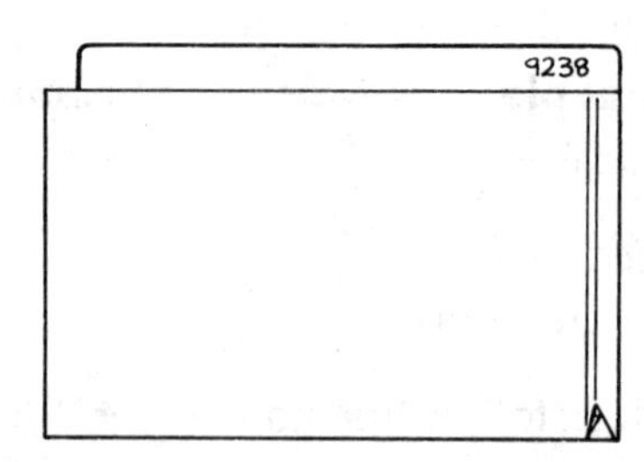

Numerical

Used by: large organisations and expanding companies
Examples: customer records
Because: it is easy to expand.

SPECIAL NOTE

- A separate alphabetical index is needed to identify numerical files.
- The number is often used as a reference on correspondence.

TAYLOR & BRIGGS LTD 523

Rules to follow

1. Consult the alphabetical index to find the number.
2. Read the number carefully and copy it *accurately* onto the document to be filed.

Remember – most mistakes are made through transposing figures!

TEST YOURSELF

Change the following list into numerical order:

Bakewell M	482311	Gibbs P	41372	Jones R	478963
Berkovitz T	47321	Hacking M	423314	Kay G	462834
Bolton T	477914	Houldsworth S	473213	Patel W	41329
Driver R	477712	Jallucci K	479836	Sanderson D	475712

Subject

Used by: organisations wanting to file under *topics*
Examples: chain stores (under type of stock)
insurance companies (under type of insurance)
director's files (under subjects)
Because: all related material is kept in the same file.

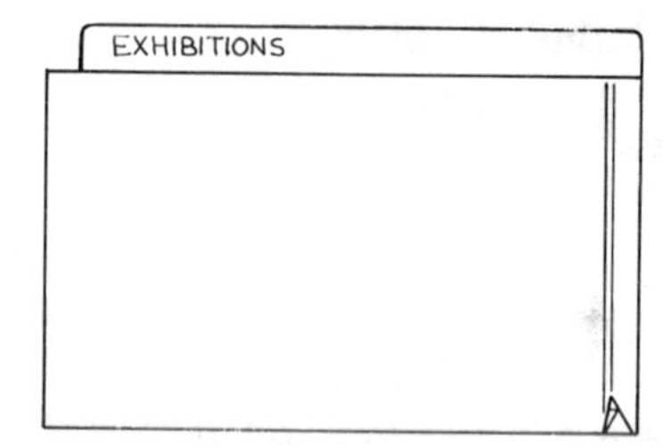

Rules to follow

1 Subjects are filed in alphabetical order –

Canaries
Cats
Dogs

2 Broad subjects are usually sub-divided –

Footwear – Boots
Sandals
Slippers
Trainers

TEST YOURSELF

Put the following into subject order:

Seminars	Publicity – Exhibitions
Publicity – Open Days	Personnel – Health and Safety
Personnel – Training	Personnel – Appraisals
Publicity – Leaflets	Conferences
Travel	Publicity – Advertising
Publicity – Displays	Personnel – Welfare
Personnel – Staff Records	Personnel – Recruitment

Chronological

Used by: organisations issuing documents in *date order*
Examples: petty cash vouchers
birth and death certificates
Because: date is more important than name or place.

SPECIAL NOTE

- *Correspondence* received by a company is stored in *date order* in a file.
- The most recent correspondence is always at the *top*.

Rules to follow

1 When writing out a list put the earliest date *first*.

2 Keep the date style consistent – 24 March 19__ *or* 24.03.__ – *not* a mixture!

TEST YOURSELF

Change the following list to chronological order using a consistent date style:

Name	*Date of Birth*	*Name*	*Date of Birth*
James Baird	29.11.74	Roberta Fletcher	13/3/74
K Barnes	04.11.73	P Ormerod	October 12 1974
Peter Best	March 4th 1974	John Taylor	01/06/74
Gemma Brooks	18 August 1973	Nicola Walker	23:07:73
Vincent Chang	December 3rd 1973	F Williams	5 Nov 1974
Janice Cruikshank	9 April 1972	K Yates	20.9.74

Geographical

Used by: organisations which prefer to file under *area*

Examples: sales companies
mail order companies
gas and electricity boards

Because: mail shots or visits can be carried out by region.

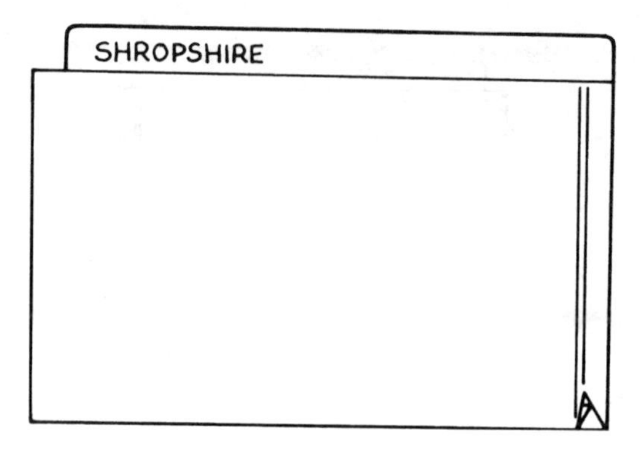

RULES TO FOLLOW

1. Alphabetical order is used within each region.
2. Files can be divided into countries, counties, towns or districts.
3. Large regions (eg counties) may be sub-divided (eg into towns).

Remember – not only the main regions but also the sub-regions are in alphabetical order!

TEST YOURSELF

Rearrange the following counties and branches into geographical order:

Cornwall	*Devon*	*Cheshire*	*Kent*
Truro	Plymouth	Altrincham	Maidstone
Penzance	Paignton	Chester	Canterbury
Falmouth	Torquay	Nantwich	Faversham
Newquay	Exmouth	Hale	Ashford
Bude	Exeter	Crewe	Sidcup
	Teignmouth		Sevenoaks

THE GOLDEN RULES OF FILING

Do file daily – to avoid a backlog and staff having to work with outdated information

Do ensure all documents are placed in the correct file. If in doubt *ask*, don't guess!

Don't let files become too bulky – split into two folders, each clearly marked with the dates covered by the folder.

Don't pull out folders by the tabs – they break off!

Do remove paper clips and pins (which may 'hook' other papers) and staple related documents if necessary

Do pre-sort and group all documents before starting filing.

Do repair any torn papers.

Do punch documents *squarely* by aligning them with the guide ruler on the punch. Or line up the centre of the papers with the centre arrow on the punch so the holes are *always* in the same place.

Don't lend out individual documents – photocopy the one required *or* lend the whole file and substitute an absent card (see page 35).

Don't make a new file for every new correspondent – check with your supervisor whether it should be filed in the miscellaneous file or a new folder made out.

Don't overload a filing cabinet. When it becomes too full consult your supervisor. Dead files are usually removed to transfer boxes and taken to a storeroom or cellar.

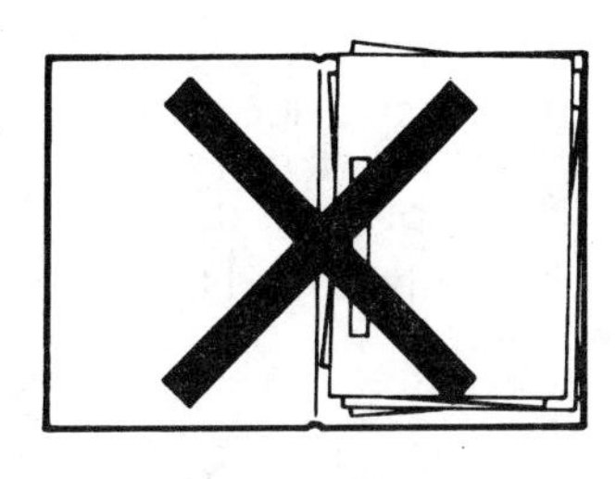

FILING PROCEDURES

The release mark

Carbon copies of documents are usually for filing. Original documents (received from another organisation) should be marked with a small tick or other sign to show when they are to be filed. This tells the filing staff that those working on the papers have finished with them.

Confidential files

Many files in an office are confidential, eg personnel records. These are usually kept in a separate cabinet, under lock and key, and are accessed only by those with authority to read the contents.

They should *never* be left open on desks or taken into public areas, eg reception.

Top secret documents and files in some establishments may be:

- kept in a safe
- only issued to someone with security clearance.

Cross-reference cards

Why use?

- To find a file quickly which could logically be placed under two (or more) names.

Rules to follow

1. Make out the cross-reference card *at the same time* you make up the new file.
2. Store the cross-reference card in the *opposite* place to the file.

EXAMPLE

R Brown trading as Kurlywig Hair Design

Under B – The cross-reference card
Under K – The file itself

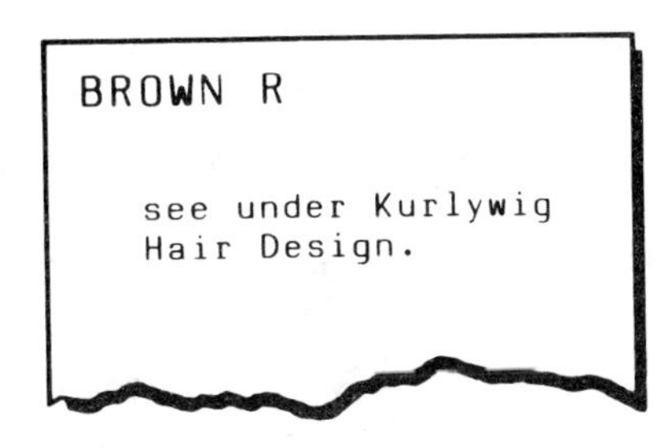

CHECK IT YOURSELF

Your local Yellow Pages is a very good example of cross-referencing.

Look up each of the categories given below and note down (from the information you will find under each one) where the entries can be found.

- keep fit
- cable television
- customs and excise office
- adult education centres

Absent or out cards

Why use?

- To keep a check on borrowed files

Rules to follow

1. No file should be lent without an absent card being completed.
2. Enter the name of the borrower, date borrowed and department, if a large organisation.
3. Place the absent card where the file is usually kept.
4. Check regularly and chase up late returns.

EXAMPLE

Name of file	Date Borrowed	Borrower	Date Returned
R Jones & co Ltd	24 April	R Taylor	26 April
J Woodstock plc	27 April	M Cowell	27 April
Berry & Wilson	28 April	J Barnes	

Tickler or reminder systems

These are used to remind filing staff which files to chase up because they are overdue for return. The system used will often depend on whether the organisation is large or small.

Small companies may keep a record in:

- **card index boxes**. A card is made out for each file. When a file is borrowed the card is filed in the box *under the date of return*. Cards are removed when files come back into the system and any cards remaining under due dates indicate files still outstanding.
- a **file diary** or **returns book**. This is kept in diary form with the files listed under the date of return. They are crossed out as they are handed in and those names remaining indicate files overdue.

Large organisations may use:

- large **absent cards** colour coded for the date of return (eg 14 colours for a 14 day cycle). These protrude from a lateral filing system and outstanding files are easy to see.
- a **computer database**. Files going out and coming in are logged into the computer. A check can be run automatically on any files still outstanding.

Types of files

Concertina	– used to pre-sort alphabetical documents
Box file	– used to keep documents which cannot or must not be punched, eg catalogues, contracts etc
Lever arch	– a large version of a ring binder with a spring clip to keep papers secure
Document wallet	– used for storing documents on a temporary basis
Manilla folders	– used to keep papers safe in a suspension filing system
	– papers are usually secured inside them with a metal or plastic pronged clip.

Indexing Systems

Many indexing systems are used in conjunction with a filing system, for instance, an alphabetical index showing the number of numerical files.
However, indexing systems are also used independently to store a variety of information – customer or supplier names and addresses, telephone numbers, stock etc. There are four main systems which can be used.

Card index

cards can be added or removed or information changed easily without disturbing the overall arrangement

inexpensive

guide cards can be added for quick identification

Visible edge	cards can be updated whilst still in the tray
	visible edge provides information at a glance
	coloured signals can be used for quick identification
Rotary index	compact enough for desk top use
	the wheel is rotated to find the correct card
	cards can be individually extracted quite easily for updating
Strip index	any line can be removed and a new strip inserted easily
	additional strips can be added at any point in the frame
	coloured strips aid easy identification

CHECK IT YOURSELF

Discuss with your tutor the **type** of information which would be kept on each type of index card.

Filing equipment

Vertical	Files stored one behind the other in drawers
	different sizes of cabinet available – 4-drawers the most popular
	folders can be suspended or free-standing
Lateral	Files stored like books on a shelf, usually in suspended pockets

	cupboards can be multi-purpose eg for files, computer print-outs, books etc
	space saving
Horizontal	Files stored in shallow drawers
	often used for large documents, photographs or plans which must not be folded
Rotary	Files stored on a revolving stand
	gives all round access to files
	space saving

Safety first

- Modern cabinets can only be opened one drawer at a time to prevent tilting.
- Use a filing stool to reach high shelves – never a swivel chair!
- Avoid carrying so many files that you obscure your view – especially on stairs.
- Steel cabinets are usually flame-proof to protect documents in a fire.

DOCUMENT RETENTION

Obviously files can't be kept forever or all organisations would eventually run out of space! Most companies operate a retention policy, ie after a certain length of time documents are either:

- retained in the current files
- transferred to a dormant file
- transferred to long term storage (often in the basement)
- transferred onto another means of storage which takes up less space, eg microfiche or computer

- destroyed. Confidential files should always be destroyed by putting them through a shredding machine so that they become completely unreadable.

How long to keep a document will depend on:

- what it is, or relates to
- whether there is a legal requirement covering the time for which it must be kept.

Generally, ordinary correspondence is kept for the shortest period of time (eg one or two years). Accounts and VAT documents *must*, by law, be retained for a minimum of six years in case of any disputes arising, as within this time a legal claim can still be made. Legal documents, such as Contracts and Agreements, are also retained for at least six years after they cease to be valid, as a legal claim could be pursued within six years of the alleged breach of the contract. Other legal documents may be kept even longer, eg those governing child custody.

SPECIAL NOTE

Never clear out files or destroy any papers without *specific* instructions from your supervisor on what, exactly, must be removed – and what, exactly, must be done with it.

CHECK IT YOURSELF

The type of retention policy in operation will often depend on the type of business an organisation undertakes.

Discuss with your tutor how the retention policy would differ for

- a solicitor
- an hotel
- an accountant
- a doctor.

OTHER METHODS OF STORAGE

So far this chapter has been concerned with paper-based methods of storage, but other systems may also be used, eg microfiche and computer based filing.

1 Microfiche

Microfilm is a method of keeping information by photographing records to produce them as miniature films. The films are negative copies and can only be viewed through a **reader**.

Microfiche is the most popular form of microfilm and consists of a rectangular sheet of microfilm with rows of images – usually about 100 photographed pages fit onto one sheet of microfiche. The reader enlarges the images to make them readable to the viewer. Some readers also incorporate a printer so that the fiche can be printed out if a hard (paper) copy is required.

The system saves a great deal of space and, if the originals are retained as well, they last much longer as they are handled less frequently.

Mainframe computers will usually print out direct onto microfiche if required (known as COM – Computer Output to Microfilm). Companies without this facility or their own processing unit will usually send their paper records away to a microfilm bureau who will produce the microfiche for them.

2 Computer based filing systems

Records and files may be kept on computer, again to save space. This type of filing is known as **electronic filing**. Companies who wish to set up an electronic filing system will usually input all their records by using a document scanner, which automatically converts any text or graphics into images which the computer can understand. Keying in the information would take too long and every document would need checking carefully for errors.

Special computer software is needed to manage the files, ie store the documents in the order required, retrieve them on command, etc. Anyone wishing to view the files needs access to a computer terminal and, if the files are confidential, a special password.

The major difficulty with electronic filing is that people are apt to keep a hard (paper) copy as well – either just to be on the safe side in case of computer breakdowns, or to write notes on. This defeats the major objective – that of saving space.

Documents and files kept on computer, which relate to personal information on any individuals other than employees, are covered by the Data Protection Act. Details of the Act are given in the chapter on Information processing.

CHECK IT YOURSELF

- Most bookshops and reference libraries keep their book lists on microfiche today. Why do you think this is so? Visit your local bookshop and enquire about a book to watch the system in operation.
- Check if the organisation where you work, or visit on work experience, keeps any of its files on microfiche or computer. Find out what type of information is stored in this way, and why, and the security systems in operation to prevent unauthorised access of confidential or special files.

SECTION REVIEW

Having completed this section, you should now be able to:

1. Identify and interpret the various classification systems used when filing documents.
2. Describe the correct procedure for sorting, handling and storing documents.
3. File documents accurately using alphabetical, numerical, chronological and subject classification systems.
4. Explain the difference in storage and access between confidential files and ordinary files.

5 Describe the term 'retention policy' and explain how this is affected by organisational and legal constraints.

6 Explain how and why a tickler system is operated.

7 Describe the function of absent cards and cross-reference cards and their role in file management.

8 List the main advantages and disadvantages of operating either microfiche or computer based filing as alternative systems of storage.

REVIEW QUIZ

True or false?

1 St Edward's Hospital would be filed under E.

2 Numerical filing is simple to use because no index is required.

3 A box file is used to keep documents which cannot or must not be punched.

4 Numerical filing is often used by rapidly growing companies because it can be expanded easily.

5 Files should be updated regularly by throwing old papers away.

Complete the blanks ...

6 Chronological filing means filing in .... order.

7 A cross reference card should always be filed in the .... place to the file.

8 Accounts and VAT documents must be kept for a minimum of .... years.

Identify the correct list

In each case below state which list is in the correct order for an alphabetical filing system – A, B or C.

9a

A	B	C
Jacquard Fabrics	JBL Computers	JBL Computers
JBL Computers	Jacquard Fabrics	Jacquard Fabrics
Barry Johnston	Alan Johnson	Alan Johnson
A Johnstone	A Johnstone	Barry Johnston
Alan Johnson	Barry Johnston	A Johnstone

9b

A	B	C
MTZ Corporation	G MacBride	McDuff & Evans
Alan MacBridge	Alan MacBridge	G MacBride
G MacBride	McDuff & Evans	Alan MacBridge
McDuff & Evans	MTZ Corporation	Main & Waring
Maine & Jones	Main & Waring	Maine & Jones
Main & Waring	Maine & Jones	Hotel Metropole
Hotel Metropole	Hotel Metropole	MTZ Corporation

10 A new employee has started work in your office and will be helping to operate the existing filing system. Draw up a short list of key points she must bear in mind under the following headings:

- **a** opening a new file
- **b** lending files
- **c** confidential files
- **d** document retention.

Section 2 – Researching, supplying and presenting information

RESEARCHING INFORMATION

Requests for information can range from the simple 'What is the telephone number of the local College?' to the quite difficult 'What is the climate like in May in Brazil?' to the more obscure 'Can you find out if it is possible to go on a day trip on Concorde?'

Often the more difficult the query, the more challenging it can be to find the answer! To deal effectively with any request for information you need to know

- where to look or go for help
- how to identify and abstract the information you need
- how to present this in the most appropriate form.

SOURCES OF INFORMATION

There are a wide variety of sources you can access and your choice will depend on what you need to find out. Options include

- your colleagues within the organisation
- friends and contacts in other organisations
- paper-based files, computer based files and microfiche
- viewdata systems (eg Prestel)
- organisation chart, company handbook, advertising literature, price lists, stock lists etc.
- reference books
- local specialist organisations
- national specialist organisations.

If you are regularly asked for information it is a good idea to keep a personal file of useful telephone numbers and addresses.

The human resource

Probably your best source of help on a regular basis is *people* – the 'human resource'. Your colleagues at work will know a tremendous amount of information about your customers, products, recent events and so on. Equally, you may have a friend or relation involved in or knowledgeable about an area you are investigating. Therefore, in many cases your first option may be to

- ask someone if they know the answer
- ask someone if they know where you can find the answer.

SPECIAL NOTE

There is a world of difference between asking others for help or information and becoming a nuisance! The difference lies in

- asking politely
- not asking unless it is necessary (ie if you could easily find out yourself by looking in a file or the telephone directory)

- not asking the same question twice (ie remembering or noting down the answers)
- saying thank you!

CHECK IT YOURSELF

Discuss with your tutor the type of information that staff in the following departments may be able to give you:

Purchasing	Sales
Accounts	Personnel

TEST YOURSELF

Below are given several queries which can be answered by accessing internal sources of information. Match each query against the most appropriate source:

1 Extension number for the Chief Accountant	**A** Accounts files
2 Details of company pension fund	**B** Organisation chart
3 The dates the receptionist is away on holiday	**C** Customer files
4 The registered office of your own company	**D** Company handbook
5 The VAT number of one of your suppliers	**E** Company advertising literature
6 The name of the Sales Director of one of your customers	**F** Internal telephone list
7 Details of one of your products	**G** Company letter headed paper
8 The executive responsible for the security staff	**H** Holiday rota

Information on Computer

The amount of information held on computer will vary from one organisation to another and may include

- mailing lists of customers
- customer records
- employee records
- stock records
- price lists
- sales statistics.

To find this information you obviously need access to a computer and you also need to know how to use the software package which holds the information to search for what you need.

Most of this type of information is held on database packages, which can be set up to hold virtually all types of records. Alternatively, companies with a special requirement can pay to have access to an 'on-line', commercial database. For instance, specialist databases are available for those in the legal profession, and many travel agencies are linked to Gallileo, which not only gives them travel information at the touch of a button, but enables them to make a booking and print out the tickets immediately. Such a system is known as an **interactive** system.

Prestel

The most common interactive computer information system is Prestel – known as a viewdata service because the information can be viewed on screen. The system links computer based information to adapted television sets or micro computers over an ordinary telephone line.

The information on Prestel is organised in 'pages' – a page being a screenful of information. Through Prestel you can call up these pages to be displayed on your computer screen.

An easy to follow index shows lists of information headings with a route number to be followed until you find the page you want.

Information provided includes:

- travel information eg airline and flight times
- financial information
- export information
- tax guides
- company information
- government statistics.

This is in addition to sports and entertainment information (similar to that found on Ceefax and Oracle).

Because Prestel is interactive (ie a two-way information service) not only can you call up information on hotels, flights etc but you can book your reservation via your keyboard or special keypad (or merely send for more information!)

SPECIAL NOTE

Prestel also offers an electronic mail service known as Mailbox. This can be used by firms so that their own executives can access the system from their homes (via their home computers or TV sets) to transmit and receive information from their head or branch offices.

CHECK IT YOURSELF

- Try to see Prestel in operation and access several of the information pages – eg those on travel.
- You can experiment by sending away for certain types of information – eg on hotels abroad – via Prestel.

Local specialist sources

Often you can find out what you need to know by telephoning an organisation which can deal with your query. Many of these are to be found locally, eg

Police
Reference Library
Local council/town hall
The Department of Social Security
British Telecom
Citizen's Advice Bureau
Chamber of Commerce
Insurance companies
Office equipment suppliers
Inland Revenue
Local radio station
Local paper
Post Office
Your company's solicitor
Your company's bank
Your company's accountant
VAT office
Insurance broker

National specialist sources

In other cases the organisation most likely to help you only operates on a national basis or has only a limited number of regional offices eg

The Department of Trade and Industry
The Consumers' Association
Tourist Information Offices
English Tourist Board
Trade Associations
AA or RAC
Foreign embassies or
National tourist offices

CHECK IT YOURSELF

- Discuss with your tutor the type of information which could be supplied by *each* of the above sources.
- Discuss with your colleagues any occasions when you have contacted a local (or national) source for information – and why.

TEST YOURSELF

Below are given several queries. In each case state the source of information which would be able to help you. Note that there may be more than one answer – to help you the total number of possible answers is given in brackets. See if you can find each one.

1. The cost of insuring your company's petty cash against theft. (2)
2. The date Blackpool illuminations start next year (1)
3. Information on exporting to Poland (3)
4. The annual turnover a company must not exceed before it is liable to register for VAT (2)
5. The date of a forthcoming Trade Fair in your town (4)
6. The address of a Japanese interpreter (1)

SPECIAL NOTE

You may find that in one or two cases you have actually identified *more* sources than are indicated in brackets. Generally, this can be a good sign as it shows you are prepared to think about a problem thoroughly and *try* several places. Even if your first contact cannot help you, they may be able to suggest somewhere else to try.

It is a useful exercise to discuss with your tutor *all* your alternatives and order them, with your most likely (or cheapest!) source listed *first*.

Personal files

The type of information you collect in your personal file will depend on

- your job
- the department in which you work
- the size of your organisation.

If you work in Sales, for example, you may find it useful to keep full details of your company's products and a price list in your file. In a small organisation your file may contain a wide variety of miscellaneous contacts, eg

maintenance contacts	eg	electrician, plumber, heating engineer, locksmith, glazier, office equipment servicing etc.
office suppliers	eg	of office stationery or equipment
agencies used by your company	eg	travel agent, shipping and forwarding agent, express delivery companies, translation bureau, advertising agency etc.

SPECIAL NOTE

Do be aware that no matter who you contact you cannot expect to be given confidential information, for instance you cannot ring a bank and find out about someone's account! Two points to note are:

- Always try to avoid asking people for information which is confidential – as a refusal can be embarrassing for both parties.
- If your boss gives you specific authority to access confidential information in your organisation – and clears this with, say, the other department concerned, do *not* repeat what you know to other people – or leave any written notes lying about.

Reference Books

The number and type of reference books kept by a company will depend on its size and the type of business it is in. Those kept by an accountant would be different to those kept by a large engineering company. Any which are not held 'in house' can be accessed by visiting the local reference library – if your query is not very straightforward you are better visiting them than telephoning.

Reference books which are useful to any organisation include:

- *Telephone, telex and fax directories*, including the *Yellow Pages* and *Business Pages* (similar to the Yellow Pages but listing manufacturers and wholesalers).
- A good *dictionary* – for meanings and spellings of words, their pronunciation and the meaning of commonly used abbreviations.
- *Road maps* and A–Z *street guides* – invaluable for executives who travel a lot or for representatives.
- AA/RAC *Handbooks* – give details of towns and cities in Britain, mileage distances, names of recommended hotels and garages and maps
- *Good Food Guide/Hotels and Restaurants in Great Britain* – for executives who regularly entertain.
- A good general reference book, eg *Whitaker's Almanack*. This gives worldwide information on governments, statesmen, population, industry and commerce and the arts, plus many useful names and addresses.

Specialist Books and Information

Specialist information can often be kept in abbreviated form as leaflets or specific timetables, rather than buying expensive books. There are 6 main specialist areas:

Travel

ABC *Rail, Coach and Airways Guides* which give detailed timetable information. In reality most offices will keep on hand timetables for rail services/airlines most frequently used and would telephone either British Rail, the coach operator or travel agent for confirmation of times and availability.

Hints to Businessmen booklets. These are

produced by the Department of Trade and Industry and cover various countries. They give invaluable advice on local holidays, climate, customs regulations, entry regulations, hotels etc.

English Usage and Secretarial work

Roget's Thesaurus gives alternative meanings (synonyms) for a wide variety of words.

Black's Titles and Forms of Address – gives the correct form of address for someone who is highly ranked or holds an official position – from the Queen to the Lord Mayor. It includes both the correct wording for when writing or speaking.

Fowler's Modern English Usage – gives guidance on difficult points of grammar and punctuation.

A good *secretarial desk book* (from a wide range available).

People

Who's Who and *Who Was Who* – provide information on famous people in Britain. The first book deals with those who are still living, the second with those who have died.

Burke's Peerage and *Debrett's Peerage and Baronetage* give details on the peers of the realm.

Vacher's Parliamentary Companion – gives details of MPs and members of the House of Lords.

Books on specific professions include *The Medical Register* (medical practitioners), *The Dentists' Register*, *The Solicitors Diary*, the *Directory of Directors* (lists prominent company directors).

Business

UK *Kompass* is issued in two volumes – the first gives a detailed guide to products and their manufacturers, the second gives information on companies in the UK. European volumes are also available.

The Stock Exchange Official Year Book – gives details of organisations and membership. It includes a short history and description of each company listed.

Guide to Key British Enterprises (Dun and Bradstreet) – gives information about prominent British companies.

British Middle Market Directory (Dun and Bradstreet) – similar to the 'Key' but this time listing mainly private and smaller companies.

Croner's Reference Books – various books are available, eg for exporters, importers and small businesses.

Current Affairs

Britain, An Official Handbook – gives information about all aspects of British industry and the economy.

Hansard – gives daily and weekly verbatim reports of proceedings in the House of Commons and House of Lords.

Keesing's Contemporary Archives – are newsheets issued weekly for insertion in a binder. They consist of reports and statistics summarised from the world's press and news services.

General reference

The *Royal Mail Guide* and the *Parcelforce Guide* give information on services provided by the Post Office.

Post Office leaflets on various postal services with the current rates.

The *British Telecom Guide* – gives information on all telecommunications services.

Willing's Press Guide – lists all British newspapers and publications and gives details of advertising rates and circulation figures.

Kelly's Directory – not only lists all manufacturers, merchants, wholesalers and firms in the UK both alphabetically and in trade order but also gives details of international exporters and services relating to different products.

Postcode Directories.

Newspapers and Magazines

Many offices take a daily newspaper and also subscribe to several business magazines. Not only will a good newspaper give information on current affairs, share prices and exchange rates but many contain information about road works in progress and other useful travel details.

The type of magazines to be found in an organisation will often vary according to the business of the organisation – many trades have their own specialist magazines. Firms which receive many foreign visitors may keep on hand a supply of foreign language journals and periodicals for reception. General magazines purchased by many companies include

Office Equipment News – gives up-to-date information on business equipment

What to Buy for Business – gives test reports on equipment and recommendations on 'best buys'

Business Traveller – contains articles of special interest to executives who travel frequently.

Magazines such as *Management Today*, *Personnel Management* and *Management Accounting* all contain specific articles of interest to these managers.

SPECIAL NOTE

Reference libraries also keep copies of periodicals and newspapers and many have back copies available (though these may be stored on microfiche). Bear in mind reference libraries have a vast amount of other useful information eg local maps dating back many years, local Council reports and surveys, Government reports etc.

Remember that in most cases books in reference libraries are *not* for loan. You will therefore either have to be prepared to take notes *or* take photocopies of the pages you need. Virtually all reference libraries operate a chargeable photocopying service – so take some small change with you!

TEST YOURSELF

From the books listed, can you identify where you would look to find out the following:

1. the cost of a full page advertisement in the Radio Times
2. a synonym for the word 'premonition'
3. information on typing layouts
4. the correct way of addressing a letter to the Duke of York
5. a list of the Directors of ICI
6. the name of a good hotel in Inverness
7. the name of the MP for Hyndburn
8. a list of plumbers in your area
9. unemployment figures for last year
10. public holidays in Japan.

CHECK IT YOURSELF

What would you do if

- you cannot find the information you need anywhere
- you cannot find the information you need in time for a specified deadline to be met
- the exact option you are trying to find out about is not available?

Coping with difficulties

The trick to coping with problems is always to put yourself in the shoes of the person who issued the request in the first place. If it was *you* who wanted the information, wouldn't you like to be

– kept informed of progress or problems

– offered alternatives if your original request was not feasible

– warned if the search was taking longer than expected?

In this way you would be able to

- make other suggestions/offer additional help
- decide on other methods of doing what you wanted to do
- make contingency plans or reschedule your plans to cope with any delay.

The golden rule to remember is *keep the person who made the request informed if everything doesn't go smoothly.*

SPECIAL NOTE

Coping with an urgent deadline always puts pressure on all of us. You will operate at maximum speed if you

- keep calm
- *think* the problem through before you start
- *avoid* getting distracted (eg reading all the other interesting entries in a reference book!)
- pass the information on immediately.

SUPPLYING AND PRESENTING INFORMATION

Having ascertained the information you need, you now have to choose how to present it to the recipient. You may decide to give the information verbally or in written form.

Verbally

Only give information verbally if it is:

- short and straightforward and/or
- wanted urgently.

Think about what you are going to say first – your aim is to inform the recipient – not confuse him! Try to avoid giving important *figures* verbally, eg train times, amounts of money – even telephone numbers – unless the person receiving the information can make a note of them immediately.

In written form

Your main decision here is whether the information is better presented in writing or visually. If you write down the information this may be in the form of a short note, a memo or a letter. Details of written methods are given in the chapter on Communicating Information.

However, there are many occasions when presenting information in words is *not* the best method. This is especially true when there are many figures, when comparisons need to be made or when people need to glance at information and understand it quickly. In all these cases it is far better to present the information *visually*.

VISUAL INFORMATION

There are various ways of presenting information visually:

- tables
- line graphs
- bar charts and histograms
- pie charts
- pictograms
- flow charts
- diagrams.

SPECIAL NOTE

Extracting the correct information from books, lists and files is usually not too difficult if you concentrate on what you are doing. However, abstracting information from tables and charts can be more tricky. For this reason this section is designed to give you practice in both presenting information visually and abstracting information from visual sources.

Tables

If you are a typist you will probably know these as 'tabs' and will either love or hate them! But have you ever considered how much easier they are for the reader than detailed written information?

CHECK IT YOURSELF

Look at the information presented in A & B below and then answer the following questions:

1. Which of the following do you find the easier to understand?
2. If you were asked to state the percentage increase for home sales in March, which document would you look at?
3. To which document could even more figures be added, eg totals, quickly and easily?

a Both home and export sales have shown continuous growth to date this year. The January home sales were £125 000, an increase of 3%, in February this increased a further 2.4% as sales reached £128 000. In March we touched £130 000 for the first time, showing an increase of 1.56% on the February figure.
Export sales in January were £75 000, an increase of 1%, in February they were £78 000, a further increase of 4% and in March they were £82 000, yet another increase – this time of 5.13%.

b

	JANUARY		FEBRUARY		MARCH	
	Sales £	%+/–	Sales £	%+/–	Sales £	%+/–
Home Sales	125 000	+3%	128 000	+2.4%	130 000	+1.56%
Exports	75 000	+1%	78 000	+4%	82 000	+5.13%

TEST YOURSELF

1. From the following written information compile a table which will be more easily read by your representatives travelling on the Continent.

   Temperatures vary throughout Europe. The average monthly figures in Celsius for four cities and for four months of the year are given as a guide. In Hamburg it is 2° in January, 13° in April, 23° in July but 13° in October. In Munich it is only 1° in January but this increases to 14° in April, then to 23° in July and back to 13° in October. In Vienna it is the same as Munich in both January and April but is 25° in July and then 14° in October. In Zurich it is the same as Hamburg in January, then 15° in April, and the same as Vienna in July and October.

2 Look at the following table and answer the questions which follow.

Temperatures in France

Average air temperature (Celsius)

	Mar/Apr.	May/June	July/Aug.	Sept/Oct.
Brittany	12.9°C	18.9°C	22.6°C	19.6°C
Loire Valley	13.9°C	21.8°C	25.4°C	18.9°C
Paris	13.2°C	21.1°C	24.3°C	17.8°C
Southern France	16.8°C	24.8°C	29.7°C	22.7°C

Average sea temperature (Celsius)

	May	June	July	Aug.	Sept.	Oct.
Channel Coast	10.8°C	13.3°C	16.2°C	16.9°C	16.2°C	14.4°C
Atlantic Coast	13.9°C	15.4°C	17.4°C	18.9°C	17.8°C	16.4°C
Mediterranean	14.4°C	15.6°C	18.9°C	19.9°C	19.4°C	16.7°C

- Where is the water coldest?
- When is the best month to go swimming in the Atlantic?
- How much hotter is the South of France than Paris in June?
- During which month is there the greatest difference in water temperature between the Atlantic and the Mediterranean?
- Which region has an average air temperature of 20°C between March and October?
- During which two months does the sea temperature on the Channel coast change the most, and by how much?

Line graphs

Line graphs may be composed of either a single line or more than one line, in which case they are called a multiline graph.

Graphs are usually used to show trends – as the lines go up and down the increases and decreases can be seen at a glance.

Line graphs can be used for most kinds of statistical information, eg

- profit figures
- imports and exports
- average prices
- purchases and sales
- population growth/decline
- crime rates.

Creating a line graph

- The x axis goes across (think of ticks and crosses – a cross = x) and y axis goes down. *Both* must be labelled clearly.
- Work out the spacing for your x axis – remember you are starting at the extreme left. This always represents the time period.
- Work out your spacing for the y axis – work in units which will correspond to the squares on your graph paper.
- Remember your spacing must be *even* throughout.
- Insert your labels so they are centred on the mid-point which represents each one.
- Decide on either different colours or different types of line for each line of a multiline graph.
- Put in dots in pencil to mark the points, join up in pencil using a ruler and ink, or colour in, afterwards.
- Don't forget the key – so the reader knows which line represents what.

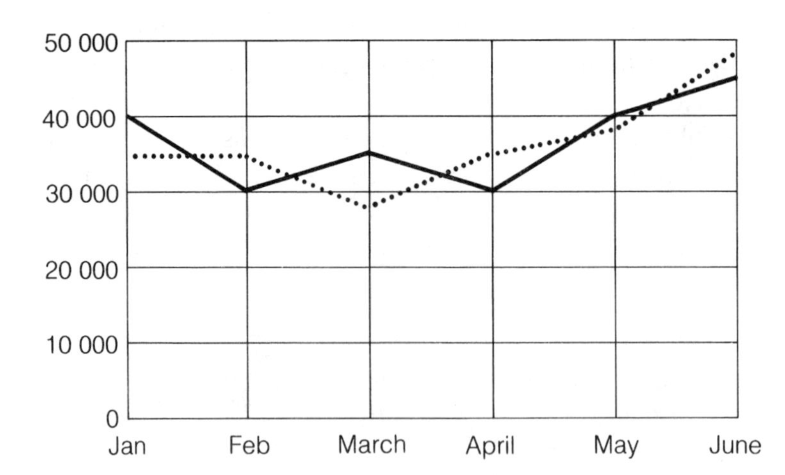

TEST YOURSELF

1 From the graph shown on the previous page can you state:

- which months home sales were at their lowest?
- by how much export sales rose between March and April?
- the two months between which home sales rose the most?
- by how much home sales rose between March and June?
- this company manufactures sunglasses and ski goggles. What trends on the graph support this?

2 Construct a graph to show the output on two machines A and B between July and December. The figures are as follows:

	July	Aug.	Sept.	Oct.	Nov.	Dec.
Machine A	2500	2000	2400	3000	3400	3000
Machine B	4000	3600	3500	3800	4500	4800

3 If you are feeling ambitious construct two more graphs – to record the sea and air temperatures for France as shown in the tables on page 59.

SPECIAL NOTE

Remember – graphs do not have to start at zero. If you are recording very small differences, eg between 52 and 78, then you could start your *y* axis at 50 and end at 80.

Don't forget the *y* axis always shows *units*, the x axis always shows *time*.

Bar charts

In this case individual bars are used instead of continuous lines, but the effect is the same – increases and decreases are shown clearly.

A bar chart can be comprised of single bars or multiple bars. A multiple bar chart compares more than one item (see the next page). Shading or colour can be used but you *must* include a key. The axes are drawn in the same way as for a line graph.

If the bars are joined together at the top of each to form a continuous line then this is known as a **histogram**.

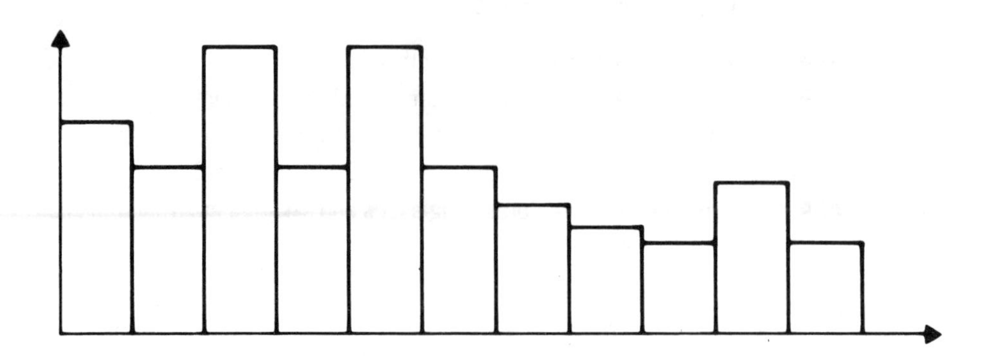

SPECIAL NOTE

Bar charts can be vertical or horizontal. In the latter case the lines are built up across the page from the *y* axis, rather than up the page from the *x* axis.

TEST YOURSELF

1 The following bar chart shows the sales made by two representatives between January and June. From studying it answer the following questions:

- In which two months did Rep A sell the most?
- Which was Rep B's worst month and which was his best month?
- How much did Rep B sell in his worst month?
- In which month was Rep A ill for two weeks?
- The company gives an award to the Rep with the best sales figures. Who is the winner?

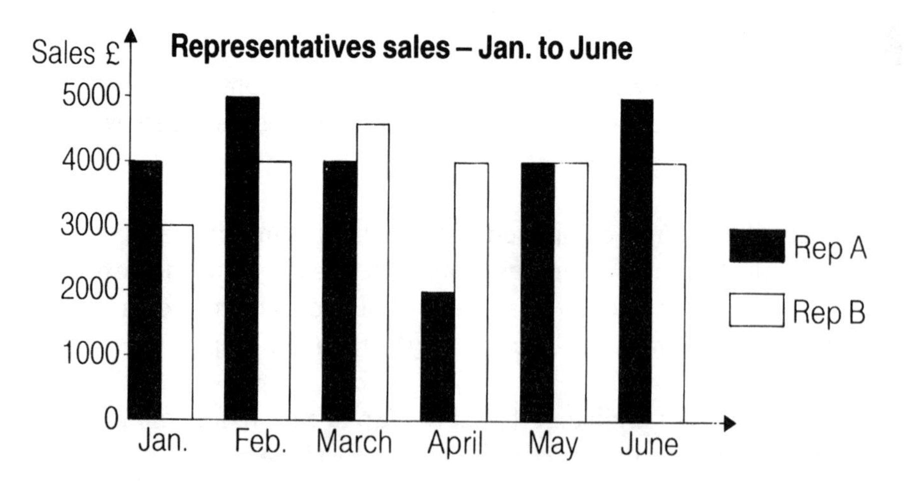

2 Convert the graph you constructed in question 2 on page 61, showing machine output from July to December into a bar chart.

Pie charts

A pie chart is always drawn as a circle with each wedge showing the portion of the whole it represents. The size of the wedge is therefore proportional to the percentage it represents.

The example below shows advertising expenditure for an organisation during November. Note that a clear key is *vital*.

November advertising expenditure by type of media

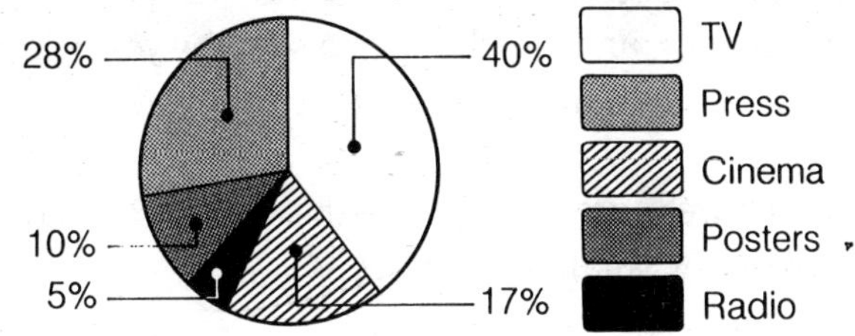

Hints on construction

- Mark off your circle into quarters (like a clock), each will equal 25%.
- Sub-divide one of these quarters if you want smaller amounts – as a rough guide aim for 10%, 10% and 5% and work from there.
- Remember your wedges *must* equal 100%!

SPECIAL NOTE

For an additional effect you can show one wedge slightly separated from the whole, as shown below.

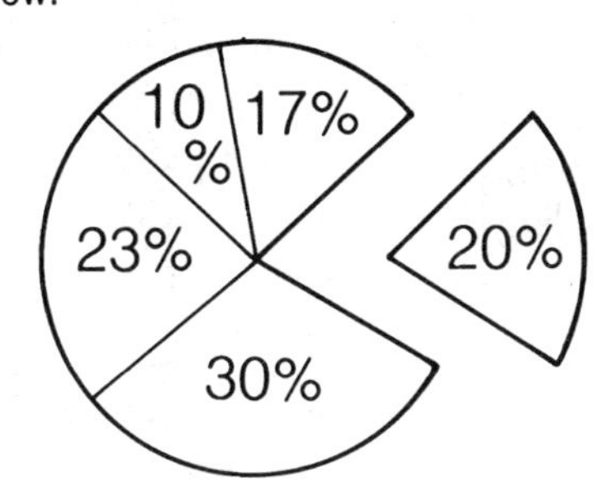

TEST YOURSELF

The following month, December, expenditure had changed as follows:

52% – TV
26% – Press
8% – Posters
3% – Radio
11% – Cinema

Construct the pie chart for that month.

Pictograms

These are pictures drawn to represent an item, and are usually used to illustrate statistics which do not have to be interpreted very precisely, and which may be seen by young people or those not familiar with the type of figures being presented.

Each picture represents a certain quantity, with parts of pictures used to show smaller amounts.

Technology update

With the exception of pictograms, all the different types of visual displays mentioned so far in this chapter can be created on a computer by using a spreadsheet package. (See Business Application Packages chapter, pages 302–333).

Flow charts

Flow charts are used to show the way in which a procedure or system operates or is followed from start to finish. They are commonly used in designing computer programs. In this book an example of a simple flow chart is that on dealing with callers in the chapter Liaising with Callers and Colleagues.

Diagrams

Diagrams are often used to present information. A car user's handbook will contain diagrams showing the controls on the dashboard and parts of the engine. Electronic circuit diagrams and those showing the components of a machine are common in industry. A diagram is a useful way of indicating the layout of furniture in a room, but should be drawn to scale so that the size of the furniture is accurately represented in relation to the size of the room.

SECTION REVIEW

Having completed this section you should now be able to:

1 Identify and select a variety of reference sources.

2 Describe the use and features of common reference books.

3 Identify suitable sources of information for particular enquiries.

4 Explain suitable alternative forms of action to take if you encounter difficulties.

5 Identify, select and communicate suitable alternatives where appropriate.

6 Explain the importance of operating within a deadline.

7 Abstract and present information in a suitable format.

REVIEW QUIZ

NB Your challenge in this section is to find out any answers you do not know!

True or false?

1 Reference libraries also keep back copies of magazines and periodicals.

2 Graphs must start at zero at the bottom left-hand side.

3 Roget's Thesaurus gives details of prominent British companies.

4 The y axis of a graph is the vertical axis.

5 If you want information about National Insurance rates you should contact the Department of Health.

Complete the blanks . . .

6 .... is an interactive Viewdata system.

7 .... is a reference book which gives information on famous people in Britain who are still living.

8 If the bars on a bar chart are joined together at the top to form a continuous line then this is known as a ....

Work it out

9 **a** Your boss has asked you to quickly find out the following. What sources are available to you in each case?

- i the exact time
- ii the up-to-date exchange rate of pounds sterling for American dollars
- iii the price of a car road fund licence
- iv the date(s) of next year's Motor Show
- v the innoculations needed for people visiting Nigeria

b An important visitor from abroad is visiting your firm, together with his wife. His wife's family come from Bath and she wants to visit the city for two days during her stay. How would you find out:

- i the name of a suitable hotel
- ii the opening times/days and names of local historic buildings
- iii the name of a good restaurant
- iv the times and connections of suitable trains

(It is suggested that students living in Bath substitute the city of Nottingham as an alternative.)

c Your boss has lost the key to his desk drawer. In his drawer is his passport – and he is due at the airport in 2 hours' time. How many alternative forms of action can you think of to solve this problem (apart from breaking open his desk!)

10 You work for an ice cream manufacturer. Sales of the three types of ice cream produced are given below for the last twelve months in units sold.

a Select a suitable form of visual presentation for this information and prepare this neatly and clearly.

	Jan.	Feb.	Mar.	Apr.	May	Jun.	Jul.	Aug.	Sep.	Oct.	Nov.	Dec.
Vanilla	4200	4000	4100	4500	5200	7400	9200	8700	5100	5000	4000	4400
Chocolate Chip	3000	2600	2800	3000	3500	5200	6000	5400	3400	3600	2800	3200
Raspberry Ripple	2600	3200	4000	3600	3800	6100	5800	6800	4400	4400	3100	2800

b From the information given above, and now shown on your visual presentation, answer the following questions:

- How much ice-cream was sold in April?
- Which is the best selling flavour?
- Which flavour often didn't follow the same trend as the other two varieties?
- Which months did it vary from the main trend, and in which direction?
- During which month was the most ice-cream sold?
- What type of summer do you think we had that year?
- Why do you think sales fell in September and yet rose again in December?
- How much ice-cream, in *each* variety, was sold altogether that year?
- What are the monthly average sales figures for each variety? (Round to the nearest whole number.)

Weight

Do you know how much you weigh? And, if so, do you know your weight in stones and pounds or in kilogrammes?

It is likely you answered stones and pounds, even though in school and college you were probably taught metric weights.

Britain, unfortunately, uses a mixture of weights at the moment. You can buy fruit and vegetables in pounds, and weigh a parcel for posting in kilogrammes (otherwise you can't work out the cost of sending it from the Post Office chart).

Metric weights

You should already know the following!

1000 grammes = 1 kilogramme
1000 kilogrammes = 1 metric **tonne** (note the spelling!)

You should also know that grammes are abbreviated to **g** and kilogrammes to **kg**.

Imperial weights

16 ounces (**oz**) = 1 pound (**lb**)
14 pounds (lb) = 1 stone
8 stones = 1 hundredweight (**cwt**)
20 hundredweights = 1 **ton** (note the difference in spelling!)

CHECK IT YOURSELF

- Americans always give their weights in pounds, which can be confusing to the British. If you met an American who said he weighed 140 lb, this would be equal to 10 stone (140 ÷ 14).

  If the figure (in pounds) won't divide accurately by 14, the remainder left are pounds, therefore 156 lb = 11 stone 2 lb.

  How much, then, will the following people weigh in stones and pounds? (Forget your calculator for these, it will mess you up completely as it will give you the answer in tenths, not fourteenths!)

  188 lb   115 lb   162 lb   137 lb

- From the weights tables above it is easy to work out other quantities by using multiplication, eg ounces in a stone = 16 × 14 = 224.

  Can you work out:

  – how many pounds there are in a hundredweight?
  – how many pounds there are in a ton?

Converting from imperial to metric

If you are told a parcel weighs 25 lb, yet the Post Office rates are given in kilogrammes you will obviously have to convert your imperial weight to metric.

You do this by simply **dividing by 2.2**. Always round your answer to either whole kilogrammes or to three decimal places to give the answer in kilogrammes and grammes, eg

25 lb in kg $\rightarrow$ 25 ÷ 2.2 = 11.363636 = 11 kg or 11 kg 364 g

TEST YOURSELF 1

Convert the following to kg:

1 16 lb
2 84 lb
3 62 lb
4 160 lb
5 52 lb

Convert the following to kg and g:

6 18 lb
7 92 lb
8 146 lb
9 22 lb
10 39 lb

Converting from metric to imperial

In this case you **multiply by 2.2**. Normally you will want your answer to the nearest pound (round to lose the decimals). At the most you will want your answer to one decimal place – but remember that this does *not* represent the number of ounces! It represents tenths of a pound, eg

21 kg in lb $\rightarrow$ 21 × 2.2 = 46.2 lb = 46 lb or
46 (and two tenths of a pound) = 46.2 lb

TEST YOURSELF 2

Convert the following to the nearest pound:

1 12 kg
2 27 kg
3 183 kg
4 16 kg
5 92 kg

Convert the following to pounds with one decimal place:

6 32 kg
7 19 kg
8 137 kg
9 62 kg
10 19 kg

Estimating

You will have noticed by now that a kilogramme is just over *twice* as heavy as a pound, and a pound is nearly *half* as heavy as a kilogramme! Because of these relationships you can become quite good at *estimating* the converted weight – to give someone who doesn't know a good idea of approximately how many pounds or kg their parcel (or whatever) will weigh.

TEST YOURSELF 3

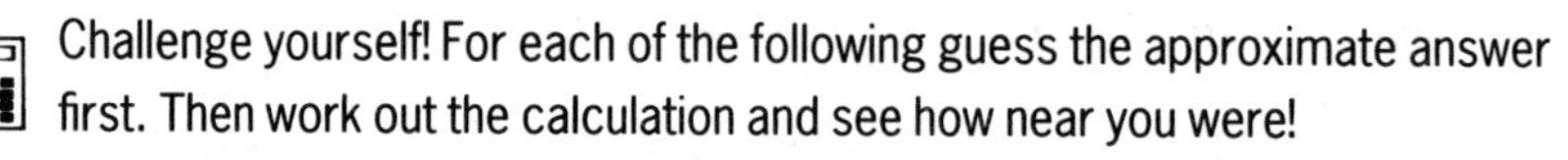

Challenge yourself! For each of the following guess the approximate answer first. Then work out the calculation and see how near you were!

Convert lb to kg: (rather less than half)		**Convert kg to lb:** (rather more than double)	
1	9 lb	**6**	5 kg
2	110 lb	**7**	20 kg
3	58 lb	**8**	108 kg
4	22 lb	**9**	82 kg
5	95 lb	**10**	12.5 kg

Simple sum trick

How to multiply a two-digit number by 11 in your head and stun your friends!

Add the two digits together and put the result in the middle, eg

$43 \times 11 \rightarrow 4 + 3 = 7 \rightarrow 473$
$62 \times 11 \rightarrow 6 + 2 = 8 \rightarrow 682$

If the two digits added together come to more than 9, add on the 1 to the first digit, eg

$76 \times 11 \rightarrow 7 + 6 = 13 \rightarrow 7\,(13)\,6 \rightarrow 836$
$98 \times 11 \rightarrow 9 + 8 = 17 \rightarrow 9\,(17)\,8 \rightarrow 1078$

Practise a bit before you try to impress anyone!

Reprographics

What is reprography?

Reprography refers to making copies of documents so that everyone who needs to have a copy can have one. Without being able to reproduce documents quickly and accurately an organisation's communications network would suffer.

REPROGRAPHIC SYSTEMS

Documents may be **duplicated** or **copied**.

The main difference is that all duplicating systems need a **master** to be made of the original document first. This *must* be carefully checked against the original before any printing is done.

Normally copying is carried out on a **photocopier**. The original document is used so that once this has been proofread carefully, no further checking is required.

SPECIAL NOTE

A vital factor all organisations must consider is *cost*. This can be broken down in various ways:

- the cost of the equipment itself (which may be bought, rented or leased)
- the cost of materials required – mainly paper
- the copy cost, if this is an extra item
- the cost of machinery repairs or maintenance contracts
- wastage!!
- unauthorised copying for private use.

Throughout this section you should take special note of *all* tips to keep costs *down*.

DUPLICATING SYSTEMS

There are two main duplicating systems which are in use in offices today, **ink** duplicating and **offset litho** duplicating.

Offset litho is the most commonly used because the quality is comparable with outside printing at a fraction of the cost, although colour work is difficult. Ink duplicators are generally used today only by very small organisations and some educational establishments.

TECHNOLOGY UPDATE

Modern technological developments have affected duplicating in the type of machines on the market and the functions they can carry out automatically.

Many machines are now **electronic**. This means they contain a silicon chip and some routine operations are pre-programmed into the machine to save the operator having to do them manually.

Comparison chart

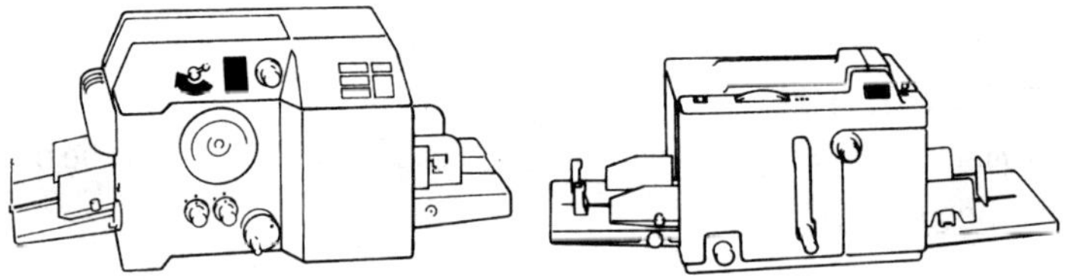

	Offset litho duplicating	**Ink duplicating**
Master	Paper or metal plate	Wax, scanner or memory (sensitive) stencil
Methods of producing masters	Typing direct onto paper plates* Photocopying onto paper plates Photographically onto metal plates Printing out onto paper plates from a computer or word processor*	Typing direct onto wax stencils* Scanning using an electronic scanner Printing out onto memory stencils from a computer or word processor

*carbon ribbon essential

*ribbon must be disengaged or removed

Paper	Bond paper (offset quality)	Semi-absorbent duplicating paper.
Other materials required	Ink, etch, fountain solution, blanket wash, blanket reviver, offset corrector	Ink, correcting fluid (red for wax, blue for scanner stencils), blotting folders for storage, stylus pens and backing plates if drawing direct onto stencil.
Principle of operation	Oil and water do not mix. The image on the plate is greasy. After the plate is placed on the machine, water is applied to dampen the non-image areas. Ink then only sticks to the areas which are not damp. The image is offset onto a blanket cylinder and the paper is fed between this cylinder and an impression roller. The reverse print of a reverse print is the right way round.	Holes are cut in an otherwise ink-proof wax stencil. The stencil is placed on the duplicator and ink is forced through the holes onto semi-absorbent paper. An electronic scanner makes a stencil by 'reading' (via a photo-electric cell) an original which is placed at one end of a long cylinder. It transmits a signal to a stylus which cuts a hole in the stencil at the other end of the

		cylinder every time it sees a black area. Because the black areas are the print the stencil becomes a 'cut out' replica of the original.
Artwork	Excellent – will produce line drawings easily and photographs via a metal plate.	Needs a scanner to reproduce line drawings. Photographs are unsuitable for reproduction.
Advantages	Superb quality at a low price Metal plates can be stored indefinitely Large quantities from one metal plate Good quality copy paper	Relatively good quality reproduction Cheap copy paper Relatively easy to operate Stencils may be stored and reused
Disadvantages	Machinery quite expensive Not economical for short runs Operator needs training to use and clean machine Colour work difficult and time consuming	Reproduction not suitable for promotional work Colours very difficult Absorbent paper not very good quality and unsuitable for handwriting

Operating a duplicator

The only way you can learn how to use a duplicator is to be shown properly and to practise.

However, the following are tips to help you.

1. Listen and watch *carefully* while the process is being explained and demonstrated.
2. Remember that paper is usually **fanned** before being placed in the feed tray to prevent it going through in clumps.
3. Trial copies are *essential* to avoid wastage. Only when you are certain that the lining up of the text *and* the quality of the reproduction cannot be improved should you start printing.
4. If a number of trial copies are required then instead of using new paper you can run the old trial copies through again on the reverse.
5. At the end of printing remove the copies to a clear and clean area.
6. **Always ask if you are unsure of anything!**

Safety first

- *Never* poke about inside the machine for any reason.
- Find out where the **stop** switch is for use in an emergency.
- *Never* operate a duplicator whilst wearing long, dangling jewellery, a scarf or loose tie. Keep long hair back off your face.

CHECK IT YOURSELF

All machines can go wrong – often when you are in the middle of a rush job! The type of fault which may occur will depend on the kind of duplicator you are using.

- Discuss with your tutor the type of common faults which may occur on the machine you will be using.
- Refer to the instruction manual and note down the action to take.
- Make a special note of those faults you must *not* attempt to rectify yourself.

PHOTOCOPIERS

Today most photocopiers:

- use **plain** paper, which is cheaper. These photocopiers will also accept labels, offset paper plates etc.
- are **flat bed**, a rubberised lid is lifted to show a transparent glass plate. Books and other large items can be laid open on the glass for copying.

However, the facilities offered, the speed they operate at and their cost can vary enormously.

Large (more expensive) copiers usually

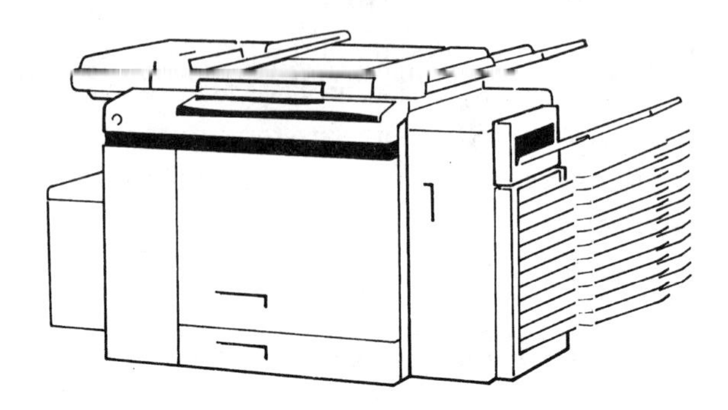

- Accept various sizes of paper.
- Accept card, labels, offset paper plates and OHP transparencies.
- Print quickly.
- Take originals placed in a document feeder so that they are fed in *automatically* one by one.
- Enlarge and reduce – with a variety of ratios available.
- Have an interrupt function.
- Have at least one auxiliary paper tray (sometimes called a by-pass function).
- Collate at the touch of a button (and may staple as well, if required).
- Have adjustments for copy density (to compensate for very light or dark originals) *or* have the ability to 'scan' an original and make automatic density adjustments.
- Have an automatic duplexing* facility.

In addition, some machines

- Print in two colours, eg black and red.

*Duplexing = printing on both sides of the paper.

- Allow special user numbers to be programmed in against a specified allocation of copies. Each user must key in his or her own number before copying can commence and the machine will refuse to print more than the allocation.
- Print out the usage for each user over a given period and the total cost.
- Insert special covers and dividers at pre-set intervals in a collated document. Special jobs such as this can often be programmed into the machine so that they can be repeated at the touch of a button.
- Have a self-diagnostic panel to signal what is wrong so that the engineer can be informed which parts are required before his visit.

CHECK IT YOURSELF

How does the photocopier you use compare against the list? Check each function you can carry out on your machine and compare your list with other members of your group.

Bear in mind that the very largest copiers are only cost effective in a centralised printroom where thousands of copies are done each month.

Technology update

Two main types of advance are being made in relation to copiers.

'Smart' copiers

- These contain their own microprocessor. They can store in memory: form layouts, letter and memo headings, signatures, graphics, and standard paragraphs.
- The operator can recall any of these at the touch of a button to print out on the paper in addition to the text of the original.
- These copiers can also be networked (linked) to computers and word processors and receive and transmit information to remote locations.

Colour copying

- Very expensive colour copiers are now on the market but are not yet common even in large organisations. Generally they are offered as a print 'service' by external printers or graphic designers.
- The machines will accept a range of coloured originals – posters, photographs and even slides and copy these onto A4, A3, A2 or even A1 paper.

Both types of copier owe their existence to new developments in laser technology.

SPECIAL NOTE

Be careful what you copy or you could be breaking the law! The Copyright, Designs and Patents Act 1988 covers authors, playwrights and composers against people 'infringing copy'. In plain English this means that you are not allowed to borrow a published document or book and photocopy it, rather than buy your own copy!

There are some exceptions – schools and colleges are allowed to copy a very small amount out of some set books without infringing copyright. Some books can be purchased which are *not* covered by copyright (the same is true of some articles in magazines) and these can be copied freely. The activity pack which accompanies this Handbook is covered by special copyright conditions so that tutors can photocopy any activities they need without breaking the law.

Copying costs

- Most copiers are rented for a specific sum each month. This means they can be traded in for a more up-to-date or faster model if required.
- The rental will include such items as **toner** (the 'ink' used in photocopiers which usually comes as a black powder) and the **silicone oil**. Servicing of the machine will also be included.
- Machine part replacement through damage and normal wear and tear will have to be paid for by the company.
- As well as the rental the company will have to pay a cost per copy made of about 1.1p.
- Paper also has to be paid for by the company.

SPECIAL NOTE

Assume an organisation pays 1p for each photocopy produced. Paper is £3 a ream (500 sheets). If someone makes 100 faulty copies (for whatever reason) in a week the cost to the organisation of their mistakes is £1.60.

If 20 people do this each week the cost now becomes £32 and if this goes on all year the organisation will have to pay £1664 more than it needs to for photocopying!

All this is *waste* – money simply thrown away.

Tips for photocopying

1. Place the original *face down* on the glass.
2. The original *must* be clean. Dirty marks will show up on the copy. You can use liquid paper to whiten any dirty areas but it is far better to use the special photocopy correction fluid which never sticks to the glass.
3. Learn to recognise unsuitable quality documents and refer these to the originator.
4. The glass must be kept spotless.
5. If you are photocopying a small (less than A4) original onto A4 paper, put a sheet of white A4 paper *behind* your original.
6. Check your alignment is perfectly accurate with the scale on the machine.
7. If your copy is too light or too dark then alter your copy density control. Some machines do this automatically. This will also need adjusting if you are copying from coloured paper.
8. If you are doing a long run take *one* copy first and check it before taking more.
9. If you are photocopying an A5 original on to A4 paper then photocopy it *once*. Put the original next to the copy (side by side) and then run through half the number you need and cut the A4 copies in half.
10. If you have made a 'paste-up' to be copied use the *minimum* amount of sticky tape on the original, or, better still, use double-sided sticky tape or mounting adhesive.
11. If you are photocopying a thick book, replace the lid and press down (gently) to make sure no light can get in where the pages meet in the centre.

12 *Don't* take an extra copy 'just for spare'!
13 *Don't* use the copier for personal copies unless you have permission.

Machine care

1 *Don't* try to refill the paper tray unless you have been shown how to do so.
2 If the machine signals a paper jam, more toner required or any other fault, then call the main operator. Do *not* try to mend it yourself, unless you have been shown the *correct* procedure as detailed in the operating manual.
3 If the machine will not work *ask for help*.
4 *Never* put anything sharp on the glass which may scratch it.
5 Keep any liquids well away from the copier.

SPECIAL NOTE

Photocopiers are normally switched on *once* at the start of the day and kept running until the end of the day. Most machines take several minutes to warm up when they are first switched on.

Safety first

- Any copier should have a free flow of air all round it. *Never* push it flat against a wall.
- *Never* open the door and poke about inside it, for *any* reason.
- If you get toner on your hands or clothes wash it off with *cold* water (hot water makes it set).

Copier records

To monitor usage most copiers will only work when a 'key' is inserted in the machine. (Don't always expect this to look like an ordinary key – it may be like a small plastic box.) Either the machine, or the key itself, has a counter which goes up by one each time a copy is made. The counter therefore always shows the current number of copies taken.

Many organisations balance this number against a **photocopy record book** which will show headings such as date, name, department and total allowance (usually per month). The operator keeps a check on usage and notifies those who are coming close to their limit.

As mentioned earlier, more sophisticated machines can be programmed with an allowance per user, and will give a print-out of the copies taken, and by whom. In this case, a manual record is not required.

Multi-page documents

Multi-page documents, eg reports and sales presentations, can be collated automatically on most photocopiers. If a duplicator is used then a separate collating machine may be purchased.

- Each page should be *numbered*. The numbers may be placed at the left, middle or right hand side of the page – top or bottom. The placement must be consistent throughout the document.
- The pages must be assembled in the correct order before collating is started! Back-to-back documents need special care.
- The first document out of the collator should be checked carefully to ensure that
  - all pages are included
  - all pages are in the correct order.
- Random checking of subsequent documents is strongly advised.
- On completion the document may be stapled or bound (see next section).

SPECIAL NOTE

There is no worse advert for your firm than a document with pages out of order (or even upside down!) And the worst job in the world is de-collating dozens of multi-page documents and having to start again. Five minutes checking in the early stages can save hours of very boring and unpleasant work later!

ANCILLARY PRINT-ROOM EQUIPMENT

A range of equipment, large and small, is available to help print-room staff who have to compile multi-page documents.

Collating Machine
- Automatically sorts pages into sets. The simplest type are similar to a vertical or horizontal arrangement of trays and a set of each page is put into each tray. The machine will then automatically take one page from each tray to make up a set.

Jogger
- these 'jog' a set of papers until they are correctly aligned for stapling or binding. Some collators also incorporate a jogger.

Binders
- there are two main types of binders:
  - **Comb binders** automatically put a spiral binding on a set of documents. Various widths of combs are available. The combs can be cut easily to fit any size booklet.
  - **Thermal binders** fasten the pages and cover together by heat. The covers can be bought in a variety of sizes, designs, colours and widths. Down the inside of the spine is an adhesive which melts when placed in the machine.

Laminator
- this puts a protective film over a document which will be handled frequently or placed on a wall for general reference.

Guillotine
- cuts several pages at once – up to several thousand with an industrial guillotine. A guard permanently protects the blade.

Rotary cutter
- more precise than a guillotine but cuts only a few pages at once. A small blade, shaped like a wheel, is pushed along the edge to be cut. Again this is protected by plastic on either side.

Stapler

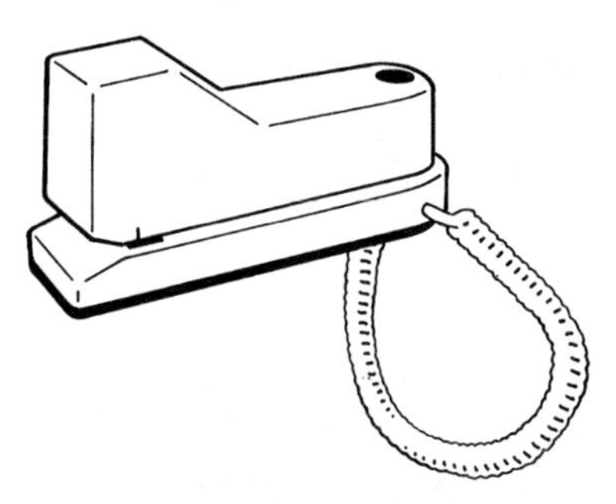

- may be manual or electric. Most fasten with a **temporary** (the prongs of the staple point outwards) or **permanent** (the prongs point inwards) fastening.
- most documents should be stapled diagonally about 1½ cm from the top left-hand corner. Text must *not* be obscured on *any page*.

Crimper

- a new variation on the stapler. Pages are crimped together in a crease so they stick together. Only about six pages can be held together and, if separated later, the pages look messy.

Punch

- can be normal or heavy duty (heavy duty take more pages at once). All have an alignment scale or arrow in the centre. The middle of the pages *must* be aligned to the centre arrow so that all pages are punched in *exactly* the same place.

Safety first

Draw up a list of safety precautions for someone operating an electric stapler for the first time.

SECTION REVIEW

Having completed this section, you should now be able to:

1. Describe the most commonly used reprographic methods and materials used.
2. Operate reprographic equipment safely and in accordance with recommended procedures.
3. Outline the range of functions available on modern photocopiers.
4. Produce copies as required quickly and accurately using a duplicator and/or photocopier.
5. Explain the importance of keeping wastage to a minimum and list the methods by which this can be achieved.

6 State the relevance of copyright law to reprography.

7 Collate and fasten multi-page documents correctly.

REVIEW QUIZ

True or false?

1 An electronic scanner produces stencils for ink duplicating

2 Offset paper plates can be produced on a photocopier.

3 Duplexing means automatic collating of documents.

4 Toner should be washed off hands or clothes with hot water.

5 Always switch off a photocopier after use to prevent overheating.

Complete the blanks . . .

6 All duplicating systems require a .... to be made from the original.

7 Dirty marks on a document which is going to be photocopied should be removed by using ....

8 A machine which puts a protective film over documents is called a ....

Work it out

9 A photocopier costs £50 a month to rent. During the month 15 000 copies are made at a cost of 1p each. Paper costs £3 a ream. What is the *total* cost of photocopying per month?

10 Your organisation has an offset litho duplicator and a photocopier. The offset litho duplicator uses paper plates at a cost of 18p each. These are produced on the photocopier. Paper is £2.50 a ream. Copies on the photocopier cost 1p each and paper is also £2.50 a ream.

Your boss is concerned that people are using the copier when the offset machine would be cheaper and wants to know the *number* of copies at which it is more cost effective for staff to put their work in to be duplicated. What number is it?

NUMERACY GUIDE 4

Decimals – multiplication and division

In the numeracy guide on pages 22–25 you were calculating decimals and rounding, and you multiplied and divided a decimal number. This is often necessary in business as not everything is multiplied or divided by whole numbers.

Multiplication

The number of decimal places in the answer must always be the *total* of the decimal places shown in the calculation, eg:

14.25	×	15.1	=	215.175
(2 decimal places)		(1 decimal place)		(3 decimal places)
16.782	×	3.67	=	61.58994
(3 decimal places)		(2 decimal places)		(5 decimal places)

To do this *without* a calculator:

- take out all the decimals and multiply the two numbers, eg 9.87 × 4.3 = 987 × 43 = 42441
- count the total number of decimal places in the two original numbers – 9.87 has 2, 4.3 has 1. Therefore 3 in total.
- count back from the *right* of the figure and insert the point 4 2 . 4 4 1

TEST YOURSELF 1

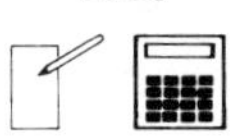

Do these first without a calculator and then check your answers:

1 5.8 × 6.23
2 17 × 2.855
3 15.23 × 14.85
4 17.8 × 16.23
5 6.372 × 8.42
6 0.21 × 14.35

Rounding

Of course you may be asked to give your answer to a specified number of decimal places. In that case you will have to round your answers up or down according to the figure you reached.

TEST YOURSELF 2

Convert all the answers you reached before to two decimal places by rounding.

Division

This is made much easier if the **divisor** (the number you are dividing by) is made into a whole number by multiplying it by 10, 100 or 1000, etc. The number being divided – the **dividend** – must then be multiplied by the same number so it is still in the same ratio to the divisor, eg:

To find the value of 27.71 ÷ 1.63, without a calculator:

- convert the divisor (1.63) to a whole number by multiplying by 100
  1.63 × 100 = 163
- multiply the dividend (27.71) by the same number
  27.71 × 100 = 2771
- find the answer by normal long division

```
       17
    ______
163 | 2771
      163
      ____
      1141
      1141
      ____
         –
      ____
```

TEST YOURSELF 3

Calculate these first without a calculator and then check them on a calculator.

1 11.2 ÷ 0.8 =
2 25.2 ÷ 1.4 =
3 34.8 ÷ 0.3 =
4 299.2 ÷ 2.2 =
5 20.40 ÷ 1.36 =
6 328.8 ÷ 2.74 =

Time

Most timetables today are written using the 24-hour clock so that there is no confusion between am and pm. Because you may be given a time to look up using the 12-hour clock it is important that you can convert the times quickly and accurately. If you convert 1700 hours to 7 o'clock there will be problems for everyone!

- Convert **to** the 24-hour clock by **adding 12**.
- Convert **from** the 24-hour clock by **subtracting 12**.

SPECIAL NOTE

Many people have problems expressing midnight in 24 hour clock time. Digital clocks and displays usually show this as 0000 hours. One minute past midnight is then 0001 and so on. However, it is usually clearer when speaking to refer to midnight as 2400 hours.

TEST YOURSELF 4

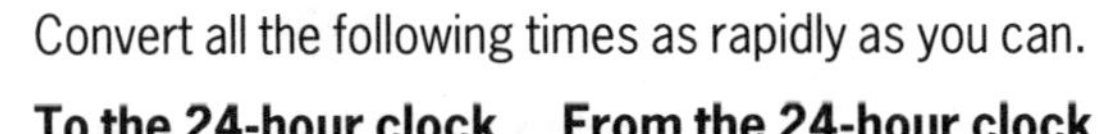

Convert all the following times as rapidly as you can.

To the 24-hour clock		From the 24-hour clock	
1	6 am	**10**	1600 hours
2	8 pm	**11**	0230 hours
3	5.15 pm	**12**	2120 hours
4	10.30 pm	**13**	1745 hours
5	8.15 am	**14**	0950 hours
6	3.45 pm	**15**	1916 hours
7	11.45 pm	**16**	1410 hours
8	5.20 am	**17**	2020 hours
9	7.40 pm	**18**	1802 hours

Travelling times

In addition to converting times you may also need to be able to work out how long journeys may take. This usually means adding or subtracting times.

However, you *must* remember that

60 minutes = 1 hour
24 hours = 1 day
7 days = 1 week

This may seem very obvious but, as with pounds and stones, it makes your calculator useless for working out most times, eg:

- A journey comprises a bus ride of 24 minutes, a train journey of 3 hours and 26 minutes and a taxi ride of about 20 minutes. Allowing an extra 30 minutes for walking/waiting etc how long does the whole journey take?

  24 mins + 3 hrs 26 mins + 20 mins + 30 mins = 4 hours 40 minutes
- A train departs at 9.50 am and arrives at 3.22 pm, how long does the journey take?

  Convert to 24-hour clock times (it's easier) and then do as a subtraction:

  1522 – 0950 = 15.22
  –09.50
  5.32

  Remember: when you 'borrow' from the hours column, you have 60 minutes.

  Put the full stop in to divide the hours and the minutes and remember that the minutes column can only go up to 60!

TEST YOURSELF 5

How long do each of the following journeys last?

1. Car 2 hrs 5 mins, wait at airport 35 mins, plane journey 2 hrs 10 mins, car journey from airport 47 mins.
2. Train 1 hr 45 mins, walking 28 mins, tube 32 mins, walking 7 minutes.
3. Car journey 5 hours 20 minutes, two stops – 22 minutes and 36 minutes, parking/walking 16 minutes.
4. Car 17 minutes, train 1 hour 19 minutes, train 2 hours 43 minutes, car 25 minutes plus an extra 30 minutes for waiting, changing trains etc.
5. Car 68 minutes, wait at airport 40 minutes, plane flight 33 hours 15 mins plus two refuelling stops of 45 minutes each, customs clearance etc 30 minutes, car 2 hours 18 minutes.
6. A train leaves at 0745 and arrives at 1420 hours.
7. A car leaves at 11.35 am and arrives at 7.25 in the evening.
8. A plane leaves London at 4.15 pm and arrives at 2.30 am (British time) the day after.
9. A bus leaves at 10.55 am and arrives at 3.10 pm.
10. A plane leaves London at 6.50 pm and arrives at 12.30 am (British time) two days later.

SPECIAL NOTE

The term British time has been used because anyone travelling a long distance will travel through various time zones and the time of arrival usually quoted is the time it will be at their destination. Time zones are covered on pages 260.

Information processing

SPECIAL NOTE

Information on computers is covered in two separate chapters:

- An Introduction to Information Technology (pages 90–111)
- Business Application Packages, which covers word processing, spreadsheets and database packages, (pages 302–333).

You should read the Introduction to Information Technology, *before* you begin to work on any computers *or* word processors.

The Business Application Packages chapter (pages 302–333) should be used for *reference*. Read the information on a particular type of package, eg word processing, just before you start to use it, so that you are familiar with the general principles of:

- how it works
- what it can do
- its main uses
- the main terms and functions used in its operation.

You will find references to the Business Applications Packages chapter throughout this book. These references occur when you have been involved in doing a particular job manually which can also be carried out by using a specific type of computer package.

INTRODUCTION TO INFORMATION TECHNOLOGY

Thousands of computers are used every day in business because they can undertake a wide range of routine office tasks very quickly and very accurately.

Although computers come in a variety of shapes and sizes, the majority found in offices are **micro** computers – small stand-alone systems which function independently.

CHECK IT YOURSELF

You are probably already familiar with micro computers either because:

- you have used them at school or college or
- you have a computer at home.

You may, however, have only seen computer equipment in use in shops and stores and have never actually operated one.

The actual equipment is called the **hardware.** If you went into a shop to buy a micro computer, could you identify the different kinds of equipment (or hardware) you would need to buy to have a complete system?

COMPUTER HARDWARE

A computer system includes:

- a **keyboard**
- a **screen** – called a **visual display unit** (**VDU**)
- a **central processing unit** (**CPU**)
- a **disk drive**
- a **printer**

Some office installations may share a disk drive or printer between a number of terminals, but the principle of operation is still the same.

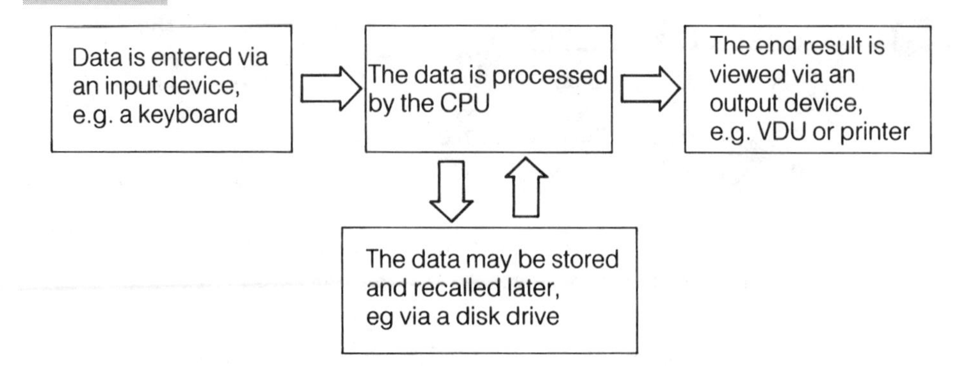

Memory

The amount of data which can be processed by a computer at any one time is determined by the size of its **memory**. The memory size is measured by the number of characters or **bytes** which the computer can store at one time.

The memory capacity of *micro* computers is measured in Kilobytes (K). (Kilo = 1000.) Therefore a small games computer with a 64K memory can handle approximately 64 000 characters at once.

TEST YOURSELF

Most business micro computers have a base memory size of 640K. Optional extended memory can add up to a further 1024K. How many characters can be stored at one time in

a base memory

b extended memory?

RAM

The proper term for a computer's 'working' memory is **RAM – random access memory** – so-called because you can access any part of your data as you are working and overwrite it with something new if you want to.

RAM only operates on a *temporary* basis – when the computer is *switched off* any data held in RAM is lost. For this reason you need a **backing store** – usually a disk drive – so that data can be saved until it is next required.

SPECIAL NOTE

Very large, powerful computer installations, which are situated centrally to cope with all an organisation's requirements, are called **mainframe** computers.

Office staff have access to the mainframe computer through a terminal (usually comprising a keyboard and a VDU) on their desk.

Memory capacity of *mainframe* computers is measured in:

- megabytes (Mega = 1 million)
- gigabytes (Giga = 1000 million)

TEST YOURSELF

1 At an interview for a job you are told that the organisation has a '64 Meg mainframe computer'. Approximately how many characters can this computer store simultaneously?

2 In offices the main method of inputting data is by a keyboard but there are other ways. How many other methods can you think of before you read the following text?

Input devices

How many methods did you think of? Alternatives to a keyboard include:

Bar code readers
- These are now a common sight in many large stores to put sales information into computerised electronic cash registers.

Touch sensitive screens
- Found in banks, hospitals and other organisations where personnel who are not typists need to input data. The operator just touches the screen next to the option he or she wants.

A mouse
- A mouse is a small box which can be moved around the work surface to make the cursor on the screen move. Again they are useful for non-typists and are also sometimes used with graphics programs.

Light pens
- These can be used to wipe over bar codes or – more often – to produce graphics on screen by 'drawing' with a pen to create pictures and designs. Design using a computer is called CAD – Computer Aided Design.

Digitisers
- These enable sophisticated graphics to be produced on a computer by

converting drawings, photographs and video stills to a series of digital impulses which can be shown on the screen.

Graphics tablets
- These are used extensively in CAD as they enable shapes to be drawn on them (with a light pen) and also enable the operator to undertake other functions automatically, eg changing the angle of the drawing.

Optical character recognition (OCR)
- Machines which automatically read text are also known as document readers. These automatically scan a document and put the text into the computer. This saves the time which would be spent keying it in.

Computer maintenance

To work well a computer *must* be kept clean. Various cleaning materials are available including

- screen wipes (to reduce static which attracts dust to the screen)
- keyboard brushes (to remove the fluff which gets trapped between the keys)
- special cleaning foam for the machine itself. *Never* use anything other than products specially made for computers.

TEST YOURSELF

Having identified a variety of devices to input information into a computer, how many methods of *output* can you think of – ways in which the processed information is eventually produced, before you read the following section?

Output devices

The two most common output devices are, of course, a VDU and a printer. Despite talk of the paperless office, most people want to see processed information on a piece of paper so that they can refer to it whenever they want, make notes on it, amend it and so on. In computer terms this is called taking a **hard copy** and there are a variety of computer printers on the market. The type purchased will depend on many factors including copy quality required, whether graphics are used and so on.

Other methods of output include:

Plotters

- These are used to produce graphs, charts and a variety of other graphics. Colour can be used (although the number is limited except on very expensive machines) and some can produce two-dimensional drawings.

Computer output microfilm (COM)

- The computer output can automatically be produced as microfilm or microfiche so that large amounts of information can be stored in a small area.

Alternatively the processed information can be transmitted to other computers via a communications link, eg a **LAN (local area network)** or a **WAN (wide area network)**.

COMPUTER PRINTERS

There are two main types of printers:

- **impact printers** (such as dot matrix or daisywheel, where direct contact is made with the paper)
- **non-impact printers** (such as ink jet or laser, where ink is placed on the paper without any contact being made).

Types of printer

Impact printers

Dot matrix

- The image is formed by a series of dots placed on the paper. Quality is only fair but printing is quite rapid. Quality can be improved on most dot matrix printers by using the NLQ (near letter quality) function which means the printer goes over each character twice to improve the density.
- Graphics can also be printed with a dot matrix printer.

Daisywheel

- These are most commonly used with word processors as the quality is very good. Printing can be quite rapid if the printer is bi-directional (goes in one direction and then in the other).

- The daisywheel is a small wheel in the machine consisting of 'petals' which fan outwards. At the end of each petal is a character and the wheel spins to print out. Different daisywheels can be used with a variety of type styles and special characters (eg for foreign language work).

Non-impact printers

Ink jet

- These spray tiny droplets of ink onto virtually any surface – paper, glass, plastic or metal. The quality is excellent – both for graphics and text.

Laser

- These printers use laser beams to transfer the original image onto a drum which then transfers it onto paper. Laser printers vary from quite compact and relatively slow printers to very large, very fast printers used with mainframe computers.
- The copy quality is excellent both for text and graphics. A variety of typestyles (or fonts) is available for printing especially if a Postscript laser printer is used which stores fonts in memory, digitally. They are therefore used extensively for desktop publishing work.

CHECK IT YOURSELF

Did you know many newspapers are prepared by using **desk top publishing** and laser printers? Discuss with your tutor how developments in technology have revolutionised the printing trade – if you live near the offices of a national newspaper you may be able to visit them to see the system in operation.

Printer costs

- The cheapest printers are dot matrix. They are therefore often used for routine internal office work.
- Daisywheel are the next most expensive. They are used for word processing and other work which has to be sent to customers.
- Ink jet are similarly priced. Desk top models are being used more extensively for both graphics and word processing as prices have become more competitive.
- Laser printers have also been falling in price recently and small versions are now within the reach of most offices. They are relatively slow, especially for graphics and artwork, and it is usual to take one master copy on the laser printer and photocopy the remainder required.
- Massive 'smart' laser printers cost many thousands of pounds and are mainly used in computer centres. Forms, letter headings, etc., can be memorized by the printer and the printing is so rapid that hundreds of copies can be produced each minute.

Using a printer

1 First find out how to **stop** the printer if there is a problem.

2 Check the type of paper being used. This could be either:
   - continuous stationery (with perforations between each sheet). This paper has sprocket holes in the sides which are placed over the sprockets to keep it in position. After printing the paper is split into individual sheets and the sprocket hole sections removed (called **bursting** and **decollating**).
     If continuous stationery is used you *must* make sure that the paper is in the right place (ie at the top of the next sheet before printing).
   - single sheet paper. This is usually placed in a single sheet feeder and a new sheet is fed into the printer automatically for each new page.

3 Most printers have a **TOF** (**top of form**) or **FF** (**form feed**) button which will turn up the paper automatically to the top

of the next sheet. The **LF** (**line feed**) button will turn up the paper by one line at a time.

4 The printer must be **on line** before printing can be carried out. Making any paper adjustments by using either TOF/FF or LF buttons will normally cancel out the 'on line' facility. 'On line' will therefore have to be pressed again for printing to recommence.

5 Commands to start printing are normally given by the computer or word processor.

Printer problems

Printer difficulties can have many causes ranging from simple problems, such as running out of paper, to more complex ones, such as incorrect computer-to-printer configurations (ie the computer and printer cannot understand one another).

To some extent the type of problem you encounter will depend on the type of printer, ribbon or paper feed system you are using. All printers have their own operating manual which contains a 'troubleshooting' section. You should always refer to this if difficulties occur, so that you never, inadvertently, make the problem worse. Equally you should know how to stop the printer, in case of an emergency.
The most common types of problems, and the action to take, are given on page 99 for guidance – but please note that this chart is no substitute for your own user manual!

SPECIAL NOTE

Some laser printers have an indicator panel or fault lights which illuminate if errors occur. If this is the case for your printer then check the printer manual to diagnose the exact error and the correct action to take.

HEALTH AND SAFETY

There has been much concern about whether working with computers for long periods can be a danger to health, especially for vulnerable operators, eg pregnant women and epileptics. Much evidence has been collected on this subject, none of which has proved that computers are, in themselves, dangerous. The

Printer problems

Fault	Probable Cause	Action
No response from printer when command to print given	No power to printer Printer not switched on Printer not connected to computer Printer not 'on line' Wrong command given	Check plug lead Switch on Check printer lead Press 'on line' key Check software manual
Print is gibberish	Printer set in test mode Software and printer incompatible Printer lead faulty	Set test mode function to 'off' Call supervisor Test with another printer lead
Print quality poor	Fabric ribbon needs changing Ribbon set too near/too far from paper Ink jet/laser – cartridge needs changing laser – paper wrong specification or internal cleaning required	Replace with new ribbon Adjust ribbon setting Replace with new ink/ toner cartridge Check printer manual
Print wrong size	Printer 'remembering' command from other software	Switch printer off and on again to clear memory
Characters omitted	Daisywheel – petals may be damaged Laser – wrong font selected	Replace with new daisywheel Check manual
Paper jam	Document feed – paper wrong specification/inserted wrongly Tractor feed – printed/unused sheet 'backing up' into printer ink jet/laser – in-tray overfull/ paper specification incorrect	Change paper and reinsert – check document feeder instruction book Stop printer and use paper release to unjam. Clear area behind printer. Reduce paper in in-tray/ change to correct paper/check printer manual
Print crooked on paper	Tractor feed – paper dislodged from sprocket holes	Stop printer and realign paper and sprocket holes correctly
Printing with incorrect pitch or line spacing	Software over-riding printer settings	Check software manual

worst problems are likely to be connected with eye strain and posture and these can be alleviated by:

- keeping glare to a minimum – no bright lights, white walls, over-bright or flickering screens, no reflective surfaces
- regular cleaning plus wool carpets (*not* nylon) to reduce static
- properly designed work stations which are comfortable to sit at, provide channels for electric cables and sufficient working surface for books and papers
- adjustable chairs
- noise reduced by using acoustic hoods on printers and sound-absorbent materials on floors, walls and ceilings. Acoustic screens both reduce noise and give privacy
- slightly higher temperature than normal – most operators sit for long periods rather than move around. However, good ventilation is also necessary, especially in summer, as the machines themselves give off heat
- regular rest breaks and medical screening for operators.

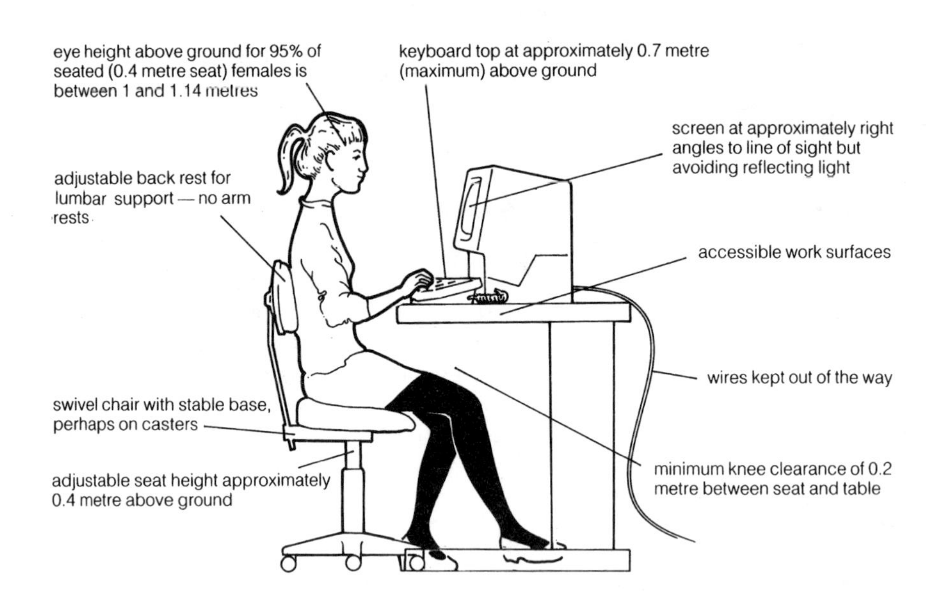

SPECIAL NOTE

- Most VDUs are available with a brightness control and a swivel base. The brightness can therefore be adjusted to suit the operator and the screen itself turned to avoid glare.

- A computer needs 'clean' power lines to function properly. This means no surges in electricity which will affect its operation.

COMPUTER SOFTWARE

Software refers to the programs which are loaded into the computer to tell it what to do.

There are two types of program used with micro computers:

Systems program
- This is the operating system which controls the computer's operation and instructs it how to function. The most common is **DOS (Disk Operating System)** used with IBM PCs and IBM compatible machines.

Applications programs
- These are the actual business programs which can be loaded so that the computer can be used for word processing as well as for graphics, spreadsheets or other business applications.

SPECIAL NOTE

Some computers already have the operating system loaded into **ROM** (the **Read Only Memory** of the computer). This means that on some machines you just switch them on and load the applications program you are using. On others you will need to load a systems program first. Always make sure you know what is required before you start!

Storage and back-up

The final piece of hardware you need is a **disk drive** to read the programs and load them into the computer. This device can also be used to:

- save data you want to keep
- back-up (make copies of) programs and data in case your original copies are damaged.

Whereas small games computers often have a cassette recorder attached to read programs from tapes, business computers use a **disk drive**. However, whereas business programs are purchased on floppy disk, computers can be bought which have disk drives for **floppy** disks and/or a **hard** disk.

Floppy disks

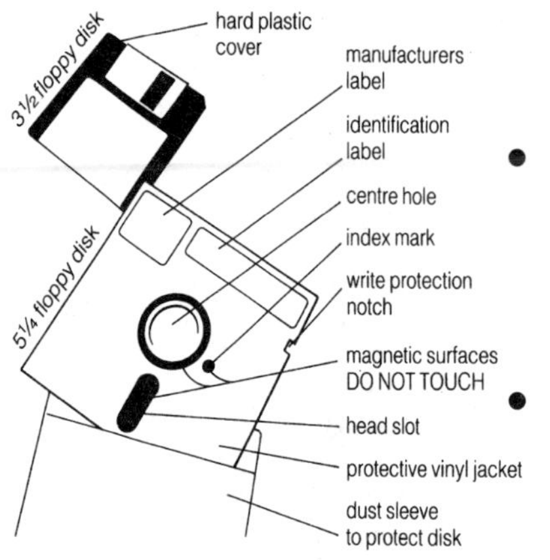

- These are available in two sizes, 5¼″ and 3½″. Obviously you need to use the size which fits the disk drive of the machine you are using.
- The amount you can store on a disk will depend on whether you are using a single or double sided disk, and whether the density is single, double or high.
- 5¼″ disks have a vinyl jacket and are provided with a dust sleeve. 3½″ disks have a hard plastic case with a metal cover which slides back when the disk is placed into the drive.

Hard disk

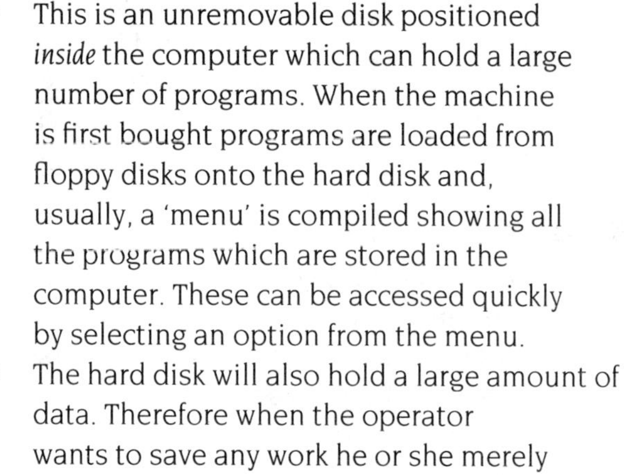

- This is an unremovable disk positioned *inside* the computer which can hold a large number of programs. When the machine is first bought programs are loaded from floppy disks onto the hard disk and, usually, a 'menu' is compiled showing all the programs which are stored in the computer. These can be accessed quickly by selecting an option from the menu.
- The hard disk will also hold a large amount of data. Therefore when the operator wants to save any work he or she merely saves it to the hard disk *without* having to load a floppy disk to hold the information.

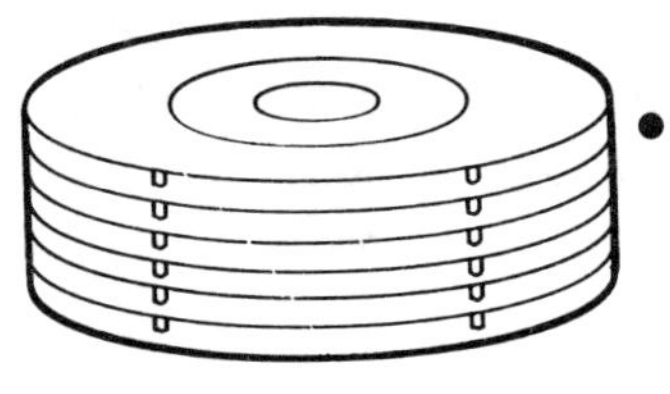

Formatting

Before a floppy disk can be used on a computer it must be **formatted**. This means simply inserting the disk into the drive and typing the formatting command. The disk is then 'compatible' to receive information from that particular computer. It is therefore not possible to use a disk which has been formatted on one type of computer on a different type without reformatting it first. Reformatting erases any information previously stored on the disk.

CHECK IT YOURSELF

What would you do in the following cases?

- You have been working on a thirty page document for the past week for your boss. It is important that this is finished and printed out by Thursday afternoon. When you insert the disk containing your work on Thursday morning your screen reads 'disk error' and refuses to load.
- You operate a computer with a hard disk. On this are several programs you use regularly, including a database of all your customers with their names, addresses, telephone numbers and other details. Information from this is requested every day by several departments. When you switch on the machine one morning it will not work. The engineer is called in and says that he can cure the fault but only at the expense of clearing all the information from the hard disk.

Back-up copies

Your answer, in both cases, should have been that you have no problem because you have a back-up copy of your work!

- Whenever you store your work on a floppy disk take an *extra* copy on another disk. If your first disk then ceases to function you simply load the second disk. The minute this loads take another copy – in case *this* one goes wrong!
- The *total* contents of a hard disk should regularly be 'backed up' by transferring the information to several floppy disks which are kept safely in case of faults with the hard disk itself. In many organisations this is done daily.

Care of floppy disks

Floppy disks can easily be damaged. To keep damage to a minimum they must be handled with care and a few golden rules followed:

- write the label for the disk *first*, then stick it on the disk. *Never* press on the disk itself with a biro to write the label.
- always keep the disk in its dust jacket when not in use and put it away in a disk box with a plastic cover to keep out dust
- don't overfill the disk box so that the disks rub against each other

- keep disks away from anything magnetic as this will wipe off the information stored on them
- keep them away from heat, eg radiators
- don't touch the exposed recording surface on 5¼″ disks.

Read/write protect

On 3½″ disks there is a small plastic clip which can be moved to prevent anyone else overwriting your disk by accident. On 5¼″ disks you have to attach a small piece of paper over the read/ write protect notch. The tabs for this are supplied with the disks.

Purging

This means clearing all information off disks to prevent them becoming unusable because they are full of outdated material. If they are your own work disks then when to purge is up to you. If you have work on them from other people it is usual to inform them first – in case they want anything saved beforehand.

TEST YOURSELF

Your boss is considering replacing your present computer with a similar model with a 40 Megabyte hard disk. He is also wondering whether or not to buy a document reader. He has asked you to:

- give him a list of all the advantages associated with these changes
- let him know if he is correct in his assumption that you will no longer need to use any floppy disks
- explain the meaning of a 40 Megabyte hard disk.

The keyboard

Because keyboards differ so much it is impossible to give you very much guidance in this book on what to expect – your tutor will go through the layout of the special function keys with you and explain what they do. Their use often varies depending on which program you are using.

However there is one fact which you must be aware of. On every keyboard there is *one* key which instructs the computer to carry out a command you have just typed onto the screen. This may be

- the carriage return key or

- an 'action' key   or
- an 'execute' key   or
- an 'enter' key.

Find this key the moment you start and *always* remember – it is never any use sitting at the computer expecting it somehow to 'know' what you have typed on the screen to ask it to do, without pressing the appropriate 'do it' key!

User-friendly programs

If a computer is marketed as being 'user-friendly' it generally means it is easy to use, even for people not used to computers. Similarly programs can be 'user-friendly' in that they are easy to understand and operate.

Many of the ideas incorporated to make a program 'user-friendly' are found in a wide variety of business application programs. The most important are

Menus • a range of choices is shown on the screen and you simply choose the one you want

Windows • these are similar to menus – when you choose a certain option (often shown across the top of the screen) a 'window' appears showing you all the alternatives you can now choose.

SPECIAL NOTE

On all computer programs you will have a **cursor** (a small block on the screen where the colours are reversed and often flashing) so that you know where you are. If you are selecting an option shown on a menu you will either:

- move the cursor to the option you want (use the cursor arrow keys)
- type the number opposite the option you want.

Sometimes you can do either – use the one you prefer.

Common features

Features which are common to many different types of program include

Status line(s) • gives information on the piece of work you are creating

- **Prompt line(s)** — gives information on what you can do next
- **Entry line** — usually identified by >. You enter your command immediately after this symbol.
- **Help feature** — on many computers you have a special *help* key. Whatever part of the program you are using, pressing this key will give you any useful information the programmer thought you might need at this point.
- **Commands** — often include Z for Zap (get rid of), Q for Quit (leave program), Esc for Escape (to undo something you have just done by accident) – there is often a specific *esc* key.

SPECIAL NOTE

Virtually all programs are designed so that important information is always shown on screen. If you are stuck the best advice is to **read your screen** – the chances are that the information you need is staring back at you!

EQUIPMENT FAULTS

It is quite possible that if a computer does not work you have to call an engineer or technician for help. However, before you do this there are a few simple checks you should make.

- If nothing works
  - check everything is plugged in
  - check the power is on at the switch
  - check there isn't a power cut
  - check the equipment is switched on
  - check the power source by plugging in something else to the same socket.
- If the VDU does not work
  - check connection between VDU and computer
  - check brightness control.
- If there is no response on screen when keyboard is used
  - check connection between keyboard and computer.

- If data does not load
  - check you have inserted a disk
  - check disk drive connections
  - try with another disk.
- Miscellaneous problems
  - remove disks, switch off, count to 15, switch on and try again
  - refer to computer manual under fault being experienced.

SPECIAL NOTE

Some software packages 'lock out' if you either give the command to print or they reach a point where they would automatically produce a print out, if the printer has not been switched on.

COMPUTER RULES

- *Never* switch a computer quickly off and on again.
- *Never* move one unless it is essential. For some hard disk machines you may need to 'park the heads' first. This means that the read/write heads above the hard disk are properly secured so that if the machine is knocked no damage will occur to the heads or hard disk.
- *Never* switch off a computer without going through the proper closing down procedure.
- *Never* try to take out a disk while the disk drive light is on – you could easily damage both the disk *and* the drive itself.
- *Never* put food, drink or other liquids near the machine – for very obvious reasons!
- If your screen shows an unknown error message check with your user manual *before* pressing any keys. If you don't know what you are doing you may make the problem worse – not better.

SECURITY

Data stored on computer is often confidential, eg

- bank account information

- staff wages and salaries
- police criminal records
- customer accounts.

For this reason only certain employees in an organisation may be able to access certain types of information and this is controlled by the use of **passwords**.

Several passwords may be needed within one program. For instance if you are using a payroll package you may find that:

- one password is required to get into the program. This may give access to hourly paid employee records
- a second password is required to access information on salaried staff
- a third password is needed for information on managers' and directors' salaries.

The rules on passwords are:

- they should be changed frequently – preferably *daily*
- they shouldn't be written down!
- they shouldn't be too obvious, eg the phone number of the company or the name of the operator! Many organisations have security problems by using a password connected to the time of the year, eg in December the password will be Xmas!

SPECIAL NOTE

- If you have to type in a password, watch your screen! You will notice that nothing you type is displayed – so no-one standing behind can read it.
- Many films and television programmes have been made about computer 'hackers'. These are people who try to gain illegal entry into a computer system by working out what the password may be.

COMPUTERS AND THE LAW

Data kept in a computer is covered by the Data Protection Act 1984, which gives legal rights to individuals regarding personal data held about them on computer. Under the requirements of this Act:

- companies who hold data on people on computer *must* register as data users with the Data Protection Registrar
- any information held on computer must have been acquired legally
- personal data must not be disclosed to others for any reason which is incompatible with the purpose for which it is held
- the data must be accurate and kept up-to-date and not excessive for the purpose for which it is required
- proper security measures must be taken against unauthorised access to the data or alteration, disclosure, loss or destruction of the information held
- personal records should not be kept longer than is necessary.

Under the provisions of the Act a person can find out the information which is held on him or her by:

- referring to the Data Protection Register (a copy is held in all major libraries) which lists all the holders of data
- writing to the holder and asking for a copy of the data held.

A holder *cannot* refuse to give the information unless the data is held for national security. In addition, information on criminal, tax, medical and social work records may also be withheld.

SPECIAL NOTE

- Finding out information is not necessarily free! It can cost about £10 a time to find out what data is being held.
- The Data Protection Act *only* covers information about 'people' held on computer – with the exception of an organisation's own payroll. Exemptions include:
  - information on companies or other topics, eg a book or car list
  - all manual systems
  - information held on personal computer systems for household use only.

CHECK IT YOURSELF

Write to the Office of the Data Protection Registrar, Springfield House, Water Lane, Wilmslow, Cheshire, SK9 5AX, or telephone them on 0625 535777, and ask for a copy of *Guideline Booklet 1 – Introduction to the Data Protection Act*.

SECTION REVIEW

Having completed this section, you should now be able to:

1. Identify the main components of a computer system.
2. Distinguish between computer hardware and computer software.
3. State the main input and output devices used in relation to computers.
4. Describe the different types of printers used.
5. Diagnose common print problems and equipment faults.
6. Explain the relevance of health and safety to Information processing.
7. Differentiate between RAM and ROM.
8. Differentiate between floppy and hard disks.
9. Explain the importance of security and back-up procedures.
10. Describe the correct procedure for handling and storing floppy disks.
11. Explain the terms **purging**, **menus**, **windows** and **cursor**.
12. Suggest suitable procedures for effective machine maintenance.
13. State the main aspects of the Data Protection Act 1984.

REVIEW QUIZ

True or false?

1. Any data stored in RAM is lost the moment the machine is switched off.
2. An applications program instructs the computer how to operate.
3. If your computer does not work the first thing you should do is contact the engineer or technician for help.
4. To zap a document means to get rid of it.

5 Under the terms of the Data Protection Act the police must give you details of any information they hold on you on their computer.

Complete the blanks . . .

6 Computer equipment is known as .... whereas computer programs are known as ....

7 Small business computers are known as micros, whereas a large centralised computer is known as a ....

8 A machine which automatically reads text by 'scanning' it to input it into the computer is known as a ....

Work it out

9 You are about to start using a computer with a 30 Megabyte hard disk. Approximately how many characters can be stored on the disk before it will be full?

10 One of your colleagues is going to use a computer printer for the first time and is worried about what she should do if anything goes wrong. To help her
- draw up a list of common printer problems and their causes
- explain to her what should be done in each case to rectify the problem.

If possible relate your answer to an actual printer you use, either at College or work, referring to the manual or handbook for guidance if required.

Money and decimal amounts

You may often be asked to calculate decimal pence, eg if you are working out petrol expenses or photocopier costs etc. For instance:

- a representative may travel 85 miles and be paid 35.4p a mile
- a photocopier may cost 1.3p a copy and make 1342 copies in one month.

The problem with using a calculator for these is that there is a great temptation to enter the numbers in the money amounts as they are written! If you do, in the examples above, you will be entering £35.40 a mile for petrol and £1.30 for each copy! You will then end up with some ridiculous amount, which, if you write it down, may keep the office laughing for a week.
To avoid this:

- *Think* about what you are doing. 35.4p is really £0.354 – zero pounds, 35 pence and *then* the point 4. You are simply working to three decimal places for pence instead of the usual two.

  Therefore 85 × 0.354 = £30.09
- 1.3p is therefore really £0.013 – again working in three decimal places.

  0.013 × 1342 = £17.446 = (rounded) £17.45

Rationality and other checks

- A rationality check should always be carried out on calculations. This is quite simply using your common sense to see if the answer is likely to be correct.

  As an example, look again at the photocopier costs above. If the copies were 1p each, and we made 1342 copies then – obviously – the bill would be for £13.42. At 1.3p a copy the amount must be slightly more than £13.42 – therefore £17.45 is rationally correct.

  If the cost had been incorrectly entered in the calculator (eg as 1.3) the answer would have been £1744.60 – which *couldn't* have been rationally correct.

- The other method of checking the answer is to work out the calculation backwards. If you re-enter the answer you got before rounding it (£17.446) and divide *this* figure by 0.013 (the cost) then you should get the number of copies as your answer. Test it out now!

TEST YOURSELF 1

Calculate the following and use a rationality check each time to make sure you are correct:

1 1621 copies at 1.2p
2 2871 copies at 1.8p
3 4021 copies at 1.3p
4 6392 copies at 1.1p
5 1875 copies at 1.4p
6 8193 copies at 1.5p

Calculate the following mileage allowances and check each one by working the calculation backwards afterwards:

7 250 miles at 31.5p a mile
8 163 miles at 30.8p a mile
9 95 miles at 34.2p a mile
10 425 miles at 32.9p a mile
11 340 miles at 33.4p a mile
12 816 miles at 35.6p a mile

Exchange rates

Multiplications involving decimal numbers are used for calculating exchange rates. If you were going on holiday to Canada and had saved £400 for spending money, you would need it changed to Canadian dollars. If you telephone the bank they will quote you an **exchange rate** of say 1.81 dollars to the pound. How many dollars will you get in exchange for your £400?

Simply *multiply* your savings by the exchange rate, ie

400 × 1.81 = $724.

If the answer does not work out to a whole number, then round it up or down. (You may like to note that banks usually round everything down!)

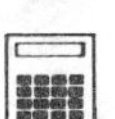

TEST YOURSELF 2

Calculate how much you would receive in each of the examples below:

1 Austria – savings £260 – rate 19.55 schillings to the pound

2	France	– savings £800	– rate 9.33 francs to the pound
3	W Germany	– savings £460	– rate 2.73 marks to the pound
4	Spain	– savings £500	– rate 175.5 pesetas to the pound
5	USA	– savings £550	– rate 1.55 dollars to the pound
6	Portugal	– savings £650	– rate 240.5 escudos to the pound

If you returned from holiday with any Canadian money you could change this back to British currency provided it is in notes and not coins. Obviously there is a charge for this (just as there is for changing your money in the first place). However, you can get a good idea of how much you have brought back if you *divide* the amount of Canadian money you have left by the current exchange rate.

TEST YOURSELF 3

Can you calculate how much you would receive if you took the following amounts of foreign currency to the bank? Remember to work out your answers to two decimal places for British currency.

1. 160 Canadian dollars – exchange rate 1.81
2. 2600 Belgian francs – exchange rate 57.40
3. 100 Swiss francs – exchange rate 2.45
4. 270 Norwegian krone – exchange rate 10.50
5. 78 Irish pounds – exchange rate 1.045
6. 800 Danish krone – exchange rate 10.65

Totals and averages

Obviously totals and total costs are calculated by adding different amounts together. For instance, a businessman travelling abroad may spend different amounts in different countries, eg £240 in Belgium, £600 in Germany, £420 in Switzerland and £400 in France.

The total amount spent is obviously £240 + £600 + £420 + £400 = £1660

If we want to know how much he spent *on average* in each country, we have to divide the total by the number of countries he visited altogether.

1660 ÷ 4 = £415.

Averages are therefore always calculated by working out

$$\frac{\textit{sum of the values}}{\textit{number of values in the set}}$$

You should note that another word for average is **mean**. If you are asked to find the mean, you do exactly the same thing.

TEST YOURSELF 4

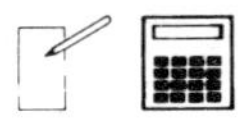

Find the average (or mean) of:

1 22, 68, 25, 43, 32
2 125, 83, 61, 126, 28, 213
3 1.64, 1.82, 1.97, 1.71, 1.81
4 £15.40, £17.28, £16.30, £19.62
5 1 hr 6 mins, 2 hrs 10 mins, 4 hrs 26 mins
6 110 kg, 250 kg, 400 kg, 210 kg, 575 kg

Now solve the following:

7 In a week the temperature was 60°F, 66°F, 61°F, 65°F, 71°F, 72°F, 67°F. What was the mean temperature for the week?
8 At an exhibition the following attendance numbers were recorded from Monday to Saturday – 2390, 1982, 1995, 2687, 3490, 5600. What was the average daily attendance?
9 Four friends weigh 8 stone 12 lb, 9 stone 4 lb, 8 stone 4 lb and 9 stone 8 lb. What is their average weight?
10 Your local town hall has been carrying out a road survey to see if a crossing is required on a fairly busy road. A clocking device has counted the number of vehicles using the road each day during the test period. From the figures given below find the average number of vehicles per day.

2190, 4187, 3990, 1780, 5990, 6709, 1890, 949, 1709, 2650, 7382, 1650.

Simple sum trick

Find out if a number is divisible by 3 *instantly* by adding together all the digits, eg

43 = 4 + 3 = 7 — 7 is not divisible by 3, so neither is 43.
204 = 2 + 4 = 6 — 6 is divisible by 3, so is 204.

This also works for 9 – try it!

Mail handling

Incoming Mail

Incoming Mail *must be* opened quickly, sorted accurately and distributed promptly, so that managers and staff can organise their work priorities for the day, know what needs 'chasing up' and act on the most up-to-date information available.

RECEIVING MAIL

Large organisations will have a specialised mail room which receives all the incoming mail. The Post Office usually deliver their mail in sacks early in the morning.

Small organisations will receive their mail from the postman and it may be opened by the manager or a senior secretary. Some organisations have post boxes at their local post office so they can collect their own mail earlier if they wish.

Incoming mail equipment

A very small office may use a paper knife to open envelopes. Most organisations will use a **letter opening machine**. This takes a thin sliver from the top of the envelope to avoid damaging the contents; the machine is adjustable for large envelopes. It is a good idea to hold the envelope the right way up and gently tap it, to make sure the contents are at the bottom, before putting it through the machine.

A **date stamp** is used to mark the incoming mail with the date received – some stamps also record the time of receipt.

MAIL ROOM PROCEDURE

1 **Sort the mail into**

- that marked *urgent* – Open *immediately*. Be prepared to either deliver it immediately or notify the addressee by telephone to collect it.
- that marked *personal* or *private and confidential* – N*ever* open. If the addressee is absent and

the letter is also marked urgent then refer it to a senior member of staff.

- that containing *remittances* (cheques, postal orders or – very rarely – cash)
  - Check the amount with that stated in the letter. (If there is any discrepancy, notify your supervisor.)
  - Write the amount, method of payment and your initials on the corner of the document.
  - Record the details in the Remittance Book.
- Recorded Delivery and Registered mail
  - This is signed for on delivery. Many firms also keep a record in an Inwards Mail Register.
- that which has been wrongly delivered
  - This should be reposted unopened. If there is a mistake on the envelope this can be changed. There is no charge for reposting.
- all other 1st and 2nd class mail
  - Open 1st class *first* – it is more likely to contain important or urgent documents.

2 **Staple or clip all enclosures to the main document**; if any are missing, check the envelope carefully and note any omissions on the main document.

3 **Date stamp all documents** (except cheques and postal orders)

4 **Sort the mail into departments**
Mail is often placed in mail baskets for distribution or collection. The order should be (from the top down)

- urgent letters
- private and confidential or personal letters
- 1st class mail
- 2nd class mail
- circulars and magazines.

5 **Check all envelopes carefully to make sure they are empty** Some organisations keep the envelopes for a day or two in case of queries.

6 **The mail is now ready to be delivered, or to be collected from the baskets.**

CHECK IT YOURSELF

- Can you think of *two* ways an enclosure is indicated in a letter or report?
- How is this information useful to someone opening the mail?

Remittance book

A written record of money received in the mail should always be kept in a **Remittance Book** and this should be counter-signed as accurate by someone in authority. An example is shown below:

Date	Name	Method of Payment	Amount £ p	Account Number	Special Notes
4 Oct	T. Baker	Cheque	43.20	48264	~
	Cole and Sons	"	164.29	97261	~
	P. McNulty	PO	15.00	~	~
	E. Allan	Cash (reg)	5.00	~	~
	M. Worthington	Cheque	22.00	48621	Should be for £26 (see letter)

Cashier's signature .... A Smith .... Date ....4 October....

CIRCULATING MAIL

Mail may be received which has to be seen by more than one person. If the item is a letter or other document, and has to be seen urgently by several people it is usual to photocopy it. Many organisations expect the mail room to note this on the top of the letter so all the recipients know who else has received a copy. To do this:

- write a neat distribution list on the top of the original letter
- count the number of people who must see the letter *in addition to* the addressee (the person to whom it is addressed) and make this number of photocopies

- tick the appropriate name on each one (remember the addressee should receive the *original*) and put all the letters in the mail baskets.

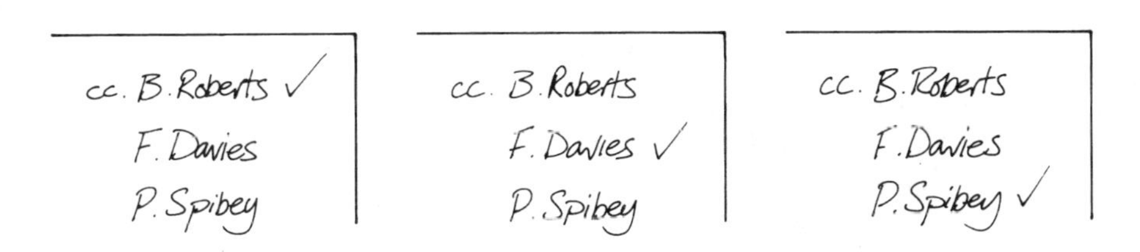

Bulky items which have to be seen by several members of staff obviously cannot be photocopied – such as a bound report, a magazine or a leaflet. In this case a **circulation** or **routing slip** is completed.

CIRCULATION SLIP

Name	Date Received	Date Passed on

Please return to .... after circulation.

Other mail

Letters delivered by hand

- should be dealt with immediately they arrive as they are usually urgent.

Parcels and packets

- These are often delivered separately to the main mail and companies differ in their policy about whether parcels should be delivered *unopened* or *opened* by mailroom staff.
- If you receive any parcels you will be expected to sign for them.

- *Unopened* parcels should be signed for as such – 'contents not checked'.
- *Damaged* parcels should be refused on delivery, if possible, and returned to the sender. If this is not possible sign for them as 'damaged on delivery'.
- *Opened* parcels should be checked carefully and a note made of any discrepancies.

Suspicious packages

Government offices, military establishments, embassies and organisations in defence work have had to face the problem, in recent years, of receiving suspicious packages in the mail. Organisations which consider they are particularly vulnerable can invest in screening equipment (similar to the type found at airports but smaller) which scans all mail before it is opened. The machine will discriminate between potentially harmful contents and routine items such as staples and paper clips. The Post Office also routinely scans mail.

Small businesses and those involved in non-sensitive areas of work are not, however, immune to the threat of a letter bomb or package arriving through the mail. The local Crime Prevention Officer for each area will willingly supply information, leaflets and posters to remind staff of the problem and the correct procedure to be followed.

Rules to follow

A letter bomb or package is designed to kill or maim when opened. There are a number of indications, any one of which should alert you to the possibility that a letter or package is an explosive device:

- grease marks on the envelope or wrapping

- an odour of marzipan or almonds
- visible wiring or tin foil, especially if the envelope or package is damaged
- the envelope or package may feel heavy for its size
- the weight distribution may be uneven; the contents may be rigid in a flexible envelope
- a package may have excessive wrapping
- there may be poor handwriting, spelling or typing
- it may be wrongly addressed or come from an unexpected source
- there may be too many stamps for the weight of the package
- it may have been posted somewhere other than Great Britain
- it may have been delivered by hand from an unknown source.

If you are suspicious

1 **Inform the supervisor immediately.**

2 If you are on your own then:

- **immediately isolate the letter or package in a locked room** (on a table if possible), away from windows and thin partition walls
- **do not poke or otherwise interfere with it**
- **do not place it in water or sand**
- **leave the building and telephone the police from a different place** (some devices can be activated by telephone signals). **Dial 999**.

SECTION REVIEW

Having completed this section, you should now be able to:

1 Describe the correct procedure for dealing with incoming mail.

2 Explain the procedure for dealing with urgent mail, private or confidential mail, registered and recorded mail and that which has been wrongly delivered.

3 State the correct procedure for handling remittances and completing a Remittance Book.

4 Explain why time constraints are important in relation to handling incoming mail.

5 Describe how documents may be circulated.

6 State how to identify a suspicious package and explain the correct action to take.

7 Describe the correct procedure for receiving parcels and packets.

? REVIEW QUIZ

True or false?

1 Registered and Recorded Delivery mail are signed for on delivery.

2 Personal letters should be opened if the addressee is absent.

3 All parcels must be opened immediately they are received.

4 The word *remittances* is used to describe payments received by an organisation.

5 Any item which arrives in the mail, which must be seen by several members of staff, must be photocopied.

Complete the blanks . . .

6 A post office box is used by organisations so that they can

. . . .

7 Any discrepancy between a remittance received and the amount stated in the document must be noted on the top of the document *and* in the . . . .

8 Advice on suspicious packages is always available from the local . . . .

Work it out

9 Check each of the following Remittance Book totals and mark them correct or incorrect. See if you can complete them all *without a calculator* within *one and a half* minutes!

£	£	£
15.25	115.80	45.31
102.32	21.87	14.59
22.14	16.86	3.29
173.24	96.30	102.43
13.90	15.20	72.84
316.85	260.13	238.46

Now rewrite them neatly putting the correct total in each case.

10 A letter has been received which states that the cheque enclosed is for £163.24, whereas the actual cheque is made out for £146.89. What is the discrepancy between the two figures?

Outgoing mail

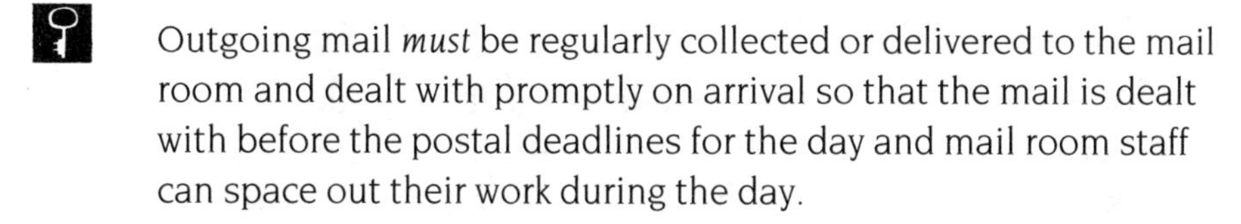

Outgoing mail *must* be regularly collected or delivered to the mail room and dealt with promptly on arrival so that the mail is dealt with before the postal deadlines for the day and mail room staff can space out their work during the day.

MAILROOM PROCEDURE

1. **Re-sort** internal mail and place in the appropriate basket.
2. **Check** all letters have been signed and the address on the envelope matches that on the document.
3. **Check** that any enclosures mentioned are attached.
4. **Fold** the documents the **minimum** number of times to fit in the envelope and seal.
5. **Separate** special mail into the following groups:
   - airmail and other foreign mail
   - Registered and Recorded Delivery mail
   - Datapost
   - compensation fee parcels
   - ordinary parcels
   - mail requiring a Certificate of Posting
6. **Weigh** any envelope containing more than two sheets of paper and note the weight **lightly** in pencil on the envelope.

7 **Calculate** the correct postage depending on whether the item is to be sent by 1st or 2nd class post.
8 **Complete** the forms for the special mail and calculate the extra postage fee required.
9 **Frank** or **stamp** the mail.

SPECIAL NOTE

Any queries about enclosures or signatures should be referred back to the typist or originator of the letter or document.

Stationery

Paper is available in several sizes, A4 being the most commonly used size for business correspondence.

Envelopes are also available in several sizes to match paper sizes, DL being the most common size used by organisations for business correspondence. These envelopes are designed to take A4 paper folded three times widthways.

Envelopes are also divided into three main styles:

Bankers • have the opening on the longer side
Pocket • have the opening on the shorter side
Window • contain a 'window' opening covered with transparent material. These save the typist time as there is no need to type the name and address on the envelope.

SPECIAL NOTE

Organisations which use window envelopes have their stationery marked with special lines to help staff fold the letters accurately so the name and address fit *clearly* and *exactly* into the window.

CHECK IT YOURSELF

- Obtain examples of as many sizes of paper and envelopes as possible.
- Obtain at least one example each of a compliment slip and a business card. Discuss with your tutor occasions when an organisation may send something through the post with a compliment slip attached.

- Obtain an example of a window envelope and a sheet of headed letter paper preferably marked for use with a window envelope (perhaps your tutor can help here). Type your own name and address between the two *dots* and then use the *fold lines* to fold the paper accurately, remembering to keep the address part on the top at the end. Check how well you have done by inserting it in the window envelope and checking that the address is clearly shown.
- Practise folding headed letter paper into DL envelopes so that the letter heading will be the *first* thing the recipient sees as the letter is unfolded.

SPECIAL NOTE

Always use a larger size envelope if you have several sheets of paper – *never* cram it in so it hardly seals!

Addressing envelopes

1. Use very neat handwriting or, better still, type them.
2. Start the address *half way down*.
3. Don't forget the name of the addressee and title (Mr, Mrs, Ms, Miss, Dr etc).
4. Start a new line for each line of the address.
5. *Always* put the postal town in *capitals*.
6. The postcode should be the last item on the envelope and preferably be on a separate line. It should *not* contain any punctuation.
7. Letters going abroad should have *both* the city (or town) *and* country in capitals.
8. Special mailing instructions, eg airmail, by hand or urgent should be typed at the top left-hand side.
9. Special addressee instructions should go two lines above the rest of the address, eg personal, private and confidential or for the attention of.

Wrapping parcels

Parcels must be wrapped securely so that the contents are not damaged, and labelled either FRAGILE or DO NOT BEND where appropriate.

Wrapping materials include:

- strong boxes available from the Post Office
- jiffy (padded) bags available from the Post Office and stationers in a variety of sizes
- corrugated paper, bubble wrap and polystyrene chips which are placed inside the package to give protection
- crushed newspaper or kitchen roll can also be used if you have nothing else to hand
- paper which has been through a shredder is used by some organisations for packing.

Rules to follow

- Wrap the article securely in one of the materials listed above for protection if it is fragile.
- If it may bend (eg a photograph), place it securely between two pieces of strong card.
- Make sure any space in the box or packet is filled with packing material if bumps or knocks could harm it.
- Put the item into a secure box and seal all flaps and edges with generous width adhesive tape. (String can be used if knotted firmly in two directions but is not as secure as tape).
- Label the parcel clearly and also include the **sender's** address at right angles to the **delivery** address. Make sure the post town is in capitals and include the post code.

SENDER:
Mr E Cawley
15 Beck Road
CARLISLE
CL3 5DT

Mr T Allan
14 Isis Way
OXFORD
OX2 8DJ

CHECK IT YOURSELF

Obtain a copy of the Post Office leaflet *Wrap up well*. Find out how to send glass, flowers, electrical equipment, records and tapes through the post.

POST OFFICE SERVICES

Registered mail

- is used to send money or articles of *monetary* value. The easiest way is to use a registered envelope which can be purchased from a Post Office. Various sizes are available, the envelope is specially strengthened and marked with a blue cross on both sides.
- all registered items automatically go by 1st class post and compensation is paid if the item is lost or damaged.

Recorded Delivery

- is used to send valuable *documents*, eg a will, passport or certificate.
- an ordinary envelope is used and the sender can choose between 1st or 2nd class post. Limited compensation is payable in the event of loss or damage.

Advice of delivery

- is a service to enable users of the Registered Mail or Recorded Delivery service to obtain proof of *delivery*.
- a special AD form is available from Post Offices which the user completes and hands in with the Registered or Recorded Delivery item. (If the AD form is completed at a later date the fee is higher.)
- the sorting office which handles the item for delivery will complete the AD form with the date delivered and return it to the sender.

Certificate of Posting

- gives proof of *posting* for either one item or several. A special form is completed listing the item(s) and this is then stamped at the Post Office.

Datapost

- provides a very fast **and** secure service and can be used for both parcels and letters being sent within the UK and abroad.
- companies who use Datapost regularly have a contract with the Post Office. Customers with an infrequent need can use the Datapost on Demand service.

Special Delivery

- with this service the Post Office undertakes to deliver the letter the next day otherwise the Special Delivery charge is refunded to the sender.

Intelpost

- is the Post Office facsimile service. British Telecom operate a similar service called **Bureaufax**.

Business reply service

- is used by companies who want their customers to be able to reply without paying any postal charges.
- envelopes or postcards are printed with a special design which shows the licence number of the company and whether the reply service is for 1st or 2nd class post.

Freepost

- again saves customers from paying postage but *all* Freepost mail is sent 2nd class unless the company has a special card printed denoting 1st class postage.

- the word Freepost is incorporated into the company's address and no special envelopes are required.

Parcel post

- parcels must be securely wrapped and a Certificate of Posting obtained before the Post Office will pay any compensation for loss or damage. Only limited compensation is obtainable for any parcels sent by ordinary parcel post.
- parcels and packets going abroad or to the Channel Islands must have a Customs Declaration Form attached to them giving information about the contents.

Compensation Fee parcel

- is used for valuable parcels. An additional fee is paid, the amount depending on the value of the goods. Higher compensation can now be claimed if there is loss or damage in transit.

Airmail

- is used to send letters and packages abroad quickly. Lightweight letters and postcards to EC countries go at a special cheap rate.
- special lightweight airmail paper and envelopes can be used to reduce the cost of postage and a blue airmail sticker must be attached to the top left of an ordinary envelope for non-European mail.

Swiftair

- for an extra charge letters can be expressed abroad using this service. All items *must* carry both a Swiftair label *and* an airmail label.

Surface mail

- is used for non-urgent letters and parcels going abroad. Although much cheaper than airmail, delivery can be up to twelve weeks to some countries.

International Business Reply Service

- special envelopes are pre-printed and sent to people abroad to enable them to reply to British organisations without paying the cost of postage.

Airstream

- used by organisations who send large quantities of mail overseas. The Post Office collects the mail, calculates the postage rates and sends it abroad by the fastest routes within hours of collection.

CHECK IT YOURSELF

- Visit the main post office in your area and get the following leaflets:

  Letter Rates – A Comprehensive Guide
  International Letter Rates – A Comprehensive Guide
  How to use your parcel service (plus the latest rates)
  International Parcels: Compendium of Prices
  How to send things you value through the post.

Whilst you are there collect as many other leaflets as you can on the services mentioned on the preceding pages.

- Ask at the counter for the following labels and forms as examples:
  - a pink Certificate of Posting form (there are two sizes)
  - a green Certificate of Posting for Compensation Fee Parcel
  - a mauve Certificate of Posting for Royal Mail Special Delivery
  - a Datapost pack
  - an orange Recorded Delivery form
  - an AD form (Advice of Delivery)
  - a Customs Declaration Form (two types – one ties on, the other is adhesive)
  - a red Swiftair label
  - a blue airmail label
- Practise completing the forms following the instructions given on each by the Post Office. Check with your tutor that you have been *neat* and *accurate* throughout.
- From magazines and newspapers try to find examples of business reply envelopes (both 1st and 2nd class) and Freepost addresses. (Sometimes the latter are read out on television.)

TEST YOURSELF

From the information given in your leaflets find out the answers to the following:

1. How much would it cost to send a parcel weighing 6.5 kg to London?
2. What would be the additional Compensation Fee charge if the parcel is valued at £200?
3. How much does the Swiftair service cost?
4. What would an 8 kg Datapost parcel cost if you were sending it to Cardiff?
5. What is the fee for Special Delivery?
6. What is the cost of the licence required to use the Freepost service?
7. How much does a letter weighing 85 g cost to send to Glasgow by
   a) 1st class post
   b) 2nd class post?
8. How much would it cost to send an 8 g letter to New York?
9. How much is the Recorded Delivery service?
10. How much would it cost to send a registered letter – in addition to 1st class postage – if you wanted compensation up to £1500?

SPECIAL NOTE

Today the Post Office no longer has the monopoly as a delivery service.

- In city areas private companies will express deliver letters and parcels.
- Nationwide there are many large private operators who will deliver packages and parcels overnight to any destination in the UK and abroad.

Look in the press and in your local Yellow Pages to see how many private companies you can find. Try to compare their charges with those of the Post Office.

Mailing lists

- Organisations sending out circulars or other advertising material usually use standard mailing lists.
- These may be purchased from a variety of organisations for specific mail shots.
- A list may be kept on a computer database and address labels printed out as required.
- Another method is to type the addresses on plain A4 paper and photocopy the lists onto photocopier labels.

Record keeping

Most organisations keep some records of outgoing mail, particularly that sent by one of the special services such as Registered Mail.

If ordinary 1st and 2nd class letters are recorded they are usually *batched* – the details are recorded in a group, rather than separately, to save time and space.

A record may also be kept of the money spent on additional charges for special services. Usually this money is withdrawn from petty cash.

This information, plus the number of stamps used, is recorded in a **postage book** which is balanced at the end of the day. Post Office receipts are clipped to the book for safe-keeping.

At the end of the day the value of the stamps remaining *must* agree with the stamp balance carried forward.

Postage Book

Date	Stamps bought	Details	Stamps used	Special mail	Fees paid on special mail from petty cash
10 Oct	£80.00	Stamps bought			
11 Oct		38 1st class letters	7.22		
		54 2nd class letters	7.56		
		McKenzie + Sons, Leeds	19	Registered	1.70
		Bright + Sons, Belfast	19	Recorded delivery	24
		Acme Laboratories Stroud	2.80	C.F. Parcel	80
		Berne + Cie, Paris	19	Swiftair	1.50
		TOTAL	18.15		
		Balance c/f	61.85		
			£80.00		

TEST YOURSELF

1 Parcels and letters are weighed in kilogrammes and grammes before the postage is calculated. How many grammes are there in one kilogramme?

2 Where would you type the instruction *first-class* on an envelope?

3 Can you quickly calculate how much you would need to take to the Post Office to buy 50 1st class stamps and 85 2nd class stamps?

CHECK IT YOURSELF

Find out the words used for Mr, Mrs and Miss on letters going to

a) France b) Germany c) Spain.

MAILROOM EQUIPMENT

Postal scales

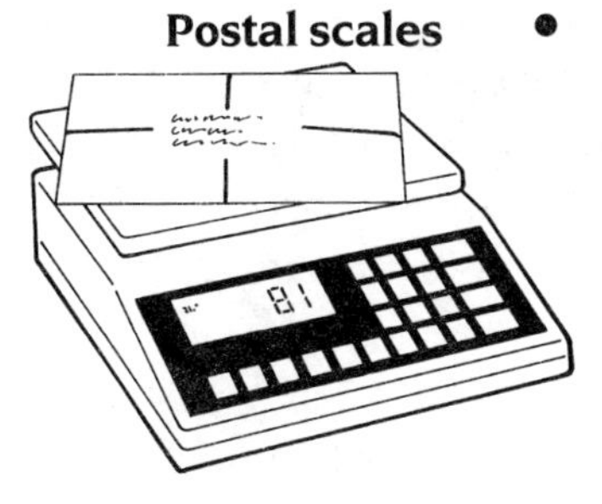

- Used to weigh and calculate postal rates quickly and easily. Most modern scales are **electronic** which means they are fitted with a special chip, programmed with the current postal rates. The scales automatically display the correct amount for the service selected.
- When postal rates change the manufacturers have to insert a new

chip in the machine with the updated rates.

Franking machine

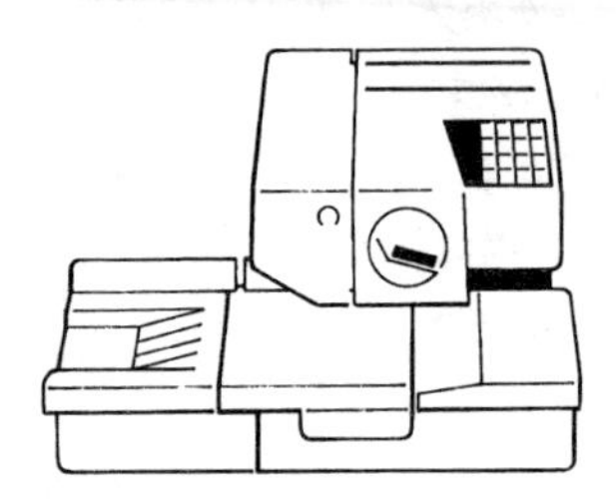

- Used to print a postal impression on either envelopes *or* a label which can be stuck on packets and parcels. This saves having to use stamps.
- Franking machines are hired or purchased from the manufacturer but a licence must be obtained from the Post Office. Postage units are purchased in advance from the Post Office and are set into the machine. The number of postage units then shows on the meter. The machine is locked when not in use.
- Every time the machine is used the units decrease until the machine is empty. The meter shows:

– the units purchased	(total deposits)
– the units used to date	(ascending register)
– the units remaining	(descending register).

- Users must complete a **franking control card** daily. The columns on the card match the registers on the meter so the operator simply fills in the numbers showing on each. This card must be sent to the Post Office weekly, even if the machine has never been used.
- Some of the latest models can have new units set into them *electronically*, after telephoning the manufacturer for a special code to key in to the machine.
- The operator must:
  - change the date daily
  - replenish the ink as required so the impression is clear
  - frank envelopes and labels as required.

- The dials are set to the amount of postage required. Any errors should be dealt with as follows:
  - if the envelope is franked with *too small* an amount a label for the difference can be franked and stuck on
  - if the envelope is franked with *too large* an amount it should be kept and returned to the Post Office for a credit.
- Franked mail must *never* be put into post boxes in the normal way. It is placed in special large envelopes marked FRANKED MAIL and handed over the post office counter.

Inserting/ Folding/ Sealing/ Machines

- Organisations which frequently send vast amounts of mail, eg mail order companies, will have a range of other automated machines to speed up outgoing mail handling.

SPECIAL NOTE

- Large organisations will have their mail collected by the Post Office each day.
- Many firms have their advertising slogan incorporated into their franked postal impressions.
- Even when organisations use a franking machine a small supply of stamps will still be kept in the mailroom for emergency use.

CHECK IT YOURSELF

- It is possible to practise using a franking machine by setting the postage dial at 0p first, *provided you are given permission to do so.*
- Practise weighing both parcels and letters on a postal weighing machine. Find out the maximum number of A4 sheets of paper which can be inserted into an envelope before the postage is more than the basic rate for 1st and 2nd class mail.
- Practise typing addresses (of your friends) on address labels. Mark your starting point with a pencil until you get used to the size.

SPECIAL NOTE

Businesses in foreign countries do not have the letters plc or Ltd after their name.

In Germany you will see the letters GmbH
In France the ending is normally 'et Cie'
In Australia many companies end 'Pty'
In America you may see 'Corp' for Corporation

Try to find out why some companies in Spain, Italy and Portugal end with the words 'y Cia' whilst others end with the letters SA. Perhaps your tutor can help.

SECTION REVIEW

Having completed this section, you should now be able to:

1. Describe the correct procedure for dealing with all categories of outgoing mail.
2. Explain the importance of deadlines in relation to outgoing mail.
3. Identify the type of envelopes used for business documents and correspondence.
4. Select suitably sized envelopes and fold documents correctly before insertion.
5. Address envelopes legibly and correctly following PO guidelines.
6. Select suitable wrapping materials and correctly wrap and address packets and parcels.
7. Describe the main PO services and the guides and leaflets available.
8. Correctly complete a range of PO forms for special services.
9. Record outgoing items in a postage book.
10. Correctly calculate postage rates for routine and special items.
11. Use postal scales and a franking machine.

? REVIEW QUIZ

True or false?

1 Registered mail can be sent by 1st or 2nd class post.

2 Datapost is an international service.

3 A registered envelope is distinctive because it has two black lines drawn across each side.

4 If a letter sent by Special Delivery is not delivered the next working day the sender can claim his Special Delivery fee back.

5 The large figures 1 or 2 on a Business Reply envelope denote the class of postage.

Complete the blanks . . .

6 Claims against the Post Office under the Compensation Fee Parcel service must be accompanied by a ....

7 An .... form must be completed if the sender wishes the Post Office to notify him when something has been delivered.

8 Franking machine control cards must be completed every ....

Work it out

9 What is the best way to send the following items through the post, assuming none of them is particularly urgent?
- **a)** the deeds to a house
- **b)** a £50 note
- **c)** a camera

10 Draw up a postage book with suitable headings and complete it with the following information:

Stamps bought yesterday = 80 1st class and 120 2nd class

Today's mail:

22 1st class letters and 38 2nd class letters (enter as two batches)

3 Recorded Delivery letters (2nd class) to Mrs K Brown, Stafford; Mr G Baker, Warrington; Frankish & Drew Ltd, Cheltenham.

1 Compensation Fee parcel weighing 5.8 kg and valued at £120 to Baker's Foods plc, Norwich.

2 airmail letters – one weighing 15 g to Cirius Enterprises, Athens and one weighing 8 g to Hudson Baker Pty, Sydney.

Look up the rates, enter the information and balance the book for today.

NUMERACY GUIDE 6

Percentages

If the amount of your income you spent on clothes was £23 out of every £100 you received, you could say that you spend 23% of your income on clothes.

SPECIAL NOTE

Do you know where the phrase 'per cent' comes from? Another way of saying one hundred is to say a century (as with runs in cricket, years etc) or centum. Originally the phrase 23 per centum was used – now shortened to 23 per cent or 23%.

The percentage of a number

You may be asked to carry out a percentage calculation where you are given the percentage and asked to find the number, eg find 12% of 340 or find 15% of £60.

The way to do this without a calculator (in case it breaks!) is to multiply the two numbers together and divide by 100, eg

$$\frac{12 \times 340}{100} = \frac{4080}{100} = 40.8$$

$$\frac{15 \times 60}{100} = \frac{900}{100} = £9$$

On a calculator you can either press the % key (if it has one) or divide by 100.

Therefore on your machine simply enter the two numbers as a multiplication and press the % key.

TEST YOURSELF 1

Calculate the following to two decimal places:

1 16% of 25
2 22% of 1830
3 30% of £180
4 62% of £98.50
5 12½% of 110 kg
6 112% of 80
7 168% of £426
8 16% of £93.24
9 74% of 2354 kg
10 81% of £12.30

11 There are 350 employees working in the offices of your company. 12% work in purchasing, 24% in office administration, 20% in sales, 14% in personnel, 18% in accounts, 2% in transport and 10% in production. From these figures calculate the number of employees in each department.

12 A company gives discounts of 5%, 8% and 12½% to grade A, B and C customers respectively. How much discount will each of the following be allowed:

- C Jones – grade A – order £126
- J Roberts – grade B – order £230.10
- B Clements – grade C – order £414.50

A quantity as a percentage

On other occasions you may be given two numbers and asked to find the percentage, eg what is 24 as a percentage of 400?

In this case we divide by the larger number and multiply by 100, if we are doing the calculation manually, eg

$\frac{24}{400} \times 100 = 6\%$

On a calculator you enter the smaller number (24) press ÷, then enter the larger number (400) and press %.

TEST YOURSELF 2

Express the following as percentages. Round to two decimal places where necessary.

1 18 as a percentage of 60
2 40p as a percentage of £3.20
3 0.134 as a percentage of 5
4 135 as a percentage of 400
5 90 kg as a percentage of 2500 kg
6 £85 as a percentage of £50
7 950 as a percentage of 500
8 106 as a percentage of 108
9 12.5 as a percentage of 20.25.
10 £36.40 as a percentage of £108.20.
11 A survey in your office regarding a proposed vending machine has shown that out of 80 people in the office, 33 want it to provide coffee, 21 prefer tea, 11 like orange juice and 8 consider hot chocolate their favourite. 5 people don't mind and 2 said they wouldn't use it anyway as they dislike vending machines. Express all the preferences as percentages and round these to the nearest whole number so that you total 100%.

Interest rates

When we *invest* money in a bank or building society we are **paid interest**. Similarly, if we *borrow* money we are **charged interest**. Knowing about percentages enables you to calculate the interest you will receive (or will be charged).

There are two types of interest – simple interest and compound interest. In this section we are only concerned with simple interest.

Imagine you have invested £500 in a building society and the current interest rate is 12%. How much interest are you owed? You can calculate this as follows:

Interest paid = 12% of £500

$\frac{12}{100} \times 500 = £60$

TEST YOURSELF 3

Your friend has £650 in the bank. How much would she receive in interest if the rate was

1 8% **2** 11.5% **3** 12.75% **4** 13.75%

Annual percentage rate

Interest charged on loans by companies has to be clearly stated to the borrower. This is done by stating the Annual Percentage Rate (APR) charged on the loan. It is calculated by adding together the interest due on the outstanding loan and administrative charges.

The lower the APR, the cheaper the loan. Always make sure you look for the APR and ignore the monthly rate (which looks so much cheaper) when calculating how much interest you would pay.

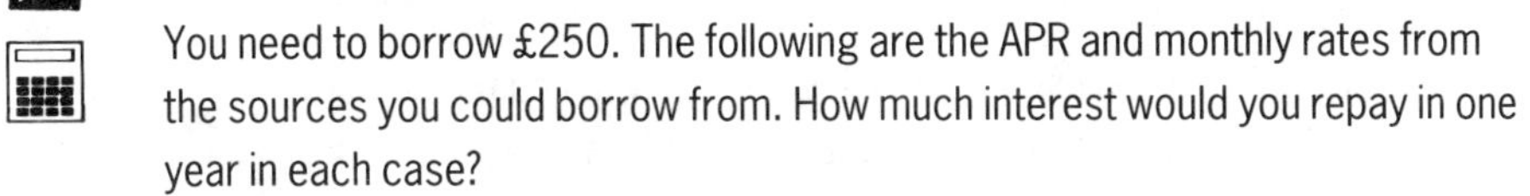

TEST YOURSELF 4

You need to borrow £250. The following are the APR and monthly rates from the sources you could borrow from. How much interest would you repay in one year in each case?

Company A – monthly interest rate 2.9% APR 41.5%
Company B – monthly interest rate 2.6% APR 35%
Company C – monthly interest rate 2.2% APR 29.8%
Company D – monthly interest rate 1.9% APR 24.65%

Value Added Tax (VAT)

Being able to calculate percentages is obviously essential to calculate VAT – currently charged at 15%.

SPECIAL NOTE

To calculate VAT quickly *without* a calculator, eg 15% of £60:

- find 10% (divide by 10) = £6
- Halve your answer (= 5%) = £3
- Add answers together = £9

TEST YOURSELF 5

Quickly work out what the VAT is on
(i) £10 (ii) £180 (iii) £42 (iv) £25

TEST YOURSELF 6

How much VAT would an organisation add on to each of the following accounts?

1 £420.40 **2** £18.60 **3** £116.80
4 £25.58 **5** £610 **6** £85.25

Adding on VAT

Obviously the organisation will send the account for the total + VAT. If you want to calculate the total quickly on most calculators, then instead of pressing the × key, press the + key instead, eg the plus VAT price of £40 =

40 + 15% = £46.

TEST YOURSELF 7

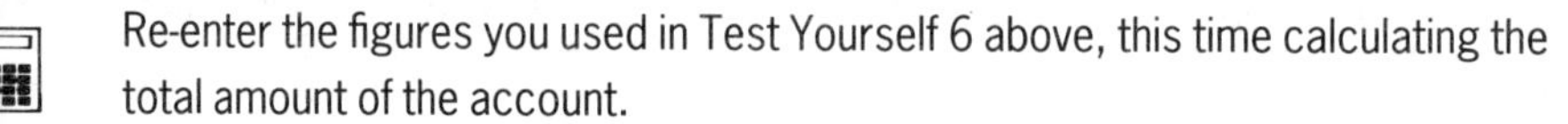

Re-enter the figures you used in Test Yourself 6 above, this time calculating the total amount of the account.

SPECIAL NOTE

The short cut you used of pressing the + key to find the amount + 15% can also be adapted for finding an amount *less* a percentage. Simply press the – key instead.

VAT inclusive accounts

In some cases the amount paid on an account is *inclusive* of VAT, eg petrol. If an expense claim is submitted for a VAT inclusive item then the amount of VAT has to be calculated so that it can be recorded separately.

Calculating VAT on inclusive accounts

to work this out use the following formula:

$$\frac{\text{rate of VAT}}{\text{VAT rate} + 100} \times \text{amount spent}$$

To see how this works, imagine a representative has spent £88 on petrol. VAT is 15%.

$$\frac{15}{15 + 100} = \frac{15}{115} \times 88 = £11.48$$

You can cancel down the fraction $\frac{15}{115}$ to $\frac{3}{23}$ to make things even easier.

Calculating the exclusive price

This is carried out either by subtracting the amount of VAT you have just worked out from the total paid (£88 – £11.48 = £76.52) or using the following formula:

$$\frac{100}{\text{VAT rate} + 100} = \frac{100}{115} = \frac{20}{23} \times \text{amount paid}$$

This is a better system as it gives you a double check on your first figure, as obviously the VAT + the exclusive price must equal the total account.

TEST YOURSELF 8

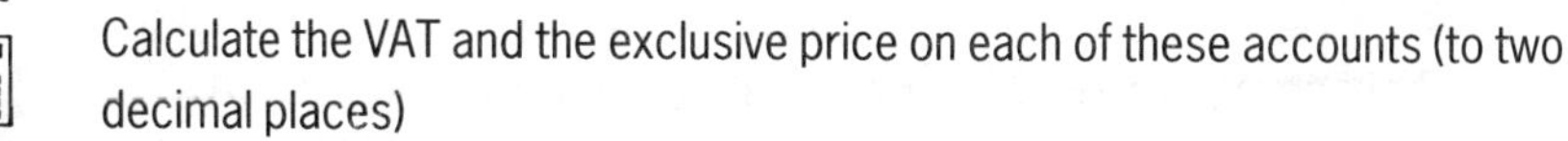

Calculate the VAT and the exclusive price on each of these accounts (to two decimal places)

1 £65.55 **2** £97.75 **3** £35.65
4 £17.63 **5** £64.50 **6** £22.60

Changing VAT rates

The formula will operate even if VAT rates changed – all you need to do is substitute different figures, eg if VAT went up to 20% the formula to calculate the VAT would be:

$$\frac{20}{120} = \frac{1}{6}$$

TEST YOURSELF 9

Calculate the cancelled down formulae if VAT was lowered to

1 5% **2** 10%

Creating and maintaining business relationships

WHAT ARE BUSINESS RELATIONSHIPS?

Business relationships refer to the professional working relationships you will be expected to create and maintain with *all* the people with whom you come into contact in your working life. In this chapter we will concentrate on your professional relationships with your colleagues and your organisation's customers and clients.

CHECK IT YOURSELF

- Discuss with your tutor the difference between a professional working relationship and a social relationship.
- How do you think this would influence the way you should act with someone and speak to someone?
- What difficulties might you encounter if you worked with someone and also knew them socially?

First encounters

We are all very influenced by first impressions. Therefore the first time we meet someone we quickly form an impression of them – from their actions, their words and the manner of speaking, the clothes they wear and whether they are friendly and approachable or distant and reserved. In the business world these 'measures' are used not only to judge the person but also the company itself – which is why an organisation is unlikely to employ anyone who does not portray the right 'image' to customers and clients. Neither is a company likely to employ anyone who would not 'fit in' with the rest of the staff.

Interview assessments

At an interview *you* will be judged – not only on obvious points such as punctuality, grooming and qualifications but also on other, less obvious, attributes, eg

- do you appear interested and enthusiastic?
- do you look pleasant and smile at the interviewer?
- do you *look* at the interviewer when you are talking to him/her?
- do you know basic business etiquette, eg were you prepared to shake hands with the interviewer on arrival or departure, if required?
- will the other members of the staff like working with you?

The last point is extremely important. An interviewer may be quite prepared to give the job to the person who will fit in the best with existing staff – even if that person is not the most well qualified!

CHECK IT YOURSELF

- With your tutor draw up a list of attributes an interviewer would assess at an interview.
- Work out how you think *you* would score under each heading.
- Discuss with your tutor how you could improve your score in other areas.
- If possible have a mock interview with your tutor and be prepared to accept any constructive criticism you receive *gracefully* – and remember it!

Good grooming – would you get the job?

Can you honestly say you:

- always look your best?
- are always 'nice to be near'?
- would project the *right* company image? (this means no way-out fashions or hairstyles!)

Good grooming has little to do with natural-born beauty and *everything* to do with attractiveness! Do the quiz below and see how you score. Give yourself one point each time you choose *sometimes*, two points each time you choose *always*. No points for *never*!

A score of 25–30 = very good, 21–24 = good. Under 20 – would you give yourself the job?

Do you:	**Always**	**Sometimes**	**Never**
have your hair trimmed regularly by a professional?			
wash your hair at least twice a week?			
change your underwear daily?			
have a bath/shower/all-over wash daily?			
always have clean, well-shaped nails?			
use an anti-perspirant all the time?			
wear lightly fragrant cologne or aftershave?			
refuse to eat strongly flavoured food (curry, garlic etc) when you are working?			
always wear clean, well pressed clothes?			
always carry a clean hanky or supply of tissues?			
clean your teeth after every meal?			
eat sensibly and watch your weight?			
visit your dentist twice a year?			
clean your shoes when they need it?			
have them repaired when they get down at heel?			

SPECIAL NOTE

Being an impoverished student is no excuse for poor grooming even if you cannot afford many new clothes or expensive products. It costs *nothing* except a little *time* to look and smell clean and fresh!

Dare you take the challenge?

Why not ask two of your best friends to score you on the quiz and see how they rate you – honestly!

Note that Job Application letters and CVs are covered in the chapter Communicating Information, pages 164–220.

Business relationships at work

Once you have obtained a job, and start work, you now have to prove that the interviewer was correct in his or her judgement in choosing you! Existing staff will be wary of you initially and sometimes may appear quite cool or remote. Do remember it takes time to build up a good working relationship with people – you cannot rush this by being over-friendly!

The best way that you can create a good impression from the outset is to always

- be courteous and tactful to everyone
- treat people who are senior to you, or older than you, with respect
- be helpful and pleasant
- make allowances for others having 'a bad day' or personal problems which may affect them at work
- communicate with people using the correct 'tone' – as well as the correct words.

Your manner and attitude is conveyed to people by the way in which you speak to them and in your gestures and facial expressions. This not only applies to the impression you give your colleagues but also the impression you give to customers and clients.

This chapter aims to make you more aware of how you appear to others and communicate with them – both verbally and non-verbally – and to help you to cope with some of the more difficult situations you may encounter in your working life.

METHODS OF COMMUNICATION

Basically we can communicate with people in two main ways – verbally or in writing. There are advantages and disadvantages to both.

Verbal

- quick, less formal and direct
- receiver can give instant feedback to check understanding
- stress can be used for emphasis
- if face-to-face then gestures and expressions help to clarify meaning.

Written

- more suitable for formal communications
- a permanent record which can be referred to again and again
- easier for difficult situations
- easier to reach a large number of people
- do not become distorted or exaggerated.

The communications cycle and problem areas

Unfortunately, when we are 'communicating', several things may go wrong. If we break down our communications into five stages we can see more easily where problems can occur.

Stage 1

We think of an idea or receive information we need to pass on.

Problems

Our idea is muddled.
We don't understand the information we received.

Stage 2

We 'encode' our idea or information into 'symbols' (usually words) we think our receiver will understand.

Problems

Our symbols are wrong. They may:

- be ambiguous
- be too difficult for the receiver to understand
- be in a language he doesn't know (eg jargon)

- be too vague
- have a different meaning to the receiver.

Stage 3

We 'transmit' our 'symbols'.

Problems

We choose the wrong method of transmission.

Our transmission is distorted.

Our transmission is interrupted.

We transmit our symbols:

- in the wrong order
- at the wrong time
- in the wrong place.

Our 'tone' is inappropriate for our receiver.

Stage 4

Our receiver 'decodes' the symbols he receives.

Problems

He doesn't understand the symbols.

He does not receive all the symbols we transmitted because:

- he was not listening
- he reacted too quickly.

He could not remember all the symbols received.

He reacts to the 'tone' of the transmission.

Stage 5

The receiver gives feedback to check he has understood the message.

Problems

He does not think this is necessary

He is in a hurry

The 'transmitter' is not present.

CHECK IT YOURSELF

- Discuss with your tutor specific examples to illustrate when *each* of the above may occur.
- What do you think could be the result in each case – and what action could you take to
  - **a** prevent the problem occurring
  - **b** put it right when it does?

VERBAL COMMUNICATIONS

This section is concerned with face-to-face communications with customers and other visitors to your organisation *plus* the people you work with every day.

To be an effective communicator and to promote good business relationships you must be able to:

- pass on information accurately and without delay, so that
  – the person concerned is aware of the current situation
  – the correct action can be taken immediately
- converse with a wide range of people with whom you have had little, if any, previous contact
- talk to your colleagues at work in a way which will promote and maintain a harmonious working atmosphere
- use a tone and style which is appropriate in terms of
  - the person you are speaking to
  - the message or information you are giving
  - the situation.

The skills you need to be a good verbal communicator include:

- a clear speaking voice
- a good speaking 'pace' (too slow and you bore people, too fast and they may not follow what you are saying)
- the ability to be a good listener
- the ability to choose the correct words and 'tone' for the person you are talking to
- the ability to put people at their ease
- an awareness and appreciation of non-verbal communication gestures and their meanings
- the confidence to talk to people you don't know.

What do you sound like?

Most people are absolutely horrified the first time they hear their voice on a tape recorder. It comes as a nasty shock to discover that we don't sound the same to other people as we sound to ourselves!

There are two aspects to our voice which affect the way we sound. The first is the **timbre** – or quality of sound – and the second is our **accent** and the way we pronounce words.

If you think your voice sounds squeaky or sharp then try to lower the pitch just a little. This may help. Try to refrain from getting excited or rushing too much as this can make us all sound more harsh.

Regional accents and dialects can be extremely attractive and no-one is suggesting that you should learn 'BBC English' before you can deal with people effectively. However, you should remember that a *very* broad regional accent may be virtually unintelligible to someone from another part of the country (or from abroad) – especially if you make matters worse by using lots of regional or slang expressions as well!

CHECK IT YOURSELF

We can all appreciate that accents and dialects make our language more rich and interesting, but these can be confusing to visitors.

Talk to your tutor about the expressions you use in *your* area which would not be suitable, and the way in which it may be necessary for you to modify your words to sound more business-like.

TEST YOURSELF

You are chairman of the students' committee at your school or college. This year the committee has raised £1200 through fund-raising activities to present to charity. The presentation will take place in front of all staff and students and you will have to present the cheque to a representative from the charity.

- Select a charity whose work you feel is worthy of receiving your cheque.
- Prepare a short speech which will last two to three minutes which would be suitable for the presentation. Mention what the charity does and why you chose it, give an idea of the hard work and type of fund-raising activities which have been undertaken and so on.
- *Tape* your speech
- Play it back and analyse it in terms of both its content and the way you sounded!
- Note that you should lose marks every time you say 'er' or 'um', and when you use slang words or expressions which would not be understood by your guest (assume he/she comes from another part of the country).
- Check the *pace* of your speech – was it gabbled or a bit hesitant and slow? How would it have sounded to someone sitting at the back of the room – would they have heard and understood every word, or not?

Listening skills

Ask yourself honestly:

- how many times do you find yourself waiting for someone else to stop speaking so that you can say the next thought that has just come into your head?
- How many times do you actually interrupt someone to say it?

Most of us are actually poor listeners. We listen to the *first* part of what we are being told, then think of something to say ourselves and spend the next few seconds waiting for the other person to stop speaking so that we can say it! During this latter part of their speech we have totally 'switched off' from what they are saying.

No-one can hold their concentration for very long – which is why *your* 'messages' shouldn't be too long. However, you should develop your listening skills so that you actively prevent yourself from switching off.

Tone

'Tone' is a common skill which you will find is equally important for good written communications too. It is so important that it should be one of the main determining factors in the words and phrases that you choose in *any* form of communication. Indeed the 'tone' of a communication can decide whether what you are saying (or writing) is acceptable or unacceptable to the receiver.

CHECK IT YOURSELF

Discuss with your tutor how your tone should vary if you were passing a message on to

- your friend
- a colleague at work
- your boss

both verbally and in writing.

NON-VERBAL COMMUNICATION

Non-verbal communication (**NVC**) is a fascinating topic and has many applications. A basic knowledge and appreciation of NVC and the way we all use it can help you to:

- realise how your own NVC is 'read' and interpreted by others
- improve the effectiveness of your own communication
- 'read' other people's NVC better – and react accordingly.

Its applications are not limited to a working environment – the next time you go out socially and meet somebody of the opposite sex you can use your knowlege of NVC to tell whether they are really interested in getting to know you better or not!

We can divide NVC into four separate areas:

- facial expressions – especially the use of the eyes
- gestures
- touching and spatial relationships (the distance between people)
- posture.

Facial expressions

These are usually the main 'give-away' on how we are feeling though we are very aware of this and may take action to 'cover up' our feelings.

Have you ever been given a present which disappointed you? Can you remember trying to make sure your disappointment wasn't reflected on your face? Therefore sometimes we have to be quite quick to read people's expressions accurately.

Generally facial expressions give us:

- continuous feedback on whether our listener understands us, is surprised at what we are saying, agrees with us and so on
- an indication of people's attitudes towards one another – people seeking approval, for instance, smile more and use more head nods and gesticulations than those who are not bothered what the other person thinks
- a clue as to how to accept a remark, eg how seriously a remark should be taken.

The eyes are very important – which is possibly one reason why we look at someone between 25%–75% of the time – noticeably more when we are listening to them than when we are speaking to them. We are all apt to consider someone has something to hide if they won't look at us when they are talking to us.

Gestures

We all use a variety of gestures to:

- communicate to someone a distance away
- accentuate what we are saying
- (subconsciously) echo what we are feeling.

Our feelings are very often shown by our gestures. The man who drums his fingers on the desk or taps his foot is signalling impatience – usually the faster he 'drums' the more impatient he is becoming! The smart, well-dressed young man who looks supremely confident may give away his inner feelings by continually touching or adjusting his cuffs – one sign of nervousness.

CHECK IT YOURSELF

How would you interpret the following gestures? Write down what you think and compare your notes with the rest of your group and your tutor.

- someone shrugging their shoulders, arms apart, palms uppermost
- the 'thumbs up' sign
- someone licking their lips
- a person rubbing his hands together (or 'washing' his hands) during a conversation with you

- a man straightening his tie and then touching his hair before moving towards a girl he has seen across the room.

Touching and spatial relationships

We subconsciously also try to maintain a certain distance between ourselves and other people – though the 'gap' we try to keep will depend on:

- which country we have been brought up in
- how well we know (or would like to know) the person next to us
- the type of event, eg business meeting or party.

We are always more wary of people being in front of us than behind us – we don't worry too much about people close to us so long as it is back to back! If we are forced to be very near to people we do not know front-to-front (eg in a crowded lift) we will do our utmost to avoid eye or body contact.

The distance we find 'comfortable' varies from one nationality to another. A British person on holiday in an Arab or Latin country can find themselves almost constantly moving backwards to try to maintain a distance which their host considers almost anti-social!

If we are with someone we know very well, or like very much, then we stand or sit much closer – often within 'touching' distance.

Posture

Posture can give various hints about your feelings.

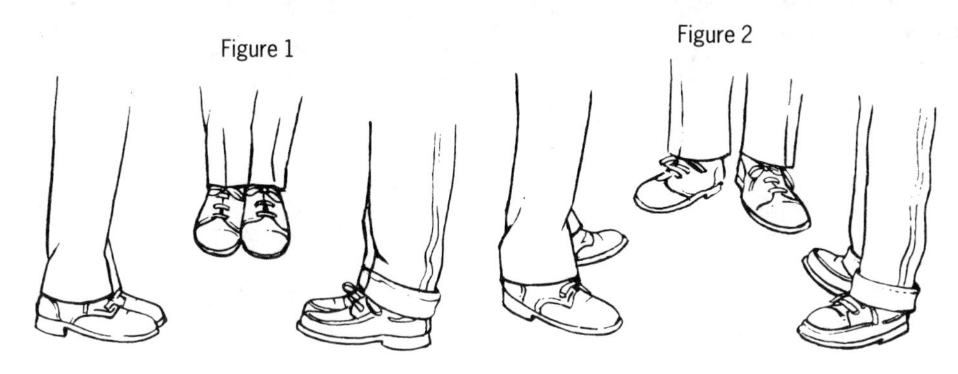

- We stand upright if we are interested or confident.
- We stand with our shoulders hunched if we are miserable, depressed or bored.
- We point our feet (and body) the way our mind wants us to go! If we are only marginally interested in someone who is passing by we will turn our heads towards them but *leave our body in the same position* (Fig. 1). We 'welcome' a newcomer into our circle by 'opening a gap' and angling our body towards them (Fig. 2).
- We unconsciously 'mirror' the position of someone we agree with.

CONFIDENTIALITY

You will be very unusual if you are never told anything at work which you are expected to keep to yourself, either by:

- a visitor
- your boss
- one of your colleagues.

Sometimes this will be in the context of a message you may have to pass on, at other times it may be in the form of a confidence which is entrusted to you. It is important that you keep such information to yourself and do not pass it on to others as 'gossip' at the earliest opportunity!

STAFF RELATIONSHIPS

Good staff relationships are important for

- staff morale and motivation
- productivity – staff who are happy at work usually work harder; colleagues who co-operate with each other are more productive.

Promoting good staff relationships is *not* just the job of senior management. You too have a part to play by:

- using the knowledge you have gained from this chapter to enable you to speak to people, and act towards them, in a mature and professional manner.
- thinking through the consequences of your words and actions before you say or do anything you may regret later.
- not bearing grudges, being moody or 'difficult' to work with.
- always carrying out requests promptly and willingly or explaining properly and politely why you cannot help.
- asking others for their help or assistance politely.
- keeping others informed about anything you have done or said on their behalf.
- knowing the difference between when *not* to 'tell tales' and when to report unethical behaviour or a problem your boss should know about.

Problems

There are a variety of situations you can meet at work where you really have to 'think on your feet'. However, by being tactful, polite, courteous and friendly – and by knowing the correct procedure to follow if you have a real problem – you will usually be able to cope.

Whilst it is impossible, in this book, to give you an example of every type of situation which may occur, the following exercise may give you some insight into what to do and what not to do.

TEST YOURSELF

1 It is suggested that you read the following situations carefully, make notes on how you would react and then discuss your answers as a group with your tutor.

What would you do if:

a you were given conflicting instructions by two senior members of staff in your company?

b you were blamed for something you hadn't done – although you knew who the culprit was?

c you overhear a colleague giving a customer the wrong information?

d the first time your boss asks you to stay late as a favour you had made arrangements to go out early that evening?

e you felt you were being continually 'picked on' by a senior member of staff?

f You forgot to pass on an urgent message to your boss.

g A colleague of the opposite sex repeatedly makes unwelcome advances towards you.

h A friend at work frequently telephones her brother, who lives in Australia, for long chats on the basis that 'no-one will ever find out'.

i The new girl you share an office with turns out to be sulky, unhelpful and uncooperative and complains whenever she is given any work to do.

j After staying late for two nights to help out with an urgent job (without pay) your boss reprimands you the following morning when you arrive 10 minutes late.

2 Discuss with your tutor when and why difficulties and problems should be reported and when officially reporting a problem may do more harm than good. If you are working you should relate this to your own experiences and discuss the procedures (if any) in your organisation for dealing with these type of problems.

SPECIAL NOTE

Customer relationships are dealt with in the chapter entitled Liaising with customers and clients and the chapter entitled Providing information to customers and clients.

SECTION REVIEW

Having completed this section, you should now be able to:

1 Differentiate between social and business relationships and state how this affects both speech and actions.

2 Describe appropriate standards for dress, appearance and behaviour in a working environment.

3 Explain the problems which can occur with everyday communications and how these can be avoided.

4 State why it is essential that information should be passed on promptly and accurately.

5 Accurately assess your own speaking and listening skills.

6 Recognise common non-verbal communication gestures.

7 Determine appropriate methods of resolving difficulties in working relationships.

8 Explain when and why unresolved difficulties and problems should be reported to higher authority and the correct procedures for doing so.

? *REVIEW QUIZ*

True or false?

1 Most people are good listeners.

2 We look at someone when we are speaking to them more than when we are listening to them.

3 Timbre refers to quality of sound.

4 Tapping our feet can signal that we are becoming impatient.

5 Regional expressions are always interesting to strangers.

Complete the blanks . . .

6 Body language is known as ....

7 Words can be thought of as .... which we use to express our thoughts and feelings.

8 A receiver of a message should give .... to check that he has understood.

Work it out

9 Write down how you would use your knowledge of NVC in the following situations.
- A business man waiting in reception is staring out of the window and, at the same time, drumming his fingers on the arm of his chair.

- You are attending an interview next week and want to give the impression you are keen and interested in the job.
- A new member of staff tells you she never feels welcome with your group when she comes over to talk at lunch time.
- A lady approaches reception with her head down and shoulders hunched. She waits patiently for you to see to her.

10 Reword each of the following statements to make them more acceptable to the receiver.

'Can you hurry up – I need it now, not in half an hour.'

'How can you expect to have your goods delivered on time when we're in the middle of a rail strike?'

'It's not my fault you've been kept waiting, we've been rushed off our feet all morning.'

'That's not how to do it – don't you know *anything*?'

'If you'd followed the directions I gave you before you wouldn't be having this problem. Why don't you listen?'

NUMERACY GUIDE 7

Cross-checking

Cross checking is an essential part of office numeracy. If you are involved in accounts or figures of any kind and you don't cross check then you will never find the mistakes you make. But someone else is bound to. Do you want that to happen to you?

Cross checking is mainly used when you have to add figures down and across. In this case there is always a **key figure** – where the sums of the amounts down and across *must* agree, eg:

20	25	28	32	61	=	166	totals of the rows
13	18	41	10	12	=	94	
19	38	62	40	29	=	188	
52	81	131	82	102		448	✓ **key figure**

totals of columns

It is very tempting, especially when you are in a hurry, not to cross check your key figure. In the above example, the steps are

- add up the rows across
- add up the columns down
- add up the totals of the columns and insert the answer (448)
- **then** to *cross check* your answer add up the totals of the rows and see if the number agrees.

If they don't agree, then you have gone wrong somewhere and you will need to repeat all the steps above.

TEST YOURSELF 1

Copy out and add up the following columns of numbers across and down and cross check your key figure both ways.

£	£	£	£
114.20	56.19	109.31	....
256.90	43.12	56.09	....
14.89	123.67	151.31	....

Calculator memory function

You may have been extremely efficient and used the memory function on your calculator to help you in the exercise above – or you may not! In which case you repeated several operations unnecessarily, eg by re-entering your column totals after adding them up the first time, to get your final total.

If you look on your calculator you will usually find three or four memory keys:

M+	add to memory	MR	recall memory
M–	subtract from memory	MC	clear memory

If your machine has three memory keys it is likely that one is marked MRC and does the work of both MR and MC.

Practise using memory

You are going to do the following exercise with the memory function to help you.

	Col. 1		Col. 2		Col. 3			
Row A	28	+	45	+	19	=	....	(E)
Row B	72	+	16	+	29	=	....	(F)
Row C	52	+	34	+	83	=	....	(G)
(A)	____	(B)	____	(C)	____	(D)	____	(D)

- Start by copying out the exercise as shown above. Don't copy out the row, column or total indicator letters – those are just references for the next stages.
- Enter the three amounts in column 1 and press total. Enter this as total A. You now need to enter this into memory by pressing M+. Your calculator should signal you that the memory is now in use. Press CE or C (this will vary according to your machine) – if you press the correct key the screen will clear with the memory signal still showing.
- Enter the three amounts in column 2, press total and enter this as total B. Now add this to your memory by pressing M+ and again clear your screen.
- Repeat the procedure for column C and again clear the screen.
- Now press MR. Your memory will now show the total of all the items you put into memory – in other words your answer for total D.
- Now press MC to clear the memory.
- Repeat the whole operation for rows A, B and C and press MR to show the sum of totals E, F and G. This should, of course, be identical to the total you entered for D before.
- **Don't forget to clear your memory**. (On some machines the memory is held for a short time even after the machine is switched off.)

SPECIAL NOTE

Calculators do vary slightly as to how the memory function works. You will certainly find a difference if you use many types of scientific calculator. If you have any difficulties then see your tutor.

TEST YOURSELF 2

Use the memory function to calculate and cross check the following:

£	£	£	£
732.48	526.98	94.52	....
66.73	5.68	325.31	....
106.40	23.89	704.05	....
6.72	189.23	8.50	....
629.38	527.14	800.00	....
81.30	14.27	680.50	....
431.26	5.01	16.70	....

Other uses for memory

The memory function can usefully be used whenever you have to carry out any numeric operation on a line of numbers and keep the total for later use, eg

47 small widgets @ £20 each + VAT	=	....
62 medium widgets @ £36 each + VAT	=	....
35 large widgets @ £42 each + VAT	=	....
Sub-total		....
Less 10% discount		....
Total		

TEST YOURSELF 3

From what you learned in the previous sections, and with what you now know about memory, you should be able to input the exercise above on your calculator with:

- each line entered as one process
- no figure entered twice – anywhere!

Can you do it?

Memory minus

Not all cross-check rows and columns are additions. The M– key enables you to subtract from memory. Study the following exercise and the notes which follow.

	In Stock	**Issued**	**Balance**
Component 1	6021	4012	....
Component 2	4150	2130	....
Component 3	231	110	....
Component 4	9216	7058	....
Component 5	2108	647	....

When the rows are calculated *across* a normal minus will be used and the balance for each component entered. The memory should be used to store the balances and recall the final total.

However, when the columns are calculated then the total of the issued stock must be *subtracted* from the total put into memory from the first column. This is done by pressing M+ after the first column (as usual) and then M– after the second column, to cross check the balance.

TEST YOURSELF 4

Can you carry out the calculation above, using memory throughout to help you?

Simple sum trick

Tell your friends to think of a number, multiply it by three, multiply the answer by three again and then add the number they first thought of.

Ask them the number they now have. It will *always* end in zero.

Take off the zero – and you can tell them the number they first thought of!

Communicating information

Communicating information accurately and clearly, using an appropriate tone, style and vocabulary is one of the most important and valuable skills you can learn. It is *essential* to the smooth running of any office so that:

- customers and clients are dealt with efficiently and correctly over the telephone
- messages are passed on promptly and accurately
- the correct information is always given to both colleagues and customers
- letters sent to customers reflect the image your organisation wishes to portray – they are well constructed and error-free.

To help you to acquire these skills, this chapter is divided into four sections.

- Section 1 – telephone skills and message taking
- Section 2 – basic writing skills
- Section 3 – business correspondence
- Section 4 – Proof-reading and text editing.

SPECIAL NOTE

Supplying information (ie visual information) is dealt with in the chapter on Supplying and Storing Information.

Section 1 – Telephone skills and message taking

There is a telephone in virtually every office in the world (often more than one!) and one of the main duties of every office worker is to deal with incoming calls from both inside and outside the organisation. In addition, you may often initiate calls on your own or someone else's behalf. Indeed, some companies conduct a major part of their business over the telephone – rather than dealing with their customers on a face-to-face basis, eg a booking agency.

In a new job most people don't like answering the telephone because they are worried they will not know what they are talking about, cannot help the caller and will look foolish.

Note – It is perfectly possible to sound competent and efficient *and* give a good impression *without* being able to give someone specific help.

Hints and tips

1. *Never* answer a telephone without a pen or pencil in your hand and a piece of paper (or preferably a message pad) nearby.
2. Answer *promptly* (the caller can't see how busy you are!).
3. Answer an outside call with 'Good morning/afternoon' and the name of your organisation.
4. Answer a call to an internal extension with either the name of your department, the extension number or your own name (whichever is usual in your organisation).
5. *Never* eat or drink when using the telephone.

6. *Always* sound pleasant and helpful.
7. If the call is for someone else who is available:
   - ask who is calling
   - ask them to hold the line a moment (*please*!). *Don't* say 'hang on'!
   - tell the person being called they are wanted and give them the name of the caller.
8. If the call is for someone else who is *not* available:
   - ask if the caller would like to speak to anyone else
   - see if *you* can help
   - suggest the caller rings back later *or* suggest the

person they want to speak to rings them back later (this will depend on the policy of your organisation)

- offer to take a message (see also page 174).

9 If the caller wants information which will take you a while to find, *don't* keep them holding on – offer to ring back when you have it to hand.

10 *Never* promise to ring someone back and let them down.

11 *Always* check with your supervisor if you are being asked for information which may be confidential.

12 Be aware that a receiver left lying on a desk top picks up the general office conversation.

13 Treat important information you receive over the telephone as confidential – *don't* pass it round the office.

SPECIAL NOTE

Sometimes callers with an enquiry need transferring to another extension. Learn the correct procedure for doing this on your telephone system so that you don't cut off anyone by mistake.

CHECK IT YOURSELF

Do you know the standard telephone tones and their meanings? If not, look them up in the phone book or dial 191 and ask the operator to demonstrate them.

The professional touch

People who sound really effective on the telephone usually know one or two things that others don't . . . such as:

- using a person's name during a conversation makes them feel important
- concluding a call by saying 'thank you for calling' has the same effect
- all forms of slang (especially OK!) do *not* sound business-like.
- if you are cut off in the middle of a conversation, the person who made the call should attempt the reconnection

- figures said in *pairs* are always easier to understand
- it is always better (if possible) to let the person who made the call conclude it
- a 'smile' in the voice is identified as being friendly on the other end of a telephone
- there is nothing wrong in asking people to repeat a name or a figure to check you have written it correctly. People with an unusual name are quite used to having to spell it out over the telephone
- it is far better to check all the details *before* ringing off than to have to ring back later
- if you are making a call then all the facts and figures should be next to you *before* you ring. If you prepare well you sound more efficient.

SPECIAL NOTE

A book, issued free by British Telecom, gives hints and tips on using the telephone correctly. If you want to know more about it, test your own telephone skills by dialling 0800 800 864 and asking for a copy. It's called *Be Your Own Boss*.

Telephone alphabet

Because you have a bad line, or you are reading an address or item name which could be misinterpreted by the listener, you may have to spell out a word to make it clear. Sometimes even spelling the word isn't sufficient – Ts, Bs and Ps, for instance, can sound very similar over the telephone.

In this case it is usual for letters to be identified using the telephone alphabet:

A – Alfred
B – Benjamin
C – Charlie
D – David
E – Edward
F – Frederick
G – George
H – Harry
I – Isaac
J – Jack
K – King
L – London
M – Mary
N – Nellie
O – Oliver
P – Peter
Q – Queen
R – Robert
S – Samuel
T – Tommy
U – Uncle
V – Victor
W – William
X – X-ray
Y – Yellow
Z – Zebra

SPECIAL NOTE

- Sometimes it isn't necessary to spell out *all* the letters – only the tricky ones in a word, eg

  PAIGNTON = P A I G for George N for Nellie T O N

- It can be useful to identify your postcode by using the telephone alphabet unless the letters in it are particularly distinctive.

DEALING WITH DIFFICULT CALLS

In addition to dealing with general enquiries you may be expected to deal with more difficult situations, eg customers calling to complain about either the service they have received or a product they have bought or perhaps a foreigner calling who speaks poor English.

The complaint/the angry caller

Listen sympathetically	**Don't** interrupt in the early stages of the conversation
Take down all the facts	**Don't** give vague excuses
Check you have these down correctly by reading them back to the caller	**Don't** put the blame on anyone
Explain to the caller you will pass on the problem to your supervisor immediately	**Don't** try to pretend the problem doesn't exist
Explain to the caller his/her complaint will be investigated	**Don't** make promises outside your control
Give a time when someone will call back	**Don't** delay in passing on the message to someone who can deal with it

The foreigner who speaks poor English/has a strong accent

Listen carefully	**Don't** speak quickly
Use simple English words	**Don't** use long sentences
Repeat carefully what you think is meant to check you are right	**Don't** shout!

Ask for help if you really cannot understand the caller at all	**Don't** become impatient

Nuisance callers (eg heavy breathing or worse!)

Stay calm and unflustered	**Don't** answer back or engage the caller in conversation
Disconnect or put the phone down	**Don't** become upset or *slam* the phone down
Report the matter immediately to your supervisor or to security	**Don't** hesitate to notify the police yourself if the calls continue and you are in a small office on your own

SPECIAL NOTE

Recorded advice on how to deal with these calls is given free if you dial 0800 888 777.

The bomb threat

Try to alert someone else while the caller is still on the line	**Don't** ring off
Listen for clues – accent, background noises, approximate age	**Don't** become excited or flustered
Try to keep the caller talking (apologise for bad line etc)	**Don't** cut off the conversation or ask for caller to 'hold'
Try to find out where the bomb has been planted and the time it will go off	**Don't** throw away any notes you make about the conversation

SPECIAL NOTE

The Metropolitan Police have issued a *Guide to Small Businesses* which includes an action checklist for anyone receiving a telephone bomb threat. Try to obtain a copy from your local Crime Prevention Officer.

Wrong numbers and misdirected calls

If you receive calls which are not routed through a switchboard then inevitably you will eventually receive a call which was not intended for your organisation. This may be because

- the caller has dialled the wrong number
- there is a telephone line or equipment fault, so that the call has been routed to you
- the caller has the wrong number noted down for the organisation he/she wants.

Do *not* become impatient or sound annoyed! Deal with the caller properly, giving your own number clearly so the caller knows where he/she went wrong. Remember – the person you are speaking to may also be an existing or future customer of your organisation!

From time to time a similar type of error may be made by the switchboard – and a call is directed to your extension which should be dealt with by someone else. Learn the procedure for either redirecting calls or referring them back to the switchboard operator using your telephone system. If several calls are received then contact the switchboard operator to inform him/her that these calls should be dealt with by another extension – and say which one, if possible. D*on't* sound annoyed or cross with the switchboard operator, who is also under pressure and may not have been told that a member of staff has transferred to another department or a type of work which is now dealt with by another office.

Emergencies

It is important that you know the procedure for making emergency calls. There are three main emergency services accessed by dialling 999 – police, fire and ambulance.

- dial the number
- state the service you require (you may need more than one)
- state the nature of the emergency and give your name, address and telephone number
- give directions if required (use churches, pubs and other landmarks as a guide).

It is useful to keep other emergency numbers close at hand, such as the number to call if there is a gas or water leak.

CHECK IT YOURSELF

Look up the number of the following services in your area

- to report a gas leak
- to report a water leak
- to report a power fault (ie no electricity)
- the nearest hospital with a casualty unit.

Telephone faults

- If your telephone is out of order then dial 151 from a nearby phone as soon as possible and report the fault.
- If you cannot obtain a particular number, dial 100 and ask the operator for assistance.
- If you have a bad connection, eg a crossed line, ring off and dial the number again rather than try to struggle through.

Confidentiality

You must be careful not to disclose confidential information which somebody may ask you for over the telephone. If you are ever in any doubt about whether you should tell a caller something always err on the side of discretion and *check first*.

TEST YOURSELF

You work in Personnel and receive a call from a young man who met a girl who worked in your office as a temp last week. He wanted to speak to her on the telephone but, because she has now left, he asks you for her address so that he can write to her. What would you say?

CHECK IT YOURSELF

How would you like someone giving out your address to anyone who asked? Whenever you receive a request for confidential information, if there is *any* doubt at all whether it should be given, say you do not know the answer and refer the problem to your supervisor.

Discuss with your tutor the type of information which must not be disclosed if you worked for the following types of organisation, and why

- an estate agent
- an accountant
- a doctor
- a solicitor

TELEPHONE REFERENCE BOOKS

In addition to the ordinary telephone directory and Yellow Pages for their area, most businesses also keep:

- telephone directories for other areas they call regularly
- Business Pages (similar to Yellow Pages but with business suppliers, not retail outlets and services, and covers a wider area)
- an internal directory showing all extensions against departments or names of staff.

You should be able to use these easily to look up numbers you need both inside and outside your organisation.

CHECK IT YOURSELF

Look through your telephone directory and find out:

- the difference between 071 and 081 when ringing London numbers
- the STD codes for Newport (Shropshire), Waterford (Southern Ireland), Castletown (Caithness), Preston (Dorset), Menai Bridge and Londonderry
- the International Direct Dialling (IDD) codes for Switzerland, Norway and Gibraltar
- the time difference between the UK and Burma
- the number of the speaking clock.

TELEPHONE SERVICES

Freefone

- is easily identifiable because the word Freefone precedes the number. Freefone callers must make their calls via the operator. There is no charge for the call. Numbers prefixed 0800 are also free and can be dialled direct. Your company may have a Freefone number itself to encourage potential customers to ring free of charge.

Directory enquiries

- dial 192 and give the name and town. If the name is a common one you will be asked for the initial or the address. Remember you are charged for this service.

Information services

- the only British Telecom information service still in operation on a regular basis is the speaking clock. All other information services are provided by private companies and the numbers all start with the prefix 0898. The services are usually advertised in the daily and Sunday papers.

International

- most international calls can now be made using the IDD service. If you have a problem getting through to an international number you can call the International Operator for assistance by dialling 155.
- the tones heard on telephones abroad are not the same as those heard in the UK, and if you are about to make a number of international calls for the first time you can ask the operator to give you a demonstration of the tones you can expect to hear.

CHECK IT YOURSELF

- You can obtain a copy of the *International Telephone Guide* from British Telecom by ringing them on 0800 800 838. The call is free and so is the guide.
- It is 9 am and soon after arriving at work one of your colleagues decides to telephone your New York office about an urgent matter which has just come up. Is this a good idea and if not, why not?

TELEPHONE CHARGES AND ECONOMIES

All organisations are usually very cost conscious in relation to the use of the telephone. Most modern equipment will provide detailed printouts of calls to help reduce costs. Private subscribers can now ask for an itemised bill showing exactly how many calls were made, where to and when.

Charges are based on:

- distance (whether the call is local, national or international)
- whether the call is made at a time and day which is classified as **cheap** rate, **standard** rate or **peak** rate
- the duration of the call.

CHECK IT YOURSELF

- Find out the times and days when calls are charged at peak rate, standard rate and cheap rate.
- In discussions with your tutor and other members of your group make out a ten point list under the heading 'Keeping Telephone Charges to a Minimum'.
- Find out the policy in your organisation (or one you visit on work experience) for making private telephone calls. If they are forbidden by a company, what facilities can be provided for employees for emergency use?

SPECIAL NOTE

Private telephone calls are not just frowned upon because of cost. *Incoming* private calls tie up a business line and you cannot be working if you are chatting to a friend on the telephone! Try to stop anyone ringing you at work unless it's important.

MESSAGE TAKING

It is, of course, quite possible that you will have to take messages from telephone callers if the person they want to speak to isn't immediately available.

Your rules should include the following:

- use simple, straightforward words
- keep your sentences short but vary the length a little so that your message 'flows'
- include all the key facts
- *don't* include irrelevant information
- ask your boss to do something – *never* tell her!
- be very specific about days, dates and times. If you give an unspecific time (eg tomorrow) add the *day* – in case your message isn't read until the following day.

Extra points you need to know:

- mark urgent messages *clearly*
- check (politely) if urgent messages have been seen later. If the person they are addressed to has not returned, someone else will then be able to deal with it.
- *never* forget to pass a message on – the results can be disastrous!

TELEPHONE MESSAGES

There are many types of pre-printed message pads on the market for telephone messages, all of which are better than scraps of paper because:

- the headings on the form help you to remember what to ask
- in many cases a duplicate copy is made automatically for reference if the original gets lost.

What to write down . . .

Basic essentials are:

- name of the caller
- telephone and extension number
- time and date of call
- message.

CHECK IT YOURSELF

Try to obtain a copy of a pre-printed message form. What other facts does it ask for besides those given above?

SPECIAL NOTE

People usually contact an organisation by telephone, telex or fax if the communication is urgent. If it was less urgent they would write a letter instead. It is therefore important that you pass on all messages, received by any of these means, *as soon as possible* – and check, later, that the person has actually received the message.

Key facts

Every message contains a number of **key facts**. If you miss these out the message will either not make sense or not make the *right* sense. You must:

- learn to listen for these and distinguish them from 'general' conversation
- write them down
- check them before ringing off.

TEST YOURSELF

Read the following carefully:

'This is Mrs Hanson of the ABC Employment Agency. Yesterday I arranged with Mr Higham, your boss, for a Miss Nicola Howarth to come to your firm for an interview at 10.30 am tomorrow. Unfortunately we have just found out that she will be unable to manage 10.30 and, if possible, we would like to re-arrange the interview for 2 pm. Do you think that will be all right? Could you ask Mr Higham to ring me back as soon as possible to let me know if he could see her at that time. My telephone number is 649783 extension 12.'

1. List the key facts in the above message – remember the interview was previously arranged for 10.30 and Mr Higham will be aware of this.
2. List the details you should check with Mrs Hanson before she rings off.
3. Is this call urgent or non-urgent? Why?
4. Write out the message neatly and clearly on a pre-printed message form. Check the message with your tutor.

Note: before you go any further check that your answers are correct by referring to Check it Yourself on page 179.

SPECIAL NOTE

The procedure for taking face-to-face messages is the same – note down the **key** facts. *But* a person's attitude, eg., worry, anger, etc, is easier to see face-to-face and you can pass this information on too, if it would be helpful.

Questioning

There are occasions when you have to ask for information from a caller which may not be offered (eg their telephone number!) There are also times when you can find out more to help the person who the message is for, eg why the person is ringing. Never be afraid to ask for additional information which will enable you to compose a clear and comprehensive message.

SPECIAL NOTE

You need to be able to develop the skill of questioning people to elicit the information you need.

- *Don't* fire questions at people and *don't* be put off asking for more information if they seem to be abrupt or nervous.
- *Do* ask politely for additional information and *do* try to think of anything else *you* would need to know if you had to follow up the call later.

TEST YOURSELF

1 Note down the key facts in the following message and then write it out for Mr Andrews, the area sales representative.

My name is John Watson and my address is 425 Glengarrow Road, Highton, telephone 48297. I have been trying to get hold of one of your products – Neutra Soap – because I have been told it is very good for sensitive skins. My mother has a problem skin and I have been to all the main shops near us but no-one has heard of your product. Can you tell me the name of your nearest stockist or even send me a sample so that my mother could try it? Can you let me have the information as quickly as possible as my mother telephones me every day to see if I have managed to get it. Thanks.

2 Read this through, identify the key facts and note what is *missing* and should be asked for:

'This is Andrew Baker of the Federated Employees Union. I've just received the information your boss John Jackson wanted. Can I call and see him in the morning?'

Check your answers with your tutor.

INITIATING A CALL

There will be occasions when you have to make a call yourself, either on your own behalf or someone else's.

- note down all the facts you must mention *first*
- make sure you have written down the correct number to call
- dial the number carefully (on most switchboard systems you need to dial '9' first to obtain an outside line)
- when the telephone is answered make sure you are through to the correct number and then ask for the person you want to speak to

- be prepared to give your own name and that of your company, eg 'This is Joanne Marsden of Walker's Plastics', in response to the question 'who is calling'
- greet the person properly when they come on the line and introduce yourself
- state the facts you need to mention – don't speak too quickly!
- make a note of the response. This may necessitate making out a message to the person who asked you to make the call, saying what happened
- tick the facts off as you say them, so that you don't repeat yourself or miss anything out
- be aware that as the caller you should be the person to conclude the call – properly!

TEST YOURSELF

Your boss, Mrs Elaine Graham, the Personnel Manager at your firm – XYZ Advertising – has asked you to telephone the Banbury Hotel, Oxford and book her a single room with bath for next Tuesday night. She wants the hotel to be aware that she will not be arriving in Oxford until about 8 pm that evening. She wants to know the cost of the room and if it will be in order for her to pay by credit card.

- List the facts you must discuss with the hotel receptionist, (in a logical order).
- Make the call with either your tutor or a colleague playing the part of the receptionist.
- Ask the person on the other end of the telephone to score you on
  - your greeting and introduction
  - the questions you ask – and the way in which you ask them!
  - the way in which you conclude the call.
- From the responses given, make out a suitable message for Mrs Graham.

Answering machines

There are some occasions when you will telephone a person – to find yourself answered by a recorded message. In the majority of cases this will ask *you* to leave a message, on the tape, after you have heard a special 'tone'. You may be asked to speak slowly and clearly and to spell out any difficult words (do you remember your telephone alphabet?)

Don't panic and replace the receiver!

- state clearly *who* you are and the name of your company
- leave a *brief* summary of your message (*or* ask the person to ring you back – if possible give them a clue why you are ringing!)
  [*Note*: the tape you are recording on is only short – if you talk too long the machine will cut you off!]
- ring off.

TEST YOURSELF

You have been asked by Mrs Graham to telephone Mr Derek Harris at Marshall and Webb Ltd to ask if he could let her have a reference on Barry Walker – who used to work as a graphic designer for their company – as soon as possible. If he wants he can fax it to her, your fax number is 663099. When you ring through you hear the pre-recorded answerphone message.

- Write out a suitable, *brief*, message you could leave on the tape.
- If possible, tape your message and play it back – then assess how it sounds with your tutor.
- Try to keep your message to within 30 seconds.

CHECK IT YOURSELF

The key facts are:

- name of caller and her organisation
- telephone number of caller and extension number
- name of interviewee
- time *and date* of original interview
- time *and date* of re-arranged interview
- request for Mr Higham to ring back and confirm

Details to check

- *All* numbers, times and dates
- spelling of interviewee's name (could be Nichola Haworth!)

Urgent/non-urgent

- Very urgent – so that the employment agency can contact Nicola Howarth and confirm the new time.

SECTION REVIEW

Having completed this section, you should now be able to:

1. Answer the telephone in a professional and confident manner.
2. Respond to telephone enquiries positively, taking a message when necessary.
3. Deal with difficult callers and emergencies.
4. Deal with wrong numbers and misdirected calls.
5. Explain the importance of confidentiality in relation to using the telephone.
6. Use telephone reference books accurately and quickly to extract information.
7. List the main telephone services and state when these would be used.
8. Describe the ways in which telephone economies can be achieved.
9. Write accurate messages, using the correct tone for the receiver.
10. Explain the importance of passing on messages quickly.
11. Initiate outgoing calls on behalf of self and others.
12. Leave messages on an answering machine.

REVIEW QUIZ

True or false?

1. It is impossible to sound efficient over the telephone unless you can give a caller specific help.

2 If a caller wants information you need to find, ask him/her to hold on whilst you look for it.

3 Figures said in pairs are always easier to note down.

4 Always return misdirected calls to the switchboard.

5 071 and 081 both preface London numbers.

Complete the blanks . . .

6 During working hours, calls are cheaper if they are made in the ....

7 Directory enquiries are accessed by dialling ....

8 The three main emergency services accessed by dialling 999 are ...., ... and ....

Work it out

9 From the following telephone conversation, make out a suitable message for your boss, Steven Jackson, the Sales Manager.

You: Sales Department, may I help you?

Caller: Yes, I hope so. My name is Gemma Pearson – I'm Paul Evans' secretary at Glendale and Walker. Mr Evans spoke to your Mr Jackson about a week ago and told him that we were having trouble with the new photocopier we bought from you last month. Mr Jackson promised that someone would come and look at it.

You: I thought that someone had been to repair it on Tuesday.

Caller: Yes, your mechanic was with us for nearly two hours. The problem is that the machine has gone faulty again – this time it's putting black streaks down every page and the collator doesn't work properly either.

You: I'm sorry about that. I'll tell Mr Jackson the moment he comes in to the office and ask him to contact you.

Caller: Can you please stress that we have an urgent job to do for a sales presentation which *must* be right. Mr

Evans has asked me to say that if we can't have the copier in perfect working order by tomorrow he would rather have the machine taken out. One of the reasons we bought a new machine in the first place was because we needed good copies for the presentation material.

You: Can you leave it with me? I'll arrange for Mr Jackson to speak to you as soon as he gets in – which should be in about half an hour. Quite obviously we'll do all we can to rectify the fault immediately. Can you give me your telephone number?

Caller: Yes, it's 663059 – my extension number is 203. We'll wait to hear from you then?

You: Yes, we'll call you back as soon as possible.

Caller: Thank you. Goodbye.

You: Goodbye.

10 Read the following dialogue and answer the questions below.

You: Good morning, Personnel Department.

Caller: I'm ringing you about my husband. He works at your firm.

You: What's his name?

Caller: His name is Robert Walker.

You: What about him?

Caller: He's had an accident and is going to be off work a bit.

You: What do you call 'a bit' – a day, a week, a month – how long?

Caller: We don't really know. The doctor said he'd have to stay in bed at least a week. I suppose two or three weeks altogether.

You: Did you get a certificate?

Caller: Yes, we've got a sick note for two weeks. I'll send it to you if you want. Will you tell his boss?

You: Who's that?

Caller: I don't know his name – Bob works in the factory.

You: Mrs Walker, we have a big factory – you'll have to

give me more to go on than that. What department?

Caller: I think it's something to do with the Stores.

You: Thank you. Send me the certificate and I'll see his foreman gets the message.

Caller: Thank you. Goodbye.

You: Goodbye.

a Can you think of at least *one* other question you could have asked to show more concern regarding the caller's message?

b What questions given above should you *not* have needed to ask – on the basis that you could have looked up the information?

c Rewrite the whole of the conversation (using the basic facts given above) in the way that you think it should have progressed.

d Write out the message for the foreman.

Section 2 – Basic writing skills

A wide variety of written communications are produced in offices every day eg memos, letters, summaries, etc. The skills essential to produce these include:

- a knowledge of the different types of written communication and the ability to select the correct type for the message and situation
- a good vocabulary
- accurate spelling
- clear and accurate punctuation
- a good knowledge of grammar
- a sense of 'order' and 'rhythm' so that the writing flows naturally from one point to the next and is never disjointed
- the ability to choose the correct words and 'tone' for the person receiving the messsage.

CHECK IT YOURSELF

Before you start to create communications of your own, it is essential that you have the basic skills or 'tools' with which to work. In each of the sections which follow:

- note the key information given and work through the examples
- apply your knowledge in the 'Test Yourself' sections which follow.

If you find anything particularly difficult to understand or apply, it is suggested that you see your tutor for additional help.

PUNCTUATION

Accurate punctuation is vital for the correct meaning of a communication to be conveyed to the reader. You should already be aware that:

- any communication of any length should be sub-divided into paragraphs and each paragraph should contain a main theme or topic. When the topic changes a new paragraph should be started.
- each paragraph is comprised of sentences. To be effective sentences should *vary* in length. Too many short sentences and your message will seem clipped and probably disjointed. Sentences which are too long become confusing for the reader and need punctuating – both to keep the sense and to allow the reader to breathe properly if he is reading out loud.

Sentences – the beginning and the end

Sentences must begin with a capital letter and end with a full stop, a question mark or an exclamation mark.

You *must* make sure every sentence you write is a **complete** sentence – it has to have a *subject* and a *verb*! The most common errors in business correspondence are sentences such as:

With reference to your letter of 15 June.

This is *not* a sentence – it is only the beginning of one! You *must* continue with your statement, eg:

With reference to your letter of 15 June, we are pleased to inform you that Mr Gray will be in your area next week.

Sub-division of sentences

Sentences can be sub-divided by the use of commas, dashes, semi-colons, colons and brackets.

Commas ,

Commas are used to:

- clarify meaning
- divide a list of items
- separate a phrase within a sentence
- separate an introductory word or phrase.

When you mark off a phrase in the middle of a sentence you must put a comma both *before* and *after* it, eg

> Rome, the capital of Italy, attracts thousands of tourists every year.

Longer pauses

Dashes –

Dashes can be substituted for commas to give a more distinct pause. Again, if the phrase being separated is in the middle of the sentence a dash must be inserted both before and after it, eg

> I hope to go to Cardiff next Wednesday – providing my car has been repaired by then – and see Philip Jones.

Semi-colons ;

A semi-colon is used to join two closely connected sentences in place of a conjunction or joining word, eg

> These boys are well-known for their athleticism; they play football, cricket and rugby.

Colons :

A colon is usually used to separate a clause which introduces a list, eg

> We sell a variety of accessories for the motorist: seat covers, floor-mats, fog lamps, sun roofs, luggage racks and child seats.

Brackets ( )
Brackets are used to sub-divide completely additional information added to a sentence, without changing the original meaning or punctuation. Occasionally an entire sentence may be enclosed in brackets if this provides purely additional information, eg:

Three suggestions were received last week (from Anne, Jayne and Sue) but we will still need more ideas.

Petty cash is the term used for small items of money. (The word petty means 'small'.)

However, note that in business correspondence brackets should be used very sparingly!

Capital letters
In addition to being used at the beginning of a sentence, initial capitals are also used for proper nouns, eg Isle of Skye, Mozart, Easter.

Capitals are *not* used for common nouns (eg company, organisation, manager, government, college, university etc) unless they are used as proper nouns, eg:

There are many universities in Britain.
I believe she will be going to Edinburgh University in the autumn.
Which manager do you work for?
The Sales Manager is Mr Watts.

Apostrophes '
Apostrophes are mainly used for two reasons:

- to indicate missing letters in a contracted word, eg:

  can't (cannot)
  didn't (did not)
  they're (they are)

Contracted words are not usually used in formal business correspondence though they may be used in informal letters and memos.

- to denote ownership, eg the manager's office

Frequently you may know that there should be an apostrophe but don't know where to put it! Try this. Change the sentence round to find out whether you have one or many owners by adding the words 'of the'. In the above example you would have 'the office of the manager' = *one* manager.

When there is one owner the apostrophe goes *before* the s, when there are several owners the apostrophe goes *after* the s. Therefore, in this case, one owner = manager's office.

Turn these around yourself, add 'of the', decide whether you have one owner or several and insert the apostrophe accordingly.

the drivers car
the girls changing room
the wasps nest
the Mayors parlour
the cats bowl
the members lounge

Your answers should have been:

the driver's car
the girls' changing room
the wasps' nest
the Mayor's parlour
the cat's bowl
the members' lounge

In many cases the spelling of a word tells you whether you are talking about one owner or many owners. In other cases you need to know the *sense* of the sentence before you can decide, eg:

the company's results (one)	the companies' results (many)
the lady's hairdresser (one)	the ladies' hairdresser (many)
the boy's caps (one boy, many caps)	the boys' caps (many boys, many caps)

In the last example you would need more information before you could make a decision.

Special plurals

When a word changes to become plural, eg child and children, see whether you need an 's' once you have added 'of the'. If you *don't* then the apostrophe comes before the 's', eg:

The childrens books = the books of the children = the children's books

If a plural word ends in 's' already (as in ladies) then simply add the apostrophe, eg the ladies' hats. However, if a *singular* word ends in 's' you need to add an apostrophe *plus* 's', eg

We are going to St James's Park (the Park of St James)

SPECIAL NOTE

Beware of its! *Its* – when possessive – has *no* apostrophe.
It's always means *it is*. Therefore

The dog drank its water. (possessive) *but* It's (it is) getting late.

Time

Units of time, eg days, months and years can also be possessive, eg

a year's pay (pay of one year)
two hours' time (time of two hours)

The same rules apply – before the 's' if singular, after the 's' if plural.

SPECIAL NOTE

Don't become so keen on apostrophes that you put them in every word which ends in 's'! By far the vast majority of words ending in an 's' are perfectly ordinary plural words, eg shops, cups, chairs, houses, which *don't* need an apostrophe at all!

Hyphens

A hyphen is used to divide complex words, eg red-haired, part-time, ill-mannered. It is also used at the end of a line to signify word division.

Today many complex words remain unhyphenated, eg swimming bath (technically this is a complex word because a bath can't swim!) However, occasionally a hyphen is essential because the unhyphenated word would mean something entirely different, eg:

It is important he re-signs the contract in the place marked.

He has said he will resign from the football team in spring.

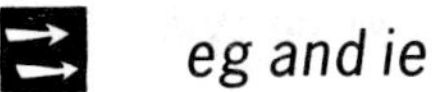

eg and ie

Do you know the difference between the abbreviations 'eg' and 'ie' – or do you consider they are interchangeable?

- **eg** should be used when you are giving some examples of *many* things – and actually stands for the words 'for example'. Read the following sentence – and instead of reading 'eg' read the abbreviation as 'for example'.

  The trader sold many unusual fruits and vegetables, eg papaya, mango and lychees.

- **ie** stands for 'that is' and is used to give a *specific* example. Read the following sentence and substitute the phrase 'that is' for the abbreviation.

  Many legal advisers (ie solicitors) have free Saturday morning consultations.

TEST YOURSELF

1 Identify which of the following are *not* complete sentences. Compose a suitable phrase to finish those which are incomplete.

- Thank you for your letter of 19 June.
- With reference to your recent memo on this topic.
- Following our telephone conversation of yesterday.

2 Put apostrophes in the correct places in the following sentences:

- Paul, my fathers friend, is visiting the miners social club next Wednesday.
- When its 7 pm we feed Billys dog and give the cat its milk in its saucer.
- Todays results were disastrous for us – its a long time since the companys finances were so adversely affected.

3 Capitalise words which should start with an initial capital letter.

- in spring we intend to visit our branch office in paris.
- leaders of the british government will meet the chinese delegation on thursday.
- many people believe that scott discovered the south pole but this is a fallacy.

4 Rewrite the following passage punctuating it correctly and dividing it into two paragraphs.

the sales managers report on the recent sales conference was interesting and informative mr owen stated that the conference had been held at the fernlea hotel near ambleside in the lake district on 26 and 27 october representatives had attended from all the uk regions including wales scotland northern ireland and eire they had been enthusiastic about the new product range for the summer especially the boys shoes and ladies sandals despite increased competition from overseas sales are expected to be above average and several firm orders have already been received from mr jamiesons region in the north of england

VOCABULARY

How many times have you been writing something and been 'stuck for words'? That is, you have known what you wanted to say, but not known – or not been able to remember – the right word to use.

Although this has happened to all of us at some time, quite obviously the more words you know the less this is likely to happen – and the more accurately you can convey the meaning you want.

There are various ways in which you can extend your vocabulary:

- by reading – newspapers, magazines and books
- by playing word games, eg Scrabble
- by doing crosswords (start with the easy ones!)
- by *always* questioning people who use a word you don't know
- by *always* looking up in a dictionary new words you hear or read.

Dictionaries

Dictionaries are not always useful for people who can't spell, especially if the beginning of a word starts with an unexpected letter or set of letters, eg lieutenant (pronounced left-tenant).

They are actually far more useful for giving you the meanings of strange words. A good dictionary will also include information on pronunciation, abbreviations and other miscellaneous information. *Reverse* dictionaries are now also available where you look up the meaning you want and a list of suitable words is given to you. Another useful reference book is a **Thesaurus** – look up a word and you can find a list of synonyms (words and phrases which mean the same thing).

TEST YOURSELF

1 How quickly can you look up *each* of the following words and write down the meaning?

candid	escalate	charisma	sceptical
unorthodox	rescind	sporadic	superfluous

2 Try *saying* these words – pronouncing them by following the spelling. You may find some suggestions made by your group very interesting! Now check the pronunciation in your dictionary and look up what they are or mean. Finally check with your tutor you are now pronouncing each one correctly!

comptroller	vehement	ptarmigan	epitome
ruse	vacillate	harbinger	blackguard

3 **Synonyms** are words which are *similar in meaning*. The problem with each of the lists is that whilst the words in column B should mean the same as their corresponding word in column A, the words in column B are mixed up. Can you rearrange the words so that they are correctly matched?

List 1		List 2	
Column A	**Column B**	**Column A**	**Column B**
pensive	= outgoing	expedite	= fair
donate	= emotionless	impartial	= shorten
stoical	= true	prognosis	= hasten
veritable	= thoughtful	authentic	= forecast
extrovert	= give	condense	= genuine

4 Homonyms are words which *sound the same* but which are different in meaning and spelling. Homonyms and other words which sound very similar are frequently confused. In the sentences below can you

- select the word which should be used
- note down the meaning of the other word.

The police will *prosecute/persecute* him after the *collusion/collision.*

It is against my *principals/principles* to *accede/exceed* to your request.

Don't *lose/loose* that *cheque/check* – *draw/drawer* the money out today.

I *accept/except there/their* are problems at the building *sight/site.*

Type a *draught/draft* of the document and go *through/threw* it carefully.

SPELLING

Generally, the more you read the better speller you are. This is because you constantly see the correct spelling and, if you write the word any other way, it automatically 'looks' wrong.

You should be able to spell basic words correctly all the time. You can check in a dictionary for longer words but it is a good idea to make a real effort to improve your spelling by consciously learning new words – and the best way to do this is to *write out* the word two or three times, concentrating on the spelling all the time.

Common errors

Errors often occur when a word can be spelt in more than one way and has more than one use. The most common areas of confusion are given below.

There/their/they're

- there = a place (eg here and there). It is also used before a verb, eg there is
- their = belonging to them (eg their coats)
- they're = a contraction – short for 'they are'

Where/wear/were

- where = a place (eg where are you?)
- wear = to put on (eg will you wear it?)
- were = a verb, the plural of 'was' (eg we were here)

To/too/two

- to = used before a verb or pronoun, (eg to go to them)
- too = as well, (eg we will go too)
- two = the number 2

Be careful also of *know* and *no*, *of* and *off*, *whose* and *who's*, *your* and *you're*!

How many words?

Although the spelling may be correct, words which should be written separately are sometimes written together in error.

- thank you – is *always* two words
- all right – *not* alright
- a lot – a poor phrase to use but still two words.

Be careful of words which are sometimes written together and sometimes separately, eg:

- may be/maybe – 'maybe' written together = perhaps

Changing the spelling

This, too, can cause confusion and errors. The most common are:

- forgetting to change a 'y' to an 'i' for the past tense, eg pay = paid (*not* payed!) try = tried (*not* tryed!)
- not understanding the difference between a noun spelt with a 'c' and a verb spelt with an 's', eg

Nouns	**verbs**	**nouns**	**verbs**
the practice	to practise	the advice	to advise
the licence	to license	the prophecy	to prophesy

Remember! If you can put the word 'the' at the front, the word is a noun and spelt with 'c'. If you can put the word 'to' in front of it, the word is a verb and spelt with an 's'.

i and e

A good *general* rule to follow is 'i before e unless after c or if the word says "a"'. Therefore

medieval (not after c) *but* receipt (after c)
rein (reign), vein, veil and weight – all words which say 'a'.

Even then there are exceptions! Examples include leisure and height – so be careful!

TEST YOURSELF

1 Below are some words used commonly in business correspondence. 20 are spelled incorrectly. Can you identify which ones?

accomodation	consistant	ommitted
advertisment	definate	parallelled
awfull	deficient	predecesser
alledge	development	questionaire
benefitted	enviroment	received
colleages	liason	referred
committee	manouvre	seperate
competant	miniture	sincerly
courteous	noticeable	underrate
conscientious	occurrance	waive

2 Rewrite the following sentences, correcting all the spelling mistakes.

- The Presidant gave a humourous speach yesterday, when he was the honorary guest at our centenery.
- The professor acknowleged that the lowest recorded temperature of –126° Celsius was almost unbelievible.
- Her boss considers she is incompetant, whoolly headed and must not be allowed to join the permanant staff.
- She has acheived a reputation for being independant, capable of guaging a situation well and forstalling any problems.

GRAMMAR

We all smile when we hear young children say sentences such as 'I is tired' and 'I bringed them to you'. We *don't* smile when we hear adults speak like this – or make similar grammatical errors when they are talking or writing.

Obviously, as we grow up, and other people correct our mistakes we stop making such basic errors – but we often make others which may sound just as bad!

TEST YOURSELF

Can you identify what is wrong in each of the following sentences?

1. Which girl is the fastest – Diane or Hilary?
2. Neither of the boys are any good at that subject.
3. Each of us, with the exception of Jim, were given a report.
4. The Government are going to debate that tomorrow.
5. We haven't been nowhere near his house.

Common grammatical errors

Some of the errors shown above may have seemed obvious – others more difficult. Look through the explanations below and study carefully those you *didn't* find in the list above.

Comparative and superlative

- If you are comparing *two* objects then add -er, if you are comparing more than two add -est.

  Therefore in sentence **1** the word should have been 'faster'.

- Some words cannot have -er or -est added to them, eg beautiful, handsome, angry. If you are comparing *two* objects put the word 'more' in front, if more than two, use the word 'most', eg

  She is the most beautiful girl I have ever seen. She is certainly more beautiful than Sarah.

Agreement

The verbs which follow singular words must also be singular, and the verbs which follow plural words must be plural. This is simple and we follow this rule every day, eg

I *am* going – we *are* going.

He *was* leaving – they *were* leaving

Our difficulties start when we are given alternatives to the basic pronouns, eg each and every, all and none, either and none.

Remember

each *one* and every *one* – therefore both are singular
either *one* or neither *one* – both are singular again
none = not *one* – another singular

With all these words the singular of the verb is used – even if a phrase is inserted in the middle of the sentence to distract you.

Neither of these bags *is* mine
None of the candidates – not even Jill or Frank – *is* suitable.

A collective noun, used to describe a group is still singular – it is *one* group, eg committee, government, society, board:

The committee *has* decided to meet next Wednesday.

Double negative

These are useless as they cancel each other out! 'I am not going nowhere' = 'I am going somewhere'! We can sometimes be guilty of using double negatives when we are speaking (and our receivers usually disregard them) – *don't* use them in written communications, eg:

He never has no time for us or I couldn't hear nobody.

Other bad errors

Word confusions which sound terrible include:

- learned and taught
- lend and borrow

Also be careful of the words due and owing to! Many people use the word 'due' when they really mean 'because'. If you can substitute the word 'because', next time you are about to write the word 'due', then use 'because' instead – it's much safer!

TEST YOURSELF

Rewrite each of the following sentences correctly.

1 Who works the hardest – Sarah or Tim?
2 None of them were prepared to take the blame.
3 I couldn't hear nobody when I called in yesterday.
4 We had to stay late due to an error in the accounts.
5 She learned me how to type.
6 The Government have decided to increase taxes next year.

SPECIAL NOTE

There are no such phrases in the English language as 'could of', 'would of' or 'should of'! If you find yourself writing any expressions like this, ending in the word 'of' you are *wrong*.

You are using the conditional form of the verb to have, therefore you should write

could have would have should have etc

Other pitfalls

Finally, two remaining traps for the unwary:

- **Ambiguity**

Can you say what is wrong with the following sentences?

The speaker, a woman, was a leading industrialist which is unusual.

You need your hair cutting badly.

In both cases the sentences are *ambiguous* – that is they have more than one meaning. Do take care that the words you write cannot be misunderstood!

- **Slang**

  Phrases such as 'fed up,' and 'leave off' have no place in business communications (either written or spoken).

USING YOUR SKILLS

Before you start to create your own documents, you can practise your new-found skills by undertaking a basic task required in every office – that of completing forms.

Form completion

Both at work and in your private life you will have many forms to fill in – and some are easier to understand than others. You may also have to help people to complete forms – especially if you work in a local government office, the civil service or in an office where you regularly deal with members of the public.

It is important that you develop the skill to be able to complete forms accurately and neatly at the first attempt. You may go for a job interview and be asked to complete an application form on the spot – if you have to ask for another because you make a mess of the first one you will hardly make a good impression!

Rules to remember

The following tips may help you to avoid the more common mistakes.

- Read the form through first.
- Look for traps! Typical ones include:
  – two lines for your name – one for your last name and one for your first name. If the lines are very long you may be tempted to write your full name on the first line and only then discover there is a blank line underneath!
  – note areas which say 'for office use only' or 'do not write in this margin' and so on.
  – look for alternatives – where you have to complete A or B but not both.
- Make sure you know basic information about yourself, eg your nationality and next of kin.
- Take care writing your date of birth – many people write the current year by mistake!
- Use BLOCK CAPITALS everywhere you are told to do so.
- If the form has no-carbon required paper (NCR) for several copies make sure you use a biro – roller ball pens, felt tips and fountain pens will not make clear copies.
- Write clearly.
- Don't leave any blanks. You can indicate you have

intentionally left an item blank by writing N/A for 'not applicable.'

- If you have to include an explanation or comment in any area it is always better if you draft it out first, so that you can be sure you word it to the best of your ability.
- *Check* the form afterwards – particularly your spelling.
- Don't forget to sign and date it, if this is required.

TEST YOURSELF

Obtain a form for a driving licence from the Post Office. Complete this with information about yourself and ask your tutor to check your work.

SECTION REVIEW

Having completed this section, you should now be able to:

1. Identify the basic writing skills required to produce business communications.
2. Punctuate sentences correctly.
3. Identify and correct incomplete sentences.
4. Identify where apostrophes are required and insert these correctly.
5. Differentiate between the abbreviations ie and eg.
6. Explain why a good vocabulary is important and how this can be achieved.
7. Use a dictionary.
8. Identify and rectify common spelling and grammatical errors.
9. Avoid common word confusions, ambiguity and slang expressions.
10. Complete forms neatly and accurately at the first attempt.

REVIEW QUIZ

True or false?

The following sentences are error-free . . .

1 In four days' time we are hoping to visit London and see St James's Palace and Cleopatra's Needle.

2 His writing is ineligible – we will have to revue his contribution to this project.

3 Is it true that there going their on they're boat.

4 Can you advise me on this as I have always found your advice very valuable?

5 She said it was alright if we pay for the goods in 3 week's time.

Rewrite any sentences containing errors correctly!

Complete the blanks . . .

6 The word 'due' is often used when the writer really means to say ....

7 Words which sound the same but are different in meaning and spelling are called ....

8 Words which are similar in meaning are called ....

Work it out

9 In each of the following examples the meaning is given for you, plus the first three letters of the word. Can you complete the gaps? (look in a dictionary for help)

able to use both hands alike	amb ....
a crime against the state	tre............................
no longer in use	obs ....
a word based on initials	acr ....
concerning the elderly	ger ....
a person who looks on the black side	pes...........................
a person who looks on the bright side	opt...........................

10 Rewrite the following paragraph without using the word 'got' once and without changing the meaning.

Keith got a new car yesterday. Immediately he got it from the garage he drove around for a while until he got used to it. When he got home he quickly got ready to go out. He got to Kathy's house at 7 o'clock, they got on the motorway and got to a little pub about 8. They got a bar snack and got a drink but when they got on the car park afterwards they noticed that one of Keith's tyres had got a puncture. They got it mended by 11 o'clock and got home at midnight.

Section 3 – Business correspondence

CONSTRUCTION AND CREATION

The next stage is to put your skills together and start to write your own business correspondence.

Before you start

Consider

- who will receive the communication (what tone/vocabulary should you use?)
- what are the important facts you need to convey?
- what response do you want?

Whilst you write

Remember:

- use words you *both* understand – forget any ideas about using unfamiliar words unless you are absolutely clear what they mean
- use simple phrases
- follow a logical order
- be concise – don't waffle
- be fussy – check your spelling and punctuation.

After you have written

- read your communication through and correct any errors
- check your 'message' is clear
- make sure your tone is correct throughout.

MEMOS

The most common form of inter-office communication is the memo – short for 'memorandum' (plural = memos or memoranda). Some organisations use these even for recording messages, rather than message forms.

Their usual use is to:

- pass on information from one person to another
- confirm arrangements
- ask for comments
- make suggestions
- report on action taken
- ask for ideas or seek clarification
- update people on the latest state of affairs.

Memo forms

Most organisations have a pre-printed memo form which may, or may not, include the name of the company. The layout is likely to vary quite considerably from one company to another but usually includes:

- **To** (for the name of the receiver)
- **From** (for the name of the sender)
- **Date** (usually typed in full, see example below)
- **Reference** (usually originator's initials/typist's initials).

Sometimes there is also a space for the subject heading. However, if this is not specified the heading can still be typed at the beginning of the text.

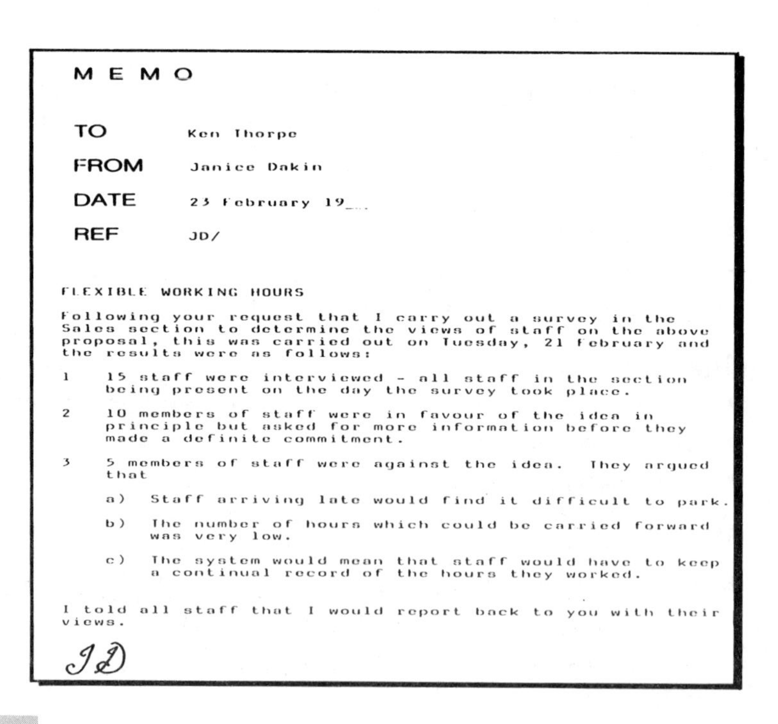

M E M O

TO Ken Thorpe

FROM Janice Dakin

DATE 23 February 19__

REF JD/

FLEXIBLE WORKING HOURS

Following your request that I carry out a survey in the Sales section to determine the views of staff on the above proposal, this was carried out on Tuesday, 21 February and the results were as follows:

1 15 staff were interviewed - all staff in the section being present on the day the survey took place.

2 10 members of staff were in favour of the idea in principle but asked for more information before they made a definite commitment.

3 5 members of staff were against the idea. They argued that

a) Staff arriving late would find it difficult to park.

b) The number of hours which could be carried forward was very low.

c) The system would mean that staff would have to keep a continual record of the hours they worked.

I told all staff that I would report back to you with their views.

JD

Additional points you should bear in mind include:

- A subject heading should always be included if possible. This makes the memo easier to file – and easier to find on a desk full of papers!
- If there is an enclosure this should be indicated beneath the space left for the initials, with the abbreviation **Enc**.
- The wording of a memo is usually relatively informal, especially between people of the same 'rank'. It is likely to be more formal if being sent to someone more senior, eg the Managing Director (or you, writing to your boss).

Confidential memos

Some memos are confidential. In this case:

- The word 'personal' or 'confidential' should be inserted as high up as possible (so that it is seen quickly), eg
  above the memo heading, or
  above the word 'to'
- The memo *must* be placed in an envelope which is *also* marked personal or confidential, and sealed.

SPECIAL NOTE

A memo containing a considerable amount of detail is usually clearer if it is divided into numbered points, rather than purely a stream of paragraphs. The idea is to keep memos *clear and simple* – so that they can be read and understood as quickly as possible.

TEST YOURSELF

Write short memos to your boss, Karen Thorpe, the Sales Director, to cover each of the following situations.

1. Before she went out of the office early today she asked you to arrange a meeting for her with Chris Maitland, the Managing Director. The MD's secretary has just telephoned you to confirm that the MD can see her for half an hour at 9.30 in the morning.
2. You have just received a telephone call from your travel agents, Speedway Ltd, that Ms Thorpe's proposed flight to Rome in 10 days' time has been confirmed. The flight number is BA385 and the departure time is 0930 hours. Her return is open-dated as requested. The agency has also queried the amount of travellers' cheques and lira which will be required by Ms Thorpe.

3 You had arranged to take a personal day off two weeks' today to go shopping with a friend. Your friend has now informed you that she can't get the day off for that day – and wants to make it a week later. You obviously need permission from Ms Thorpe before you can agree to this.

SUMMARIES

Summarising means reducing the amount of original information you are given so that you state the key facts only. You have already practised summarising in one form when you were writing messages and deliberately omitting all the irrelevant and superfluous information.

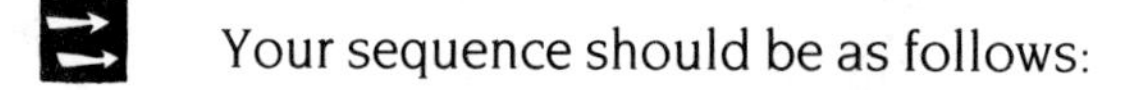

Your sequence should be as follows:

- Read your original passage at least twice to start with. You cannot summarise anything you do not understand yourself!
- Check any unfamiliar words.
- Make sure you understand the sense of the passage.
- Read the passage again either marking (if you are allowed to) or noting down the key points.
- Miss out examples and illustrations unless they are essential to the meaning. Leave out repetitious phrases (many writers 'recap' their main points at the end).
- List your key points on a separate sheet of paper.
- Draft out your corrected version. You don't have to match the order of the original but it is often easier to do this.
- Check that
  – it reads well
  – it retains the sense of the original
  – all key facts are included.

TEST YOURSELF

The following article is concerned with taking notes during a telephone conversation. Each paragraph discusses one important aspect.

- List the key facts of each paragraph in five numbered points.
- Join these together in two or three connected paragraphs.

Ask your tutor to check your work.

Note taking and the telephone

It is always ideal, of course, if a speaker states his main points clearly to make listening and note-taking as easy as possible. However, this is often not the case and the listener cannot insist on this to an important customer or client. It is therefore very important that the receiver of the call listens carefully and follows the speaker's argument.

How detailed the notes should be is obviously debatable and it is impossible to lay down hard and fast rules. If the speaker is giving very precise and detailed instructions, where every point is important, then full notes are essential. However, if the conversation mainly consists of pleasantries, repetitions and examples to illustrate each point then these should obviously be shortened.

Notes that will be used very quickly can afford to be more condensed than notes which may have to wait for a while before they are written into a more acceptable message form. With each hour that passes recollection of the exact conversation – who said what about whom – will fade. The employee who takes a message for his boss at 9.30 am but cannot pass it on until 4.30 in the afternoon may have forgotten many of the details during the intervening period.

The receiver of the message should guard against becoming flustered or not being able to keep up. Some callers speak extremely quickly and have no idea how difficult this makes things for the receiver. In this situation remember to note down only what is important and if the speaker is talking too quickly ask him politely to slow down or repeat what he has just said.

It is always advisable to check the notes with the speaker before the telephone call is concluded. This is essential for figures, dates, references, names and so on – all vital information for the message itself. Failure to clarify the details can mean an inaccurate message or having to ring the speaker back later to check the information – which can be embarrassing for both parties and give a poor impression of the person who took the call.

Business letters

Business letters are written and typed by the thousand every day of the week. Whereas organisations may differ slightly in terms of their 'house style', ie the exact layout they use, the components of a letter are always the same. Letters are always typed on an organisation's letter-headed paper.

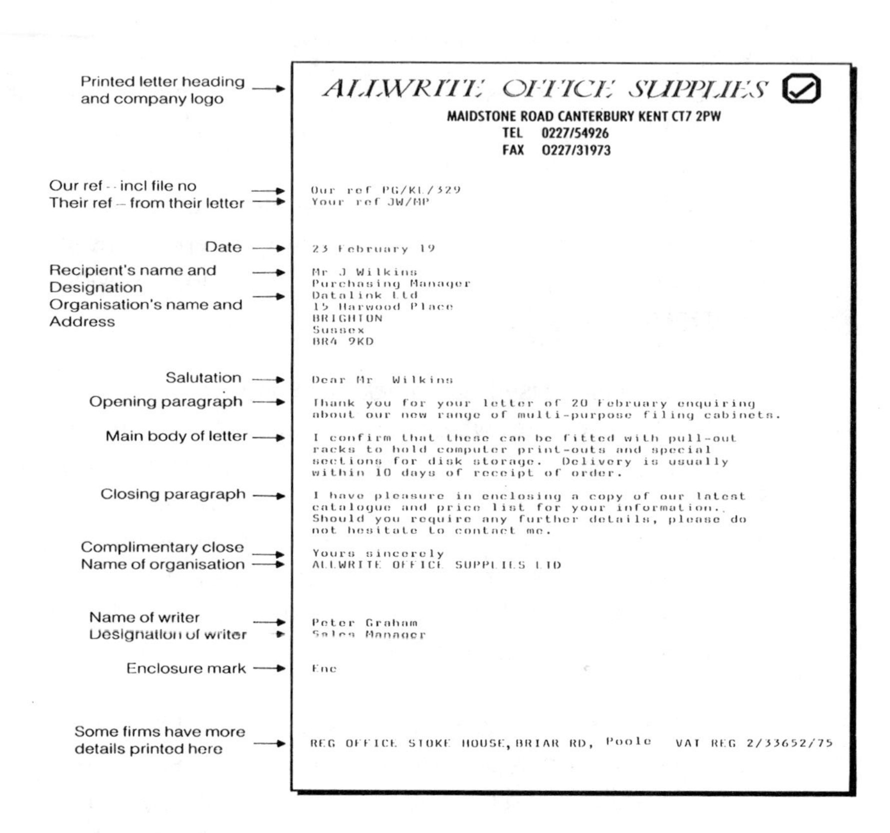

ALLWRITE OFFICE SUPPLIES

MAIDSTONE ROAD CANTERBURY KENT CT7 2PW
TEL 0227/54926
FAX 0227/31973

Our ref PG/KL/329
Your ref JW/MP

23 February 19

Mr J Wilkins
Purchasing Manager
Datalink Ltd
15 Harwood Place
BRIGHTON
Sussex
BR4 9KD

Dear Mr Wilkins

Thank you for your letter of 20 February enquiring about our new range of multi-purpose filing cabinets.

I confirm that these can be fitted with pull-out racks to hold computer print-outs and special sections for disk storage. Delivery is usually within 10 days of receipt of order.

I have pleasure in enclosing a copy of our latest catalogue and price list for your information. Should you require any further details, please do not hesitate to contact me.

Yours sincerely
ALLWRITE OFFICE SUPPLIES LTD

Peter Graham
Sales Manager

Enc

REG OFFICE STOKE HOUSE, BRIAR RD, Poole VAT REG 2/33652/75

SPECIAL NOTE

The complimentary close must always match the salutation:

Dear Sir (or Madam) = Yours faithfully

Dear Mr Brown = Yours sincerely

A woman should include details of her married status to guide the person who will be replying. If no indication is given then the reply will probably be addressed as 'Ms'.

COMPOSING A BUSINESS LETTER

Business letters should be *clear, concise* and *courteous*.

You may have noticed that the example shown consisted of three paragraphs:

- an opening paragraph giving background information as to why the letter is being written
- a second paragraph which gives further details (the information is usually too long to be given in full in the opening paragraph)
- a closing paragraph to 'round off' the letter.

Longer letters may, of course, include a further paragraph to give even more information or to state what action is now required.

Preparation stages

- Check you have all the information to hand.
- Arrange the information in a logical order – always give background information/reason for writing *first*.
- Decide on a suitable opening and a suitable conclusion.
- Draft out the letter.
- Read it through *as if you were the recipient*. Check
  – the tone
  – the order
  – whether it is 'complete' or not.
- Type it out using an appropriate layout.

Opening and concluding

Starting and ending a letter can create more problems than anything else when you first start writing letters. The following points may help you:

- If you are replying to someone else's letter always start Thank you for your letter of (date) regarding . . . .
  (*not* – 'With reference to' and *never* – 'I am writing!'

- If you are starting with a phrase such as 'Further to our recent telephone conversation . . .' or 'Following our recent telephone conversation . . .' *do make sure you complete the sentence*!

- There are several standard conclusions, eg
  – We look forward to hearing from you.
  – Please let us know if we can be of any further assistance.

– We look forward to receiving your confirmation.
– We hope this information will be useful to you.
Again, do make sure you write a complete sentence. Phrases such as 'Hoping to hear from you' are not acceptable.

SPECIAL NOTE

To be on the safe side always avoid starting your last paragraph with a word ending in -ing.

LETTERS OF ENQUIRY

To write a successful letter of enquiry you need to be concise and yet include all relevant information so that you will receive the details you want.

TEST YOURSELF

1 Make a list of your criticisms of both letters A and B shown below. Discuss your ideas with your tutor.
2 Rewrite the letters yourself, avoiding all the faults you have noted in the examples.

Datalink Ltd
15 Harwood Place
Brighton
Sussex BR4 9KD
Tel 35781
Fax 28344

DC/PT

4 March 19__

The Businessman's Digest
47 Walpole Street
LONDON
NW4 8DL

Dear Sirs

With reference to your recent advertising material on your magazine we enclose our cheque for £56.

Yours faithfully

Doreen Hayes
Receptionist

Enc

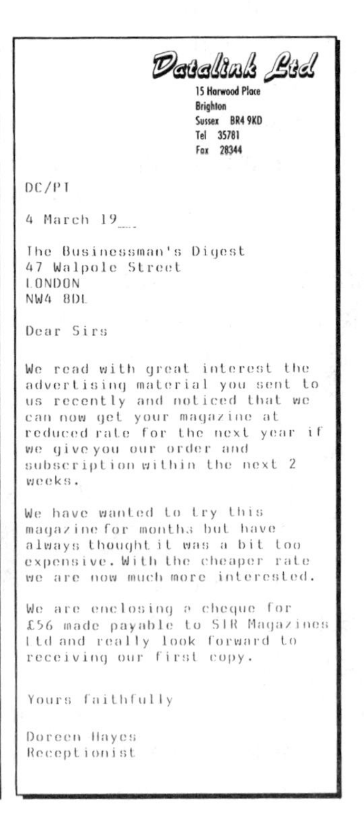

Datalink Ltd
15 Harwood Place
Brighton
Sussex BR4 9KD
Tel 35781
Fax 28344

DC/PT

4 March 19__

The Businessman's Digest
47 Walpole Street
LONDON
NW4 8DL

Dear Sirs

We read with great interest the advertising material you sent to us recently and noticed that we can now get your magazine at reduced rate for the next year if we give you our order and subscription within the next 2 weeks.

We have wanted to try this magazine for months but have always thought it was a bit too expensive. With the cheaper rate we are now much more interested.

We are enclosing a cheque for £56 made payable to SIR Magazines Ltd and really look forward to receiving our first copy.

Yours faithfully

Doreen Hayes
Receptionist

SPECIAL NOTE

If you are writing to an organisation, but don't know which individual should receive the letter, you can help their mail room by addressing it to the relevant department. In the case of the letter regarding the magazine, this could be sent to the Subscriptions Department. Other examples include:
– letter of enquiry about products to the Sales Department
– letter of booking confirmation to Reception.

TEST YOURSELF

You work for Mr Jim Edwards, Office Manager of KDT Products Ltd. Prepare the following letters for *his* signature. To help you, notes for the first reply have been given.

1. As you know, Peter Hayes and I were both supposed to attend the seminar organised by Janine Cook, Sales Manager of Bright's Office Products Ltd, Strathclyde Road, Glasgow, G4A 8DT. I couldn't go at the last minute because I had to attend a meeting elsewhere. Peter brought back a very interesting sales promotion pack on their Desk Top Publishing system which he now can't find! Write to them and ask for another. Say something like:
   - I'm sorry I couldn't attend their recent seminar – understand it was very interesting.
   - I believe they were issuing a sales promotion pack on DTP giving details of their system.
   - We are interested in introducing DTP here.
   - Could they please send us a copy of the pack for information.
2. Write to Floral Art Nurseries, Barnes Road South, Cheltenham. They apparently supply floral displays and plants on a contract basis – they maintain them, change them every so often etc. Can you ask them to send us details? This could be a good idea both for reception and the show room.

LETTERS CONTAINING INFORMATION

As well as sending letters of enquiry, your organisation will most probably also receive letters of enquiry from other people and organisations. Such letters should be replied to promptly and courteously. Often a short remark to 'personalise' the letter can be made, eg:

- I hope you find this information helpful
- If you need any more information please do not hesitate to let me know.

24 Wood Lane
LINCOLN
LC3 4PD

10 January 19__

The Public Relations Department
Livewire Advertsing Agency
4 St Anne's Square
MANCHESTER
M2 7DK

Dear Sirs

I am currently undertaking an Advertising project for my GCSE in Business Studies. To be able to do this successfully I need to obtain as much information as I can about Advertising Agencies and how they operate.

If you have any booklets or brochures on your services, could you please send me a copy? I enclose a stamped addressed envelope.

Yours faithfully

Dimitris Lemos

Enc

Livewire Advertising Agency
4 St Anne's Square
MANCHESTER
M2 7DK

KL/PS

Mr Dimitris Lemos
24 Wood Lane
LINCOLN
LC3 4PD

Dear Mr Lemos

Thank you for your letter of 10 January 19__ asking for information on our services.

We have pleasure in enclosing a copy of our sales and promotion brochure, together with several other leaflets which we hope you will find helpful.

We wish you well with your examinations.

Yours sincerely

Carolyn Parker
Public Relations Assistant

Enc

SPECIAL NOTE

Because this enquiry was from a young person, Carolyn Parker could have started her letter 'Dear Dimitris' to personalise it further. This type of approach will depend very much on the policy of the individual organisation.

TEST YOURSELF

Write letters in response to the following enquiries, all to be signed by your boss – Steven McCall – manager of the large retail store where you are employed.

1. An enquiry has been received from a young man – Mr Robert Westall, 14 Kelvin Avenue, Hightown, HG5 9DK. He would like to be considered for a Saturday job with your company as he has just reached the age of 16. Write back thanking him for his enquiry and informing him that although there are no vacancies at present you will keep his letter on file and will notify him if one occurs in the near future.
2. Mr D Isherwood, 50 Rydall Close, Hightown, HG3 5ET has written asking if you hire out large garden mowers. Reply saying that you don't offer this service at present and suggest he contacts Barton's Garden Centre of Nixon Road.

3 Your final letter is from Mrs K Temple, Matron of Barnstead Residential Home, 80 Birch Hall Road, Hightown, HG1 6LW. She wants to know if your store will be holding a pre-Christmas shopping night for the disabled, as you did last year.

Reply saying this is scheduled for the first Wednesday in December (give the date), starting at 6.15 pm and continuing until 9 pm. Helpers will be on hand all evening.

LETTERS OF CONFIRMATION

A letter of confirmation is sent after arrangements have been made verbally. It is usual to clearly state all the main points which were agreed verbally, to prevent any misunderstandings.

- If a date is involved state *both* day and date.
- If you are giving a time make sure you either use the 24-hour clock or make it clear whether it is am or pm.
- It is usual for the person who made the arrangements verbally to sign the letter of confirmation.

Livewire Advertising Agency
4 St Anne's Square
MANCHESTER
M2 7DX

MK

10 April 19__

Reception
The Fernhearst Hotel
Ashley Green
HIGHTOWN
HG9 4ST

Dear Sirs

Following our telephone conversation of today, I have pleasure in confirming our reservation for 2 single rooms with private bath for 2 nights, Tuesday and Wednesday, 23 and 24 April 19__.

The rooms should be booked in the names of Mr T Scott and Mr S Dawson.

I should be grateful if you would note that their time of arrival on Tuesday, 23 April 19 _ will be about 8.30 pm.

Yours faithfully

Margaret Kelly
Secretary

Details to note

- Alternative ways of starting the letter include
  - 'We refer to our telephone conversation of today . . .'
  - 'Further to our telephone conversation of today. . .'
- If you are confirming hotel accommodation always inform the hotel if the guests are likely to check in after 6 pm – otherwise they might find the rooms have been relet.

TEST YOURSELF

You work for Mr Michael Hirst, Sales Manager. Write the following letters to be signed by you.

1. Mr Hirst is travelling to Ipswich next week and you have booked him a private room with bath at the White House Hotel, Market Road, Ipswich, IP3 9SD. He will arrive about 7 pm on Monday and stay until Thursday. You have also asked the hotel to book a table for him in their dining room for dinner on the Tuesday night – he will be entertaining 5 guests. Confirm the reservations.
2. Whilst he is in Ipswich Mr Hirst will be visiting Mr Edward Makin, Technical Manager of Datacorp Ltd, Earl Road, Ipswich, IP5 4DT. You have arranged with Mr Makin by 'phone that Mr Hirst will see him at 10 am on the Tuesday. Confirm the meeting.

JOB APPLICATION LETTERS

If you are not employed already, you will probably be looking for a job towards the end of your course. Even if you are working there is always the possibility that you might want to change jobs to move up in the world or earn more money.

Although employment agencies are one method of finding out about jobs and getting interviews, many people also scan their local paper when they are job hunting – and most advertisers ask for applicants to write to them if they are interested in being considered.

Your application letter is an advertisement about you, your skills and what you can do. It *must* be

- neatly written or typed
- displayed in an accepted business format
- correctly spelled and punctuated

- grammatically accurate
- worded correctly.

It is usually a good idea to keep the actual letter fairly short and to the point and to include full details about yourself on an attached CV (Curriculum Vitae). Look at the formal layout on page 214.

Your letter can then consist of three or four simple paragraphs, eg:

- an opening paragraph to say where you saw the advertisement and that you would like to be considered for the position (say what it is – there may be more than one vacancy).
- a second paragraph to give general background information about yourself – are you just finishing a full-time course; are you already working – if so, how long have you been there and what is your job? Mention that full details are given on your attached CV.
- possibly a third paragraph if you have a particular reason for wanting either this type of job or to work for this particular organisation – something to make your letter seem a little special.
- a final paragraph to say you are available for interview at any time (or if you're not available at any time – when you are available).

TEST YOURSELF

Select an advertisement for a job from your local paper – one which quite interests you. Draft out a letter of application and check it with your tutor. If necessary re-draft it until you have a very good idea of what constitutes a good application letter.

CURRICULUM VITAE

The best way to prepare this is to use a word processor, then store it on disk, update it and print out copies as you need them. *Don't* send a photocopy to an organisation – always send an original.

A CV is a typed display, using either side or shoulder headings, giving information about yourself, eg

Personal details

- name, title and address
- telephone number
- date of birth

Educational details

- school(s) attended (not primary) and dates
- GCSE results
- other awards at school/positions of responsibility held etc
- further education details – college, dates and course
- examinations/awards taken or being taken and results if known
- any other details, eg member of student union/committee etc
- work experience details (from college)

Employment details

- current job held if working (brief resumé of duties)
- previous jobs and areas of responsibility (if applicable)
- details of any part-time or Saturday jobs you have done if you are a full-time student

Other useful information

- details of any hobbies/interests or sports
- details of any organisations you belong to
- any other useful information, eg car driver

Referees

- it is usual to give *two* names (ask permission first!)

SPECIAL NOTE

If an advertisement asks you to contact the organisation for an application form you usually don't send a CV as well – these are the type of details which would be required on the form.

The final touches

Paperclip your letter to the front of your CV (so your letter is on top). Type a white DL envelope neatly and accurately and include the postcode. Give the impression of being an efficient and organised worker at this stage!

CHECK IT YOURSELF

From the details just given draft out a CV for yourself and check it with your tutor before inputting it onto a word processor or typing it.

SECTION REVIEW

Having completed this section, you should now be able to:

1 Compose business letters of enquiry and confirmation and those containing information using appropriate language and tone.

2 Compose memos giving factual information and making simple requests using appropriate language and tone.

3 Use commonly accepted business formats and styles.

4 Extract key information and compose short summaries.

5 Compose job applications.

6 Create your own CV using an acceptable format and style.

REVIEW QUIZ

True or false?

State whether these sentences are correct in every detail (if not, identify the errors).

1 My sister's friend, who is an expert, considered the antique vase to be authentic.

2 We sincerly hope that when their there, they enjoy it as much as we did.

3 Whose going to be the one who will collect the licence – can you advice me?

4 Which of the following two sections do you find the easiest to understand?

5 He said he would liase with me about Mrs Smiths' contract if I agreed to wave the claws in paragraph 4 of the draught.

Complete the blanks...

6 Before a confidential memo is despatched it should be ......
....

7 The abbreviation CV stands for ....

8 If a letter starts Dear Sir it must conclude ....

Work it out

9 You have frequently said to your boss, Brian Hanson, that you feel you could be far more productive if you used a word processor to type your work, rather than the electronic typewriter you use at present.

He has now agreed that you can obtain more details to see how much one would cost. Write a letter of enquiry to Barnes Office Supplies, 15 Bridge Street, Hightown HG1 2JT. Address it to the appropriate department.

Ask them to quote you both for a dedicated word-processor *and* for a micro computer which can be used for word processing, but the printer must, of course, be letter quality (preferably ink jet or daisy wheel).

10 Brian Hanson has asked you to write a memo on his behalf to Tony Marsland, Chief Accountant, based on the following notes he took at a meeting he attended yesterday. Note that Brian Hanson is the Sales Manager.

- Barbara Yates, Purchasing Director of KLS Services not happy with credit terms offered in our last letter.
- We offered terms of 30% on delivery, balance in 4 instalments.
- KLS want to pay 25% on delivery, balance in 6 instalments.
- What does Tony think? I think OK but suggest checking credit rating first.
- Advise Tony terms were offered in response to possible order for 2 XL10 machines – total value £25 000.

Section 4 – Proof-reading and text editing

All the care in the world with grammar, spelling, punctuation and letter construction is absolutely useless if you type your documents and can't be bothered to check them.

Remember:

- nobody likes proof-reading! Most people want to carry on and tackle the next piece of work, but . . .
- a letter or memo is not good enough if it is 99% correct – it must be 100% accurate
- if your boss is the type of person who, rather than give you a document back to retype, is kind enough to alter an error in pen as she signs it, this makes her look kind, you look sloppy!
- You should always proof read a document word by word, *never* scan it rapidly, or read it as if it were an article in a magazine.

TEST YOURSELF

Read the following paragraph and *list* the number of errors you find (no grammatical errors are included).

The community charge

The community charge (usually called the poll tax) is leveid on every adult in the country over the age of 18. This is a flat rate tax on every every adult but the amount of paymnet dpends on where a person lives. the idea is to ensure that everyone who who can vote in council elections,or use local services, makes a contirbution to councill spending.

CHECK IT YOURSELF

How many did you find? Fewer than 9 and you will have to keep looking!

OTHER ERRORS

In addition to typing errors, people creating documents may:

- make spelling, punctuation or grammatical errors
- wish to change their minds regarding the layout of the document.

Checking techniques

A long or complicated piece of work is always better checked by *two* people – one person reading the original document and the other person checking the finished version. If you use this technique

- read slowly and clearly
- change over reader and checker after a while so that you don't become 'stale' and lose concentration.

If you have no option but to work alone use a ruler – especially when checking figures – so that your eyes don't wander and read the wrong line of the document.

Always

- mark the place you have reached if you are interrupted
- do a double check *before* you start making written alterations on the document itself.

PRINTER'S CORRECTION SIGNS

If you are a typist, or learning to type, you will come across these as you are working towards your typing exams. If you think you know all about correction signs then use this section for revision and then try the exercises which follow.

A variety of symbols is used so that work can be amended before it is returned to the typist, without crossing out so much of the typescript that it is unreadable.

Look at the chart on page 219 showing the principal correction signs. If you think some of them are confusing then you will find that they are usually quite clear when you read them in context, providing you use your common sense!

Sign in the margin		Sign in the text	Meaning
caps/	≡	under word(s) to be changed	spaced caps required
caps/	=	as above	closed caps required
uc/		letter(s) to be changed underlined or crossed out	upper case required
lc/		as above	lower case required
NP or Para	[	before first word of new paragraph	new paragraph
run on	~	continue text in one paragraph	no new paragraph
stet or	✓- - - -	underneath word to remain	keep as written originally
ꝺ		letter(s) or word(s) crossed out	delete
⁐	⁐	between two letters or words	close up the gap
( )	( )	between two spaced lines	as above
	↕↕	between two lines or paragraphs	reverse the order
trs	⊔⊓	drawn around letters or words – a numerical order is indicated	transpose letters or words
#	⅄	insertion mark between letter or words	space required

TEST YOURSELF 1

The following passage has been amended using common printer's correction signs. Retype this correctly as the author requires.

BUSINESS STUDIES

Business Ownership

The smallest type of business unit is the sole Proprietor
whom, although he may employ staff, is the sole (only) owner
of the business. He has several advantages - he is
independent, can keep all the profit (after paying his
Income Tax), can give a personal service and does not have
to go through a complicated procedure to start his business.
However such an under taking may be hard work. he may be
able to have very little time off, and above all he has the
problem of unlimited liability. This means that he is
personally responsible for all his debts, even to the
point of selling his house, or other possessions. He also
may not have enough capital to expand his business. He may
therefore decide to take a partner - who he will have to
consult before he can make decisions. The partner will put
capital into the business but will expect a share of the
profits.

There may be disagreements and will still be the problem of
unlimited liability. However, they will now be able to take
more time off and responsibility will be shared. If the
owners want to expand the company further still they may
decide to become a limited company. This will give them the
benefit of limited liabilty.

SECTION REVIEW

Having completed this section, you should now be able to:

1 Explain the importance of effective proof-reading.

2 Identify and use suitable reading techniques for proof-reading.

3 Identify typographical, spelling, punctuation and grammatical errors.

4 Use common printers' correction signs to mark up corrected and amended text.

NUMERACY GUIDE 8

Proportion

Quantities are said to be in **direct proportion** to each other if they increase or decrease at the same rate, eg:

- If two books cost £4, then four books will cost £8.
- If five pens cost £20, then ten pens will cost £40.

In both these examples, when the number of books and pens doubled, then so did the cost. Doubling one simply meant doubling the other.

You will not always be able to work out the calculation so easily. If you are given the cost, for instance, of a greater number of articles, eg:

- 16 pens cost £4.32, how much will 176 pens cost?

The answer is to find the cost of one and then multiply it by the number you have to work to.

$$\frac{£4.32}{16} \times 176 = 25p \times 176 = £44$$

TEST YOURSELF 1

Calculate the cost of

1. 75 ring binders if eight cost £7.68
2. 18 typing ribbons if five cost £9.20
3. 23 desks if 35 cost £1487.50
4. 430 reams of paper if 29 cost £62.06
5. 53 staplers if 19 cost £80.75

Inverse proportion

Quantities are said to be in **inverse proportion** when one increases as the other decreases, eg

- If 5 workers take 1 hour to assemble a long report, how long will 10 workers take?

Obviously it should take them *half* as long to do the job (unless they get in each other's way or talk to each other!) and the answer is therefore half an hour.

The easiest way to calculate this is to think in terms of 'man hours'. The report in the example takes 5 man hours to assemble. This figure (5) is then divided by the number of people working on the project (10) to give the time taken as half an hour.

TEST YOURSELF 2

1 If it takes 4 people 6 hours to type a report, how many people are needed if the deadline is in 4 hours' time?

2 If it takes 10 workers 5 hours to complete an urgent project, how many workers will be required to complete it in 2 hours?

Percentage increases and decreases

By now you may have thought you knew all about percentages but there are two other types of problems you should be able to cope with, eg

- An item was being sold for £16 and should be increased to £17. What is the percentage rise in price? (You have to calculate a **percentage increase**.)
- You have been asked by your boss to prepare a notice advertising sale reductions – all items have been marked down by the same amount. If £20 items are now marked £18 what is the percentage reduction? (You have to calculate a **percentage decrease**.)

Percentage increases

These are calculated by:

- finding the difference between the two prices – in the first example it is £1
- dividing this figure by the original price (lower figure)
- pressing the % key (or multiplying by 100).

Therefore:

$\frac{1}{16} \times 100 = 6.25\%$

TEST YOURSELF 3

1 On a temperature chart the temperature in March is 13.3°C and in June is 21°C. What is the percentage increase?

2 The following table shows the increase in advertising expenditure by your company from January to June this year, in various types of media. Calculate the percentage increase in each case (to two decimal places).

Media	January (£'000)	June (£'000)	Percentage increase
National newspapers	63	74	
Television	49	52	
Magazines	36	41	
Trade journals	35	37	
Cinema	14	16	
Total	197	220	

Percentage decreases

These are done in almost the same way except that now the original price is the higher figure. In the example where goods were reduced from £20 to £18, we divide 2 by 20, eg

$\frac{2}{20} \times 100 = 10\%$

TEST YOURSELF 4

Your boss has received a leaflet from a supplier showing price reductions for a variety of items. He has asked you to calculate the percentage reduction in each case.

Can you also calculate the average reduction?

Item	Original price	New price	% reduction
1	£58	£50.75	
2	£37	£33.30	
3	£65	£59.80	
4	£26	£24.83	
5	£168	£144.48	

Liaising with callers and colleagues

Whether you work in a small or large organisation it is extremely likely that you will have to deal with callers to your company on a fairly regular basis:

- In a small organisation there is unlikely to be a special receptionist – or if there is she may be busy or need help.
- callers may visit your office or department.
- in a large organisation you may be asked to help on reception.

Obviously the better you know the work of your company or department, and who deals with what, the more you are able to help people who call in.

SPECIAL NOTE

Whether it is your job or not, *never* walk past a caller to your organisation who is not being attended to without offering to help!

DEALING WITH CALLERS

Callers to your company will probably include:

- customers or clients
- representatives
- business associates
- delivery and maintenance people
- friends or relatives of your boss and/or colleagues.

In addition, if your company is a branch of a large organisation you will also be visited by people who work in other branch offices or at head office.

Some callers will be 'regulars' and you should make every effort to learn and remember their names – so that you can address them *personally*.

The exact procedure you follow when visitors arrive will, to a certain extent, depend on the policy of your company. However, the following chart should give you guidance on the action to take to create a good impression – of both yourself and your organisation.

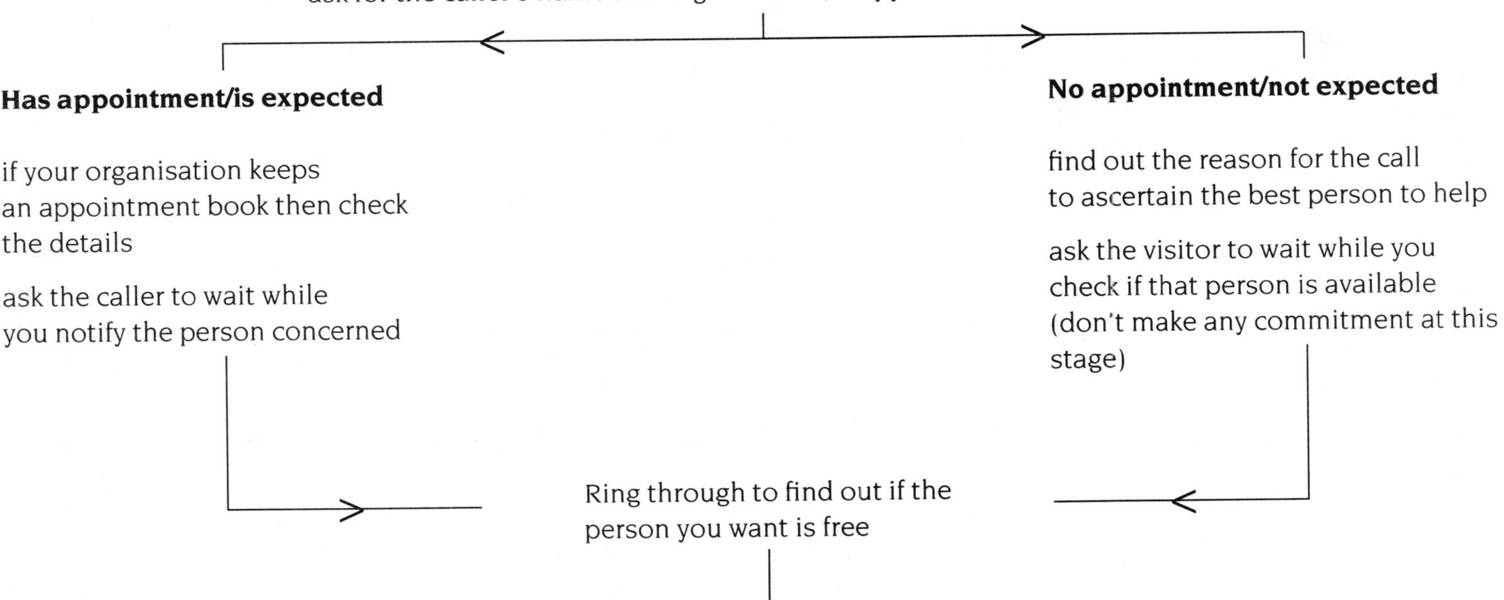
DEALING WITH CALLERS
Greet the caller promptly
smile to make him/her feel welcome
use your company's standard greeting, eg 'Good morning' or 'May I help you?'
find out if he/she has an appointment or is expected by someone
ask for the caller's name and organisation, if applicable.
Has appointment/is expected
if your organisation keeps an appointment book then check the details
ask the caller to wait while you notify the person concerned
No appointment/not expected
find out the reason for the call to ascertain the best person to help
ask the visitor to wait while you check if that person is available (don't make any commitment at this stage)
Ring through to find out if the person you want is free

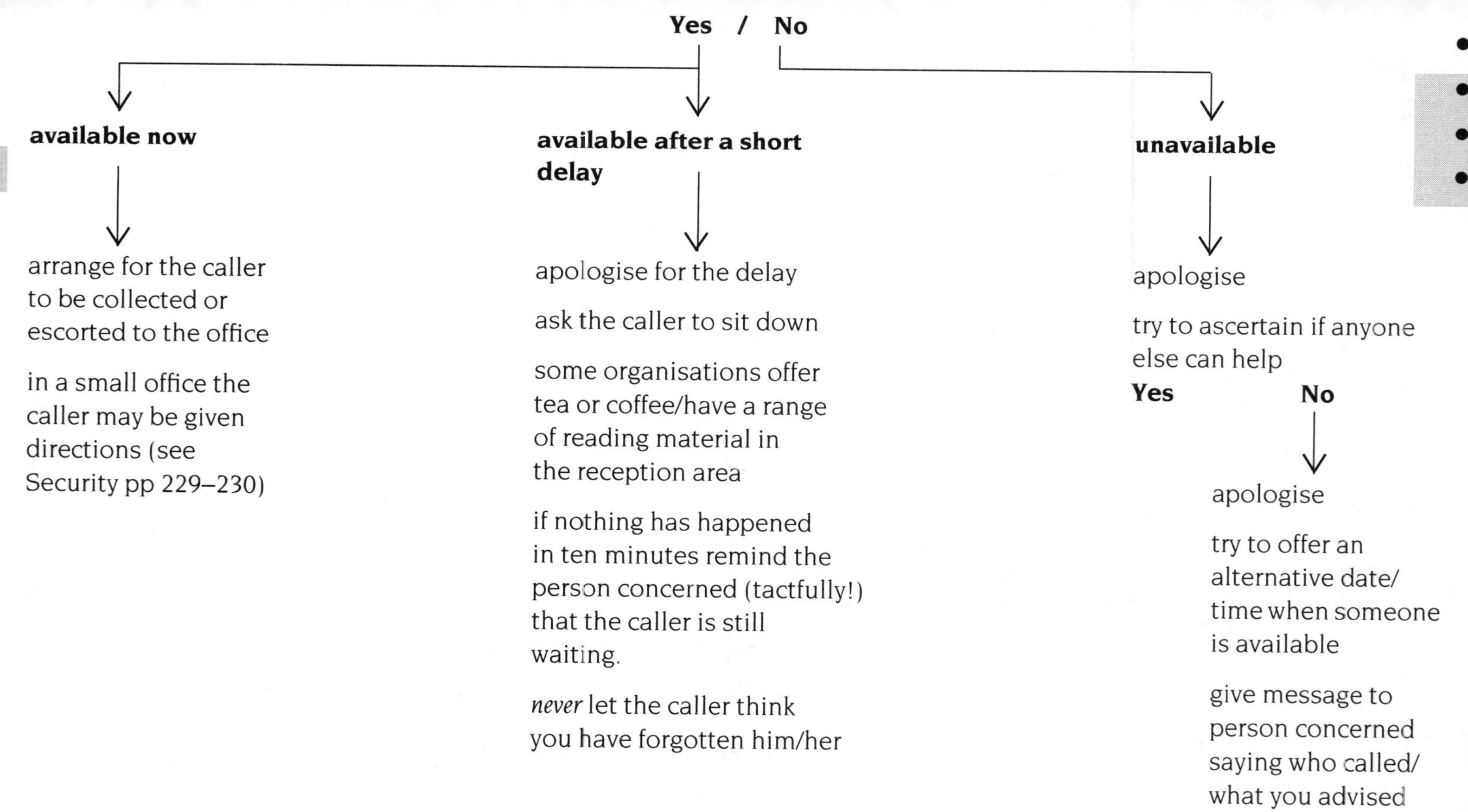
Yes / No
available now
arrange for the caller to be collected or escorted to the office
in a small office the caller may be given directions (see Security pp 229–230)
available after a short delay
apologise for the delay
ask the caller to sit down
some organisations offer tea or coffee/have a range of reading material in the reception area
if nothing has happened in ten minutes remind the person concerned (tactfully!) that the caller is still waiting.
never let the caller think you have forgotten him/her
unavailable
apologise
try to ascertain if anyone else can help
Yes
No
apologise
try to offer an alternative date/time when someone is available
give message to person concerned saying who called/what you advised

Difficult callers

Whilst most callers will be pleasant and state their requirements clearly, others may be more difficult to handle, eg

The shy or nervous caller	• Don't become impatient or try to rush them. *Don't* finish off sentences for them! Speak gently, calmly and deliberately as very nervous people often don't 'take things in' as easily.
The angry or aggressive caller	• Stay calm and don't interrupt whilst they tell you their problem. Be sympathetic *without* accepting the blame on behalf of your company or any of your colleagues. (There are two sides to every story!) Be patient, reasonable and as helpful as possible. Get help from a supervisor if you cannot handle the situation or if the caller is unduly aggressive or rude.
Persistent callers without an appointment	• Most probably these are reps trying to sell their products. Find out if your company has a policy for dealing with such callers – often they are asked to write or ring the company to make an official appointment before calling.
Callers asking for money (ie charity callers)	• Find out your organisation's policy on charity donations. *Always* check first whether any money should be given.

Callers who ask for confidential information

- *Never* give out any information which is not obviously disclosable to any caller without specific authority from a senior member of staff. Equally never discuss other callers, your colleagues *or* the business in general with casual callers.

Callers who request access to another part of the building

- Again this depends on your company's policy (see under Security). All maintenance and delivery people and *anyone* who says they have come to collect a piece of equipment should be asked for identification. If you are in any doubt at all check with your supervisor.

CHECK IT YOURSELF

Discuss with your tutor the non-verbal communication gestures which would be displayed by both nervous or aggressive visitors. How many can you remember from the chapter on Business Relationships? What typical signals are given by someone who is becoming impatient?

Handicapped Callers

Don't be patronising or treat people as if they are less intelligent because they have a physical handicap.

the deaf

- *look* at them when you speak to them to help them lip-read. Speak *relatively* slowly and clearly.

the blind

- speak when they enter – your voice will guide them towards you. *Lead* (don't drag!) them to a chair. If there are any steps say whether these are *up* or *down* and say how many there are.

the disabled

- life will be much easier for any disabled callers if there is a ramp, rather than steps, leading to your building. Be ready to open doors if necessary. *Don't* try to rush them or appear impatient. Apart from being attentive and thoughtful and prepared to offer help when necessary, concentrate on the *person* rather than the disability.

Security

- Many large organisations have a gatehouse where security staff check visitors as they enter the premises and issue a special visitor's badge.
- Very security conscious firms may insist that any large bags or holdalls are left in the gatehouse and collected on departure.
- Visitor's badges may be colour-coded to show which areas the visitor has access to and which he/she hasn't.
- The visitor will also be asked to 'sign in' in a Visitor's Book or Caller's log stating their name, company and other details of their visit. Alternatively this may be completed by security or office staff. Often the car registration number of the visitor is included if their vehicle is parked on a company car park.

CALLERS' LOG

Date ....

Time of arrival	Name of caller	Company	Car Registration Number	Business	To see	Any special action taken	Time of departure

- The gatehouse will also 'check out' visitors as they leave and retrieve their badges.

- The main entrance to the building is normally sited at the front, or adjacent to the gatehouse, so that visitors have no excuse for wandering about.
- In a large, security-conscious company visitors are usually escorted from one place to another.

TEST YOURSELF

1. Why do many firms insist that large bags are left in the gatehouse?
2. Why do you think a record is kept of car registration numbers?
3. Why would a record of all visitors be essential in the case of an emergency evacuation of the building?

'Moving' visitors

Organisations vary in the methods they use to 'move' visitors from one part of the building to another. Visitors may:

- be given verbal directions (usually only in small organisations or if the visitor is well known)
- be escorted by security staff
- be escorted by a member of the office staff
- be collected by the person they have come to see.

Escorting visitors

- Walk at a reasonable pace (bear in mind the age and fitness of the visitor).
- Don't make the trip a guided tour.
- Answer general questions and let the visitor pause briefly to look at things which interest him/her on the way.
- Give warning of hazards – steps, swinging doors, congested areas etc.
- Show courtesy by opening doors.
- Introduce the visitor on arrival.
- If no-one is in the office when you arrive then find someone or wait with the visitor until someone comes.

Introductions

If you know how to introduce people properly then the idea is not as worrying as it might at first appear. Introductions mean that the two strangers you are introducing to each other can start talking without any difficulty.

- If the two people are more or less equal in age, sex and standing you can introduce either to either. If you need to bring them together across a room you always take
  – the less important person to meet the more important one
  – the man to meet the woman.
- You introduce them on the same basis. Therefore mention the woman *first* if you are introducing her to a man.
  'Mrs Barnes, this is Mr Tatton our Chief Accountant. Mr Tatton, Mrs Barnes from the Community Council.'
- Mention the most senior person first if the two are not of equal standing. Therefore if a young man arrived for an interview with the Personnel Manager you would say:
  'Mr Wilson, this is Brian Foulds. Mr Foulds, this is Mr Wilson, our Personnel Manager.'
- If you are introducing an individual to a group of people always mention the individual first. For example:
  'Mr Trent, this is Mr Hamilton, Mr Turner and Mr Mitchell. Gentlemen, Mr Trent.'
  It is usual to go round the circle in the order people are standing or sitting.
- If you are introducing a man and his wife mention them *both*. For example:
  Mr Gray, this is Mr and Mrs Clayton. Mr and Mrs Clayton, this is Mr Gray, our Sales Manager.
- If you are on first name terms with the people concerned you can make the introduction more informal:
  'John, I'd like you to meet Susan Robbins from Brightwell Electronics. Susan, this is John Baker, one of my colleagues.'

SPECIAL NOTE

You may have wondered which way to introduce a junior woman to a senior man – if both the woman should be mentioned first and the most senior person mentioned first! This will depend on circumstances.

In a working environment it is usual to put *seniority* first – therefore if a young woman arrived for interview you would still mention the name of the Personnel Manager first, out of courtesy for his position.

Giving directions

- Be specific and clear and *don't* speak too quickly.
- Give gestures as you talk – but make sure you know your left from your right!
- If the route is long, eg from one building to another, make a quick sketch or write down the directions as a list of points.

TEST YOURSELF

Work out the clearest directions you can for

- someone arriving in the main entrance of your college or organisation and visiting a room at the other end of the building
- someone arriving in one building at your college or company who has to visit another building or a firm nearby.

Check your directions with your tutor.

LIAISING WITH CALLERS AND COLLEAGUES

When you are receiving callers on behalf of your company and your colleagues, passing on information from callers to your colleagues and vice versa, and generally acting as the 'go-between' it is your responsibility to ensure that any messages (usually oral) are passed between them accurately and without distortion, and in such a way that any problems or difficulties are minimised. This means:

- listening carefully
- making clear notes of anything you cannot be 100% certain of remembering accurately
- passing on the information promptly and accurately – preferably in person
- not leaving urgent messages on the desk of someone who is absent without checking if the message has been dealt with later.

Difficulties and problems

No matter how careful or efficient *you* are, difficulties can still occur – and some may be caused by other people, eg:

- a colleague promises you information to give to an expected caller and then forgets to give it to you
- a colleague keeps callers waiting a long time – some get very irritable and take it out on you
- a caller asks you to do, or find out, something which is outside your area of responsibility
- a caller arrives to see a member of staff, by appointment. The person concerned has obviously forgotten and gone out of the building.

Golden rules for coping

- no matter how tempted you are *never* denigrate other members of staff to outside visitors!
- stay polite and calm. Apologise to the person who has been inconvenienced (you are apologising on behalf of the company – not yourself!)
- *get help* rather than struggle on your own.

This way you cannot be held solely responsible if there is a serious problem. In addition a senior member of staff may be able to sort out the problem quickly to prevent it escalating. If you watch, and see how they handle the situation, you will be better equipped to deal with it yourself next time.

SPECIAL NOTE

If a member of staff continually makes life difficult for you, it may be worth having a quiet word with your supervisor, rather than trying to tackle the problem yourself. This is especially the case if your problems are caused by a senior member of staff. However, if the person concerned is *very* important you may have to just learn to cope – even if this means telling a small 'white lie' to keep people happy from time to time!

CHECK IT YOURSELF

Discuss with your tutor how you should handle *each* of the situations given above if, for some reason, there is no-one in the office who could help you.

Keep the caller informed

As a general rule, people are far more understanding and co-operative if they know what is happening – and why. Therefore

- if there is an unavoidable delay, explain why and give the caller the opportunity to call back later, if possible.
- if there is a problem, so far as you can, be honest about what has occurred, suggest an alternative solution or ask the *caller* what he/she wants to do.
- if you cannot help the caller at all, apologise and say so. If possible suggest somewhere else where he/she may be able to get the help they require.

However, keeping the caller informed may mean 'translating' some of the things you are told by your colleagues into a language more acceptable to a caller!

TEST YOURSELF

Assuming you were given each of the following messages over the telephone how would you rephrase them, diplomatically and tactfully, for the benefit of the caller?

1 'Oh heavens, Brian forgot he was coming. Can you find out if he can wait ten minutes?'

2 'Not her again! See if Tom will deal with her, will you?'

3 'Who on earth's asking for those – we haven't sold them for at least fifteen years. I haven't a clue where she'll get any nowadays.'

4 'When Gary Culshaw arrives make him wait in your office will you? He likes to try and wander into mine without warning and I've some papers out at the moment I don't want him to see.'

5 'Sarah Brown's a nerve asking that – she knows we never divulge that sort of information. Tell her that the goods were sold to a private buyer, and that's all we're prepared to say'.

Discuss your answers with your tutor.

SECTION REVIEW

Having completed this section, you should now be able to:

1 Greet callers promptly and courteously.

2 Identify how you can be of assistance to both routine and non-routine callers.

3 Describe the importance of confidentiality of information and security in relation to dealing with callers.

4 Explain how you would assist difficult callers.

5 Identify common non-verbal communication signals displayed by nervous, impatient or aggressive callers.

6 Escort or direct a visitor to his/her destination.

7 Identify how to deal with difficult situations and in which type of situations to ask for assistance.

8 Explain why problems or difficulties should be reported to a higher authority.

9 Complete a Caller's Log.

? *REVIEW QUIZ*

True or false?

1 Always speak more loudly to someone who is deaf.

2 A person who calls in to see someone without an appointment cannot expect to be helped there and then.

3 Visitor's badges are often colour-coded.

4 Visitors should be 'checked out' on departure.

5 Using gestures when you give directions confuses the listeners.

Complete the blanks . . .

6 Details of callers are often recorded in a ....

7 Visitors who leave their cars on a company car park may be asked for their ....

8 Information should always be passed on .... and ....

Work it out

9 Draw up a Caller's Log with the same headings as shown in the chapter. Date it for today and enter the following in *time* order, using the 24-hour clock.

2.30 pm Mr John Barnes of Wilkins Plastics (a rep) arrives to see Judith Pearson, Buyer, without an appointment. Car reg no H298 CBP

10.00 am Bridget Swindlehurst arrives for an interview with Mr Martin Webb, Personnel Officer (No car)

1.00 pm John Penny, painter, arrives to start work painting the newly refurbished canteen. Van reg no G60 KLS

3.45 pm Mr Tom Spibey calls in. He is a Director of Baker & Watts Ltd, one of your customers, and wants to see Philip Jones, your Sales Manager, urgently as some recent goods which he received were faulty. Car reg H108 PLS

10 Complete your action column, stating what action you would take if

- Ms Pearson never sees reps without an appointment
- Ms Swindlehurst should have arrived for an 11 o'clock interview
- you are informed that Mr Penny cannot start work in the canteen until tomorrow – someone got the date wrong
- Philip Jones is out of the office today on business.

NUMERACY GUIDE 9

Length and distance

If you measure a room, or a piece of cloth or paper, do you usually use metres and centimetres? You will certainly have been taught to do this at school. Yet at work you will be dealing with members of the older generation who still think in feet and inches! And no matter how 'metric' you are, we still calculate road distances in miles in Britain, not kilometres!

You therefore need a working knowledge of both systems to cope with all the situations you may meet.

Metric

Hopefully you already know that:

10 millimetres (mm) = 1 centimetre (cm)
100 centimetres = 1 metre (m)
1000 metres = 1 kilometre (km)

Imperial

Do you also know that

12 inches (in) = 1 foot (ft)
3 feet = 1 yard (yd)
1760 yards = 1 mile

Conversions

To be able to convert imperial to metric and *vice versa* you need to know equivalents. These are *approximately*:

2.5 centimetres	=	1 inch	1 metre	=	1 yd 3 in
30 centimetres	=	1 foot	1 kilometre	=	$\frac{5}{8}$ of a mile
90 centimetres	=	1 yard			

Imperial to metric

- To convert inches, feet and yards to centimetres simply multiply by the figure shown on the chart above, eg

  10 in = 10 × 2.5 = 25 cm

- To convert yards to metres, divide by 1.09.
- To convert miles to kilometres, multiply by 8 and divide by 5.

Metric to imperial

Now you need to work all the operations above in reverse:

- Convert centimetres to inches by dividing by 2.5. Then work out the correct distance in inches, feet and yards. Don't try to convert directly to feet and yards.
- Convert metres to yards by multiplying by 1.09. Remember that any decimal you are left with is a tenth of a yard (3.6 inches) and not a foot or an inch!
- Convert kilometres to miles by multiplying by 5 and dividing by 8.

TEST YOURSELF 1

Convert the following:

1 18 inches to cm
2 2 ft 6 in to cm
3 545 yards to metres
4 630 miles to km
5 1850 miles to km
6 20 cm in inches
7 180 cm in yards
8 240 cm in yards and feet
9 840 km to miles
10 2336 km to miles

Perimeter

The **perimeter** is the distance measured all the way round a shape, eg, length and breadth

length (l) = 250m

breadth (b) = 100m

$$\begin{aligned}\text{Perimeter} &= l + b + l + b \\ &= 250 + 100 + 250 + 100 \\ &= 700 \text{ m}\end{aligned}$$

The perimeter of a square can obviously be quickly calculated as the length of any side × 4, as all sides are the same length.

Shapes which are not true rectangles or squares are still calculated in the same way – by measuring each side and adding them all together.

TEST YOURSELF 2

Your company employs security guards to patrol the perimeter fence of their site with guard dogs each evening.

The combined office and warehouse block is a rectangular building 480 metres long and 300 metres in breadth. The fence is 80 metres out from the building on all sides.

1. How far will one guard and his dog walk in one tour of the fence?
2. If they patrol it three times a night on an eight hour shift, how far will they walk each night?

Area

The **area** of a shape is given by the number of square units which it contains and is calculated by multiplying the length and breadth, eg

$$\text{Area} = l \times b$$
$$= 6 \times 2.5$$
$$= 15\ \text{m}^2$$

length (l) = 6m

breadth (b) = 2.5m

Areas are expressed in square units, eg square metres in this example which are written as m^2.

Multiple shapes can be calculated by dividing up the shape into squares and/or rectangles, calculating the area of each and adding these together, eg

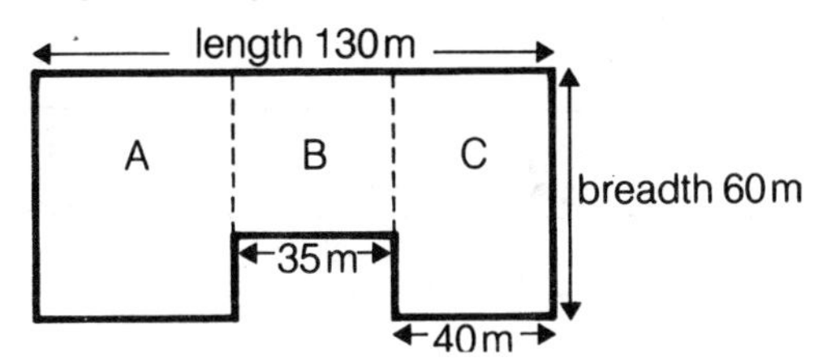

The shape above is comprised of three sub-shapes, A, B and C as shown by the dotted lines. A and C are rectangles, B is a square.

Note that you do not need to be given every figure. You can work out the additional numbers you need from the information already given:

- As you are told that B is a square then knowing one side gives you all four sides.

- If the total length is 130 m, and, on the opposite side we know that B and C are each 35 m and 40 m long, A must therefore be 55 m long.

TEST YOURSELF 3

From the information given above, calculate the area of each sub-shape – A, B and C – and then add these together to find the total area of the whole shape.

Don't forget – your answer must be expressed as m^2 as the lengths of all the sides of the component shapes are measured in metres.

TEST YOURSELF 4

Your company wishes to buy carpet tiles for the reception and surrounding office area of your building. Each tile is 1 m^2.

1. From the diagram below, can you calculate how many tiles will be needed?
2. If each tile costs £4.50, how much will it cost to tile the whole area?

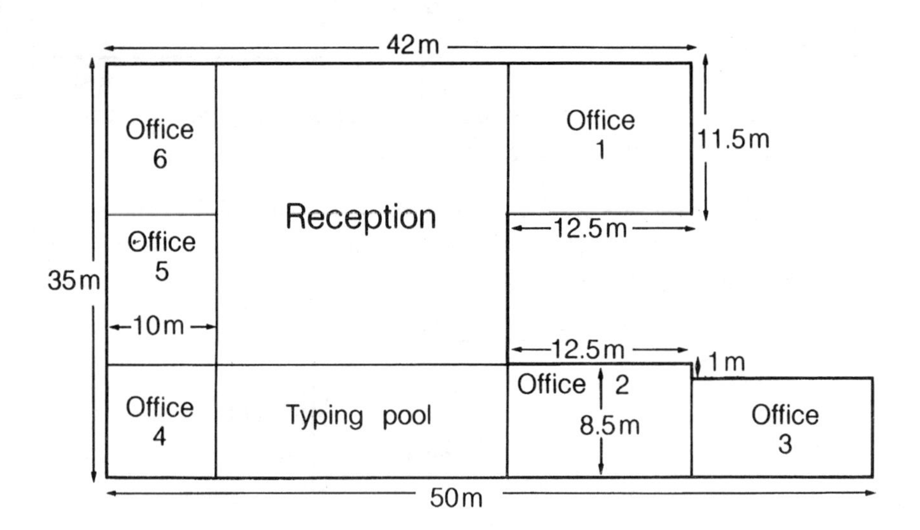

Simple sum trick

Multiply and divide by 5 instantly with even numbers!

Multiplying – halve the number and add a 0, eg 22 × 5
half of 22 = 11 + 0 = 110

Dividing – double the number and remove the 0, eg 135 ÷ 5
135 doubled = 270, remove the 0 = 27

Stock handling

OFFICE CONSUMABLES

What are consumables? 'Consumables' is the name given to office materials and supplies which are frequently used and therefore often need replacing.

Compare a box of paper clips and a typewriter. Which is the consumable item?

SPECIAL NOTE

Items which are not consumables are usually called **capital** items and an organisation will have one budget for capital expenditure (on equipment, transport, buildings etc) and one budget for consumables.

TYPES OF OFFICE CONSUMABLES

Most office consumables are **stationery** items:

Paper
- Available in reams (500 sheets)
- **Bond** paper is good quality, watermarked paper used for top copies of letters, reports etc.
- **Bank** paper is flimsy and used for carbon copies.

Carbon
- Available in quires (24 sheets)

Envelopes
- Purchased in boxes (normally 500 or 1000 per box)
- Different sizes and styles are available (see outgoing mail) in brown and white. Some have self-adhesive flaps.

Pencils and pens
- May be available in dozens (12) or by the gross (144)

Filing materials
- Filing folders, ring binders, document wallets, index cards, lever arch files, box files etc.

Printed items
- Letter headed paper, memos, compliment slips, business cards. Printed pads of standard forms may be stocked. These are often printed on IDEM or NCR paper meaning no carbons are required for copies to be made.

Miscellaneous items
- Shorthand pads, paper clips, staples, duplicating materials, bulldog clips, treasury tags, sticky tape etc.

In addition, small items of equipment are also classed as consumables, eg. staplers, punches, scissors, disk boxes, etc.

CHECK IT YOURSELF

Look through at least one stationery catalogue from a local supplier.

- Check all the items listed above, note the *catalogue reference number* for each and the *unit* in which they would be ordered (box of 12, pack of 10 etc).
- Look for other frequently used items which are not listed above.

SPECIAL NOTE

Station*e*ry = paper and envelopes, etc (*e* for envelope)
Station*a*ry = not moving (station*a*ry car)

STOCK CONTROL

The main aim of good stock control is to keep costs *down* whilst making sure that there is always an adequate supply of stock to hand.

It involves:

- checking goods carefully when they are delivered to make sure nothing is damaged or missing
- knowing which goods are **active** (frequently used – therefore a fairly high level of stock is required) and knowing which goods are **inactive** (infrequently used – therefore only a few are required). Keeping too much of the wrong type of stock means tying up capital which could be used better elsewhere

- storing stock properly and using it in rotation
- guarding against pilfering and misuse
- making sure items are ordered in good time (bearing in mind delivery times) so that essential items never run out
- storing hazardous materials safely
- having a proper stock control system for issuing stock.

In a large organisation it may be part of one person's job to act as **stock control clerk** and be in charge of the stationery supplies. His/her job entails:

- receiving orders for stationery from other people in the organisation
- booking out stock against these orders
- adjusting the stock record cards accordingly
- ordering new stock (either direct or through the Purchasing Department by means of a stationery requisition) as required
- ensuring that there are adequate amounts of stationery available
- making sure the stock cupboard is kept tidy and the stock is stored correctly to prevent wastage and deterioration
- undertaking physical stock checks to make sure the actual amount of stock agrees with the records.

SPECIAL NOTE

Many organisations use the term **requisition** to describe an order. Therefore a **purchase requisition** would be the term used to send an order to the Purchasing Department (eg to buy more stationery) and a **stationery requisition** would be the term used for orders sent by individuals to the stock control clerk.

Stock control systems

Stock control may be undertaken by using a manual system or by computer. The basic idea is very similar, except that on a manual system information is kept on cards, and checking stock for reordering and frequency of use can be quite time-consuming.

With a computerised system all the records can be brought up on screen and the computer can quickly and easily print out reports showing which stock needs reordering, the total value of stock held and so on. Computerised stock control is dealt with fully in the chapter on Business Application Packages (pages 302–333).

Stock control procedure

1. On each item of stock the management will fix a *maximum* stock level. This indicates the maximum amount of capital they are willing to have tied up in that particular item of stock and this figure must never be exceeded.
2. A *minimum* stock level will also be set. Once this level is reached an order should be raised to bring the stock back up to about its maximum level. The minimum level set should allow for a **buffer stock** to be kept until the new goods are delivered so that stocks will never completely run out. Active items will obviously need more buffer stock than inactive items.
3. When the stock control clerk makes out her order she should bear in mind that in many cases she will have used up more stock before the new order is received. Her order may therefore be slightly greater than the exact difference between her actual stock and the maximum level. In many cases the quantity ordered will depend on the *units* in which the goods are sold (dozens, per gross etc).
4. The stock control clerk will make out a **stock record card** for each item of stationery.

eg

STATIONERY RECORD CARD

ITEM: A4 White bond paper. MAXIMUM ...100 Reams.
MINIMUM ...20 Reams..

SUPPLIER: Office Supplies Ltd. UNITS............Reams...

Date	Received	Issued	Department	Order No	Balance
Nov 1					40 Reams
" 3		10 Reams	Sales	421	30 Reams
" 5		5 Reams	Personnel	164	25 Reams
" 8		10 Reams	Accounts	283	15 Reams
" 10	80 Reams				95 Reams

5 All items issued are booked out on the card, together with the order (or requisition) number and the balance is recorded.
6 Items received are booked in on the card and the new balance calculated.

TEST YOURSELF

1 Draw up three stationery record cards (or use pre-prepared cards provided by your tutor). Complete them for the following items:

shorthand notebooks
– Supplier: Ace Office Products Ltd
Max – 200 books Min – 50 books
Units 10 books

A4 white bond paper
– Supplier: Copynational Ltd
Max – 100 reams Min – 20 reams
Units – reams

DL white banker envelopes
– Supplier: Ace Office Products Ltd
Max – 50 packs Min – 10 packs
Units – pack of 10

2 Your opening balances should now be entered as at 1 December 19—.

Shorthand Notebooks – 80
A4 White bond paper – 35 reams
DL white banker envelopes – 38 packs

3 You issue stationery against authorised requisitions weekly. Your December requisitions are as follows. Book out the stock issued in each case.

3 Dec	Sales – requisition no		105	5 reams bond paper
				4 shorthand notebooks
				6 packs envelopes
	Personnel	"	217	2 shorthand notebooks
				2 reams bond paper
10 Dec	Accounts	"	521	6 reams bond paper
				5 packs envelopes
	Purchasing	"	307	5 reams bond paper
				10 packs envelopes
17 Dec	Personnel	"	218	8 packs envelopes

4 Consult the final balance for each item and decide which items you must order before the Christmas holidays.

SPECIAL NOTE

Although ordinary index cards are sometimes used, the most usual system is to keep the records on **visible edge** record cards where the stock titles are recorded at the *bottom* of the cards for quick reference.

Receiving goods

When goods are delivered they must be carefully checked against the stationery order to make sure that no item is missing or incomplete and no item is damaged. It is not sufficient just to check the Delivery Note which accompanies the goods against the order – the goods themselves must be unpacked, counted and carefully checked.

- **Missing goods** goods may be omitted because they were out of stock when ordered or because the firm forgot to send them. Out of stock goods will either be marked as 'to follow' on the delivery note (ie they will be delivered later) or noted as 'discontinued'. Sometimes a firm will substitute another similar item for a discontinued line.

  If the omission is because of a mistake on the part of the supplier then there will normally be a discrepancy between the number listed on the delivery note (which will match the order) and the actual number received.

  The stock control clerk should

  a notify the Accounts Department if the order is incomplete so that payment will not be made for goods which have not been received.

b make a note of all 'to follow' goods, notify the Accounts Department when these arrive and chase up the supplier if they don't.

c examine substitute items to see if these are suitable – and return them if not.

d contact the supplier immediately if there are any discrepancies between the quantity shown on the delivery note and the actual goods delivered.

- **Additional goods** a mistake by the packer may mean goods are received which were not ordered. These should be returned to the supplier. If the goods are recorded on the Delivery Note the Accounts Office must be informed so that these goods will not be paid for.
- **Incorrect goods** if the wrong goods are received then these, too, must be returned. It is usual to telephone the supplier to point out the error and, again, keep the Accounts Office informed.
- **Damaged or faulty goods** notify the supplier if any goods are damaged on delivery or if any items of equipment do not work. There should be little difficulty in exchanging these. The situation is, of course, different if the goods are damaged or broken *after* delivery. (See Consumer Legislation).
- **Goods you ordered in error** A problem! Much will depend on your relationship with the firm – they have no obligation to take these back. (Again see Consumer Legislation section).

Issuing stationery

Stationery must *only* be issued against an authorised requisition and a regular check should be made to ensure that orders from a certain section – or member or staff – are not excessive. If they are, then inform your supervisor.

Usually stationery will only be issued at specific times of the week and staff will have to submit orders in time for those to be made and some provision should be made for dealing with urgent requests so that work is not interrupted. Again, if too many 'urgent' requests are made from one section or one member of staff this shows bad planning on their part and you should mention the problem to your supervisor.

Stock reconciliation

At regular intervals the actual stock is reconciled (matched) with the stock records by undertaking a stock *inventory*. This involves counting the stock and matching the actual stock against the recorded stock. Any discrepancies must be reported to the supervisor or manager before the records are adjusted. The reason for the adjustment is noted on the card. Discrepancies are obviously investigated if pilferage is suspected.

Other adjustments

The stock cards will need to be adjusted if, for any reason, the stock is unusable, eg

- it is damaged (eg through water, sunlight, excess heat, carelessness etc)
- it is obsolete.

Before any stock is disposed of, the stock clerk should

- examine damaged stock carefully to see if any is still fit for use
- see if any obsolete stock could be given an alternative use, eg out-of-date office forms can be made into scrap pads
- in some cases old stock may be resaleable (cheaply) to the staff, eg if the company no longer uses 5¼" floppy disks.

The stock clerk should enter the adjustments, ensure these are authorised by a supervisor, and retain the cards (even of obsolete stock) until the end-of-year stock audit.

Stock audit

Once a year, or more frequently in some companies, an audit is carried out of all stock used and stored. This means

- carrying out a stock inventory
- calculating the *value* of stock held (usually at cost price)
- calculating how much stock has been issued during the year
- noting any adjustments
- working out the cost of the issued stock + adjustments

By this means the company can calculate how much it is spending on stationery in relation to the budget it has allowed for this. Any income (which would only be minimal) from selling obsolete stock is set against this expenditure to calculate the final total.

Care and storage of stock

- Store stock in a dry, well-ventilated room.
- Keep fast moving items where they are most easily accessible.
- Keep large and bulky items on *low* shelves to avoid lifting heavy weights.
- Label shelves clearly.
- Keep paper wrapped to avoid discolouration.
- Store stock with descriptive labels facing *outwards*.
- Ensure new stock is placed under or behind old stock so the old stock is issued first.
- Break down items supplied in large quantities (eg paper clips) to avoid wastage.
- Keep pens and pencils in boxes to avoid them rolling about/ getting knocked off shelves.
- Keep the door locked.

Safety first

- Label dangerous substances *clearly*.
- Keep inflammable liquids well away from heat and *don't* overstock.
- *Never* smoke in a stock room.
- Don't leave boxes where people can fall over them.
- Use a safety stool to reach items which are high up.
- Keep pins in boxes.

CONSUMER LEGISLATION

If you are buying or receiving goods on behalf of your company, then it is obviously sensible that you know what your legal rights are in relation to wrong deliveries, damaged goods etc.

The following section has been designed to give you *guidance* in this area, in the sense that it covers broad areas and not specific cases where exceptions might apply. Therefore, in real life, if a difficult situation occurs you should report it to your supervisor or manager who would be able to ask your company's solicitor for advice, if necessary.

Every time a customer buys something from a supplier he is entering into a **contract** which has two parts:

1 the customer's offer to buy the goods at a given price

2 the supplier's acceptance of the order and/or agreement to sell the goods.

When both parts have been completed there is a **binding contract** and neither side can simply change their minds or alter the terms of the contract. Therefore the customer cannot suddenly return the goods without good reason and expect his money back and the supplier cannot raise the price or make other changes to the agreement.

SPECIAL NOTE

A supplier has no legal obligation to accept an offer to buy from a customer, so long as his refusal is not on grounds of race or sex.

Acts covering consumers

There is a variety of consumer legislation to cover buying and selling. The main Acts you should be familiar with are

- Sale of Goods Act 1979
- Trade Descriptions Act 1968
- Consumer Protection Act 1987.

SPECIAL NOTE

The above Acts all apply to England and Wales – the situation in Scotland and Northern Ireland is broadly similar though some Acts have different names and dates. The Office of Fair Trading issue special leaflets on consumer rights in Scotland and Northern Ireland and these can be obtained by writing to the OFT, Field House, Bream Building, London EC4A 1PR.

TEST YOURSELF

The questions in this section should be attempted in four stages.

- Read through each question and attempt to answer it – if necessary with your 'best guess'. Discuss the problems as a group if this makes things easier.
- Read the information on the Acts which follows.
- Return to the questions and write down your 'informed' opinion
- Check your final answers with your tutor, before checking them with the answers at the end of this section.

1 You have taken delivery of twelve staplers. When you test these you find that the staples crumple as they are ejected and will not fasten the paper properly. When you notify the suppliers they argue that you must be using them incorrectly. You insist they must take them back. Who is right?

2 You order a large quantity of lever arch files from a local supplier. They arrive packed in flimsy boxes and the front of each file is either bent or badly scratched. Can you insist that these are returned?

3 When you check an order you discover that highlighter pens have been delivered instead of marker pens because you transposed two figures of the catalogue reference number on your order form. Your company doesn't use highlighter pens – can you insist the supplier takes them back?

4 You buy a disk box, described in a catalogue as holding 50 disks. When it arrives you find it will only hold 35 at the most. Can you return it and insist on a refund?

5 You buy a large quantity of floppy disks from a local computer shop during a sale. When staff try to use them they find none will format on their computers. The firm argue that you cannot expect the disks to be of the normal quality because they were sale goods. Are they right?

6 You contact a new supplier in the district to order stationery. He refuses to deal with you because he has heard bad reports about your organisation. Can he do this?

7 A representative persuades you to place a large order for photocopying paper with his company. You point out that your photocopier is rather temperamental and will only take good quality paper – he assures you that his paper will suit your machine. When staff try to use it they find it jams in the machine. Can you insist the paper is returned?

8 One of the two new electric staplers you have received has a damaged flex with bare wires showing. When you contact the supplier they tell you that as the fault is in the wiring of the machine you must take up your complaint with the manufacturer of the equipment. Are they correct?

The Sale of Goods Act 1979

This is probably the most important piece of legislation as far as the customer and the retailer are concerned. Under this Act, goods for sale must be:

- as described
- of merchantable quality
- fit for the purpose for which they are intended.

As described

Where there is a contract for the sale of goods there is an implied condition that the goods will correspond with the description – if you bought some scissors labelled 'Stainless Steel' and then found out they weren't you could claim your money back. The Trade Descriptions Act deals even more fully with the question of description (see page 254).

Of merchantable quality

This means the goods must work and includes goods sold at sale prices. However various points should be noted.

- If a defect is specifically drawn to the buyer's attention before the sale is completed then this is acceptable.
- If the buyer examines the goods before the sale and should have been able to see the defect easily (eg a scratch on the paintwork of a car) this is also acceptable.
- The seller must be a business seller – private sales are exempt.
- The seller can be a manufacturer, wholesaler or retailer.
- A person cannot reasonably expect the same standard of quality and durability from cheap goods as expensive goods, although if the goods were bought in a sale the price would probably not be relevant.

- Goods described as 'shop soiled', 'seconds' and 'manufacturers' rejects' cannot be expected to be of the same quality as a new or perfect product.

Fit for the purpose for which they are intended

Most goods have an implicit purpose for which they are intended, eg a hole punch should punch holes in paper. If it will not then the seller is contravening the Sale of Goods Act.

Consumers often place considerable reliance on the advice and experience of the seller or sales representative. If he or she indicates that the goods will do a particular task and they fail that purpose then the seller will be liable.

If the goods do not conform with any one of these three criteria then the purchaser is entitled to a *refund*.

- If the buyer prefers he can accept a replacement or repair but the seller is not obliged to offer anything except cash compensation.
- The buyer does *not* have to accept a credit note – if he does he may have difficulty getting his money back later if he finds nothing else he likes.
- Notices such as 'No money refunded' are illegal and should be reported to your local Trading Standards Department.
- Secondhand goods are also covered by the Act but the buyer's right to compensation will depend on many factors, eg price paid, age of the article, how it was described etc.
- Sale items are also covered by the Act but if the price is reduced *because* the item is damaged the buyer cannot complain later about that particular fault.
- There is no legal obligation on the buyer to produce a receipt and signs such as 'No refunds without a receipt' have no legal standing. However the buyer can be asked for proof of purchase, eg cheque counterfoil, credit card copy sales voucher etc.

The buyer is *not* entitled to anything if he:

- changes his mind
- decides that something does not fit
- damages the item himself

- was aware of the fault or should have seen it
- did not buy the item himself.

Trade Descriptions Act 1968

The principal offence under this Act relates to **false description of goods**. Any seller who gives a false trade description of goods or supplies or offers to supply goods which are falsely described, is guilty of an offence. This includes:

- selling goods which are wrongly described by the manufacturer
- implied descriptions, eg a picture or illustration giving a false impression
- other aspects of the goods including quantity, size, composition, method of manufacture etc

Usually the spoken word of the seller overrides the written description of the goods as the buyer can rely on the expertise of the salesman.

SPECIAL NOTE

Usually subjective comments are not covered by the Act, eg the salesman telling the buyer how much a garment suits him.

Consumer Protection Act 1987

This Act introduced two new areas to consumer protection in general.

- A person is guilty of an offence if he gives consumers an indication which is misleading as to the price at which any goods, services, accommodation or facilities are available, eg:
  - false comparisons with recommended prices (eg saying the goods are £20 less than the recommended price when they are not)
  - indications that the price is less than the real price (eg where hidden extras are added to the advertised price)
  - false comparisons with a previous price (eg a false statement that the goods were £50 and are now £25)
  - where the stated method of determining the price is different to the method actually used.
- The 1987 Act also creates a new offence – of supplying consumer goods which are not reasonably safe. An offence is

also committed by offering or agreeing to supply unsafe goods or exposing or possessing them for supply.

SPECIAL NOTE (UNFAIR CONTRACT TERMS ACT 1977)

Many organisations may try to evade their responsibility by using exclusion clauses or disclaimers on their premises, tickets, contracts or booking forms, eg articles left at the owner's risk.

None of these disclaimers are valid unless the organisation can prove that their terms are fair and reasonable. Therefore, if they lose or damage an article through their own negligence then the owner is probably entitled to compensation. This will not be the case if the organisation can prove they took reasonable care of the goods and could not be held responsible for what occurred.

Notices and disclaimers can *never* absolve an organisation from its liability to either staff or customers if personal injury or death is caused through their negligence.

CHECK IT YOURSELF

How did you cope with the questions on page 251? Check your suggested answers with the ones given below and discuss any areas where you went wrong with your tutor.

1. The staplers are not 'fit for the purpose for which they are intended' under the Sale of Goods Act 1979. You can insist they are returned.
2. The lever arch files are not 'of merchantable quality' – again under the Sale of Goods Act.
3. The buyer has fulfilled his part of the contract by supplying the goods you (inadvertently) ordered and is under no legal obligation to take them back. You may have a stronger argument if you have included a written description of the goods on your order form – otherwise you will have to rely on the goodwill of the supplier.
4. The box is not 'as described' under the Sale of Goods Act 1979 and the catalogue description contravenes the Trades Descriptions Act 1968. You can return it.
5. The term 'merchantable quality' under the Sale of Goods Act applies equally to sale goods subject to certain conditions (see page 252). The disks are not of merchantable quality and should be returned.
6. A supplier is under no legal obligation to sell to anyone providing he

is not discriminating against them on grounds of sex or race. He is within his rights to refuse to deal with you.

7 Both the Sale of Goods Act and the Trades Descriptions Act allow for the fact that the buyer will usually place considerable reliance on the advice of a sales rep, and his word will be taken to override any written description of the goods. As he has misled you then you are within your rights to return the paper.

Note that the situation may be very different if you had ordered the goods *without* mentioning your temperamental photocopier. Then, if the paper had been 'as described' the firm would have been under no obligation to take it back just because it didn't suit your machine.

8 It is an offence under the Consumer Protection Act 1987 to sell goods which are not reasonably safe. Your contract is with the supplier – not the manufacturer. He must take the goods back and is also liable under the Act for supplying unsafe goods. It is up to the supplier to take up the argument with the manufacturer – not expect the customer to do this.

SECTION REVIEW

Having completed this section, you should now be able to:

1. List the main types of consumable items used by companies.
2. Describe the job of a stock control clerk.
3. Explain the aims of good stock control and how these can be achieved.
4. Complete stock record cards, record stock movements and balance the cards correctly.
5. State how to deal with damaged and obsolete stock.
6. Check goods received against the order and delivery note and state the procedures to be followed if discrepancies occur.
7. Issue goods to staff in accordance with specified procedures, including those for emergency supplies.

8 Carry out a stock check and inventory reconciliation and explain why this is required.

9 List the procedures involved in undertaking a stock audit and explain why this is carried out.

10 List the procedures which must be followed so that stock is stored safely, securely and with minimal damage.

11 Explain how wastage can be minimised.

12 State the consumer legislation which relates to the receipt of goods and identify how this can be applied to wrong deliveries, damaged or faulty goods and wrongly completed order forms.

REVIEW QUIZ

?

True or false?

1 A gross = 124.

2 Flimsy paper is known as bond paper.

3 Stock control can be carried out on a computer.

4 Letter headed paper is classed as inactive stock.

5 On a visible edge record card the main details are written at the bottom of the card.

Complete the blanks . . .

6 The alternative word often used for a stationery order is a stationery ....

7 Stock should be stored so that the latest stock is used ....

8 Buffer stock is ....

Work it out

9 List *six* measures a company can take to ensure that they do not spend more than is necessary on their stationery requirements.

10 A company buys 12 boxes of ball-point pens. Each box contains 14 pens. If the total bill for the pens is £30.24 how much has each pen cost?

11 Pencils are bought by the gross. The maximum stock level allowed is 8 gross and the minimum level 2 gross. Today you have 302 pencils in stock. Will you order any more? If so, how many?

12 Your boss recently lost his pen and has asked you to go out and buy a new one for him. He tells you exactly which type to get and gives you the money to pay for it. The pen costs £14.50. When your boss tries to write with it he finds that the ink will not flow through the pen as there is obviously a fault in the barrel of the pen. He asks you to take the pen back to the shop and either get him another or ask for a refund.

- **a** Does the shop *have* to exchange the pen or give you a refund?
- **b** If that pen was the last one of its type in stock, could the shop have insisted that you accept a credit note?
- **c** Which Act covers problems like this?

NUMERACY GUIDE 10

Capacity

When it comes to measuring liquids, British measures are just as confusing as with length and weight! Petrol is now sold in litres, though most drivers still think in gallons. Milk is bought in litres from a shop but delivered in pints by a milkman.

You should be familiar with metric measures of capacity:

10 millilitres (ml) = 1 centilitre (cl)
100 centilitres = 1 litre (l)
1000 litres = 1 kilolitre (kl)

In imperial units the main quantities are

2 pints = 1 quart
8 pints = 1 gallon

If you work in the brewing industry you may hear the word 'hogshead'. This is equivalent to 2 gallons.

Conversions

There are two main conversion factors you need to know:

1 litre = 1.76 pints *and* 0.22 gallons

Therefore a litre is just about $1\frac{3}{4}$ pints, and just under a quarter of a gallon.

TEST YOURSELF 1

Give rough estimates of the following quantities:

1 5 litres in pints
2 30 pints in litres
3 98 litres in gallons
4 240 gallons in litres

Exact calculations

You will not be expected to convert pints to litres at work or *vice versa*, though you may have to alter gallons to litres and *vice versa*.

To convert litres to gallons *multiply* by 0.22
To convert gallons to litres *divide* by 0.22

Remember – when you are converting litres to gallons, if you end with a decimal number, this is tenths of a gallon and not pints! The easiest way to express the answer then is as a fraction, eg

35.5 = $35\frac{1}{2}$ gallons, 35.25 = $35\frac{1}{4}$ gallons and so on.

In most cases, however, it is perfectly acceptable to round up or down to the nearest whole number of gallons.

TEST YOURSELF 2

Convert to gallons (nearest whole number)

1 82 litres
2 154 litres
3 27 litres
4 68 litres
5 218 litres

Convert to litres (to two decimal places)

6 55 gallons
7 30 gallons
8 136 gallons
9 79 gallons
10 209 gallons

Time zones

Everyone has heard of jet lag – the problems people have when they travel long journeys through different time zones so that when they are wide awake they should be in bed, and *vice versa*.

If you travelled from London to New York by *Concorde* you would actually arrive before you set off! Not literally, of course, but because New York time is 5 hours behind London time, and the journey on *Concorde* takes nearly 4 hours, you arrive New York time one hour earlier than you left London time.

Airline timetables can therefore look confusing, as they are given in local times at the airports of departure and arrival. In the example of New York, above, the timetable may show the departure as 1000 and arrival as 0900!

If you travel east, instead of west, then the opposite occurs. The journey will look very long because the destination may be several hours ahead of Britain. A flight to Hong Kong may read as if it takes 23 hours from London. However, Hong Kong is 8 hours ahead of us so the flight is therefore 15 hours.

Two other factors make things even more confusing!

- Britain's time changes in March and October. During the summer we operate on BST (British Summer Time), in the winter we operate on GMT (Greenwich Mean Time). Most time differences are given in GMT which means you must *deduct* an hour in summer when we operate one hour ahead of GMT.
- If you fly over the Pacific you cross the International Date Line. If you travel east, eg from Australia to Hawaii, you gain a day – Hawaii is just starting to have the day Australia has just had! So you would have the same day twice! However, if you travel west, from Hawaii to Australia you lose a day – by the time you arrive in Australia the day Hawaii was about to have has finished!

Because of time differences, airline timetables often show a different day of arrival to the day of departure.

TEST YOURSELF 3

The following show the times of arrival and departure from various places to and from London. Assuming it is winter (GMT), allow for the time difference given in each case to calculate the actual journey time. (All times are given using the 24-hour clock.)

1. London – Montego Bay, Jamaica — 5 hours earlier than GMT
   1250 dep – 1800 arrive
2. London – Singapore — 8 hours later than GMT
   1000 dep – 0700 arrive a day later
3. London – Barbados — 4 hours earlier than GMT
   0900 dep – 1120 arrive
4. London – Bahrain — 3 hours later than GMT
   1800 dep – 0400 arrive a day later
5. London – Sydney — 10 hours later than GMT
   2100 dep – 0800 arrive 2 days later

Estimates

You practised estimating a little on pages 68–70, when you were converting lb to kg and *vice versa*. This is a useful skill to develop in an office because people often want quick estimates – the actual figures will do later. In addition, being able to estimate means you can always give your calculations a rapid 'rationality check' to make sure they are likely to be accurate. (You looked at this on pages 112–113.)

To find an estimate you:

- work to nearest numbers – rounding up or down as necessary
- always work to the order of magnitude of the original question – therefore, 0.28 = 0.3 not 3 or 30!

Estimate the area of a rectangle 16.22 m × 9.65 m
$16 \times 10 = 160\ \text{m}^2$

Estimate the cost of travelling 348 miles at 35.2p a mile
350 × 0.35 = £122.50

Estimate the cost of 3123 articles at £4.25 each
3000 × 4 = £12 000

SPECIAL NOTE

If you want a closer estimate of two numbers then bear in mind that if you lower one, and raise the other, this will often take you closer. In the last example this would have meant 3000 × 4.5 = £13500. The exact answer is £13272.75 so as you can see, the second method brings you considerably closer.

TEST YOURSELF 4

Make rough estimates of the following:

1 the value of 43.2 × 11.4
2 the cost of 985 articles at £1.80 each
3 the cost of photocopying 278 sheets of paper at 1.2p each

Make close estimates of the following:

4 the value of 19.6 × 27.4
5 the cost of 3965 articles at £3.85 each
6 the cost of travelling 517 miles at 31.5p a mile

Simple sum trick

Multiply even numbers quickly by halving and doubling, eg

16 × 16	is also	8 × 32	(too hard? then try . .)
		4 × 64	(still too hard? then try . .)
		2 × 128	(easier? – then what about)
		1 × 256!	

Useful if you've left your calculator behind!

Note – you can't always get it down to 1 = . . . but you can always make things a lot easier!

Providing information to customers and clients

Customers and clients contact an organisation for a variety of reasons:

- to obtain information on their goods and/or services
- to place an order
- to enquire about progress of their order
- to clarify details
- to query their accounts
- to complain, if they are dissatisfied with the service they have received.

ASSISTING A CUSTOMER

To be able to help a customer effectively you need to be able to convince him or her that, after contact with you, progress has been made in the area of concern. Even if you could not help the customer personally, he should feel that his call has resulted in some action being taken by your organisation. If you leave the customer feeling that he has made little, if any, progress he will probably take his business elsewhere in the future. At the very least he will be annoyed that his time has been wasted as nothing has been achieved.

Basic facts and information

What do you need to know before you can start to help someone? Ideally you should know:

- your company structure and organisation – who deals with what

- the products/services your company offers – not just a broad appreciation but details of what you can and can't offer. The expertise you can gain in this area will depend very much on the type of company you work for eg:

  – in a retail organisation sales assistants should know their stock well, its uses, the range, what can be ordered and so on

- in a service industry, eg an insurance company or solicitors, staff should know the full range of services offered and who to contact in the organisation for further information if required
- in a manufacturing industry the technical details of some products may be too intricate to be known by anyone other than the technical specialists. In this case you should have a good knowledge of the range of products manufactured and know who to contact in relation to the particular query you are asked.

- your company procedures and the main methods of communication between and within departments
- basic facts about the law in relation to your organisation and its customers, eg the Trades Description Act and the Financial Services Act
- where to go for more information, help or advice.

SPECIAL NOTE

It is perfectly natural for anyone in a new job to feel lost and rather useless when they have to deal with a customer enquiry. You become effective much more quickly if you

- read the information available
- look at the products sold (if possible)
- ask questions
- **remember the answers!**

The personal touch

Unless you work in a very large store, most organisations have their 'regular' customers. Although all customers are important to an organisation regular customers are *vital*. It can take years – and a considerable amount of hard work (and money spent on advertising) to build up a good customer relationship and yet this can be ruined in minutes with poor service or back-up.

You will always be more effective if you make a concerted effort to get to know your regular customers quickly and *remember their names*. If you can remember their likes and dislikes, who they deal with and other details, so much the better. This will enable you to give them a far more personal service which will be noticed and appreciated.

STEPS FOR GREETING CUSTOMERS AND CLIENTS

Follow this flow chart and you won't go wrong

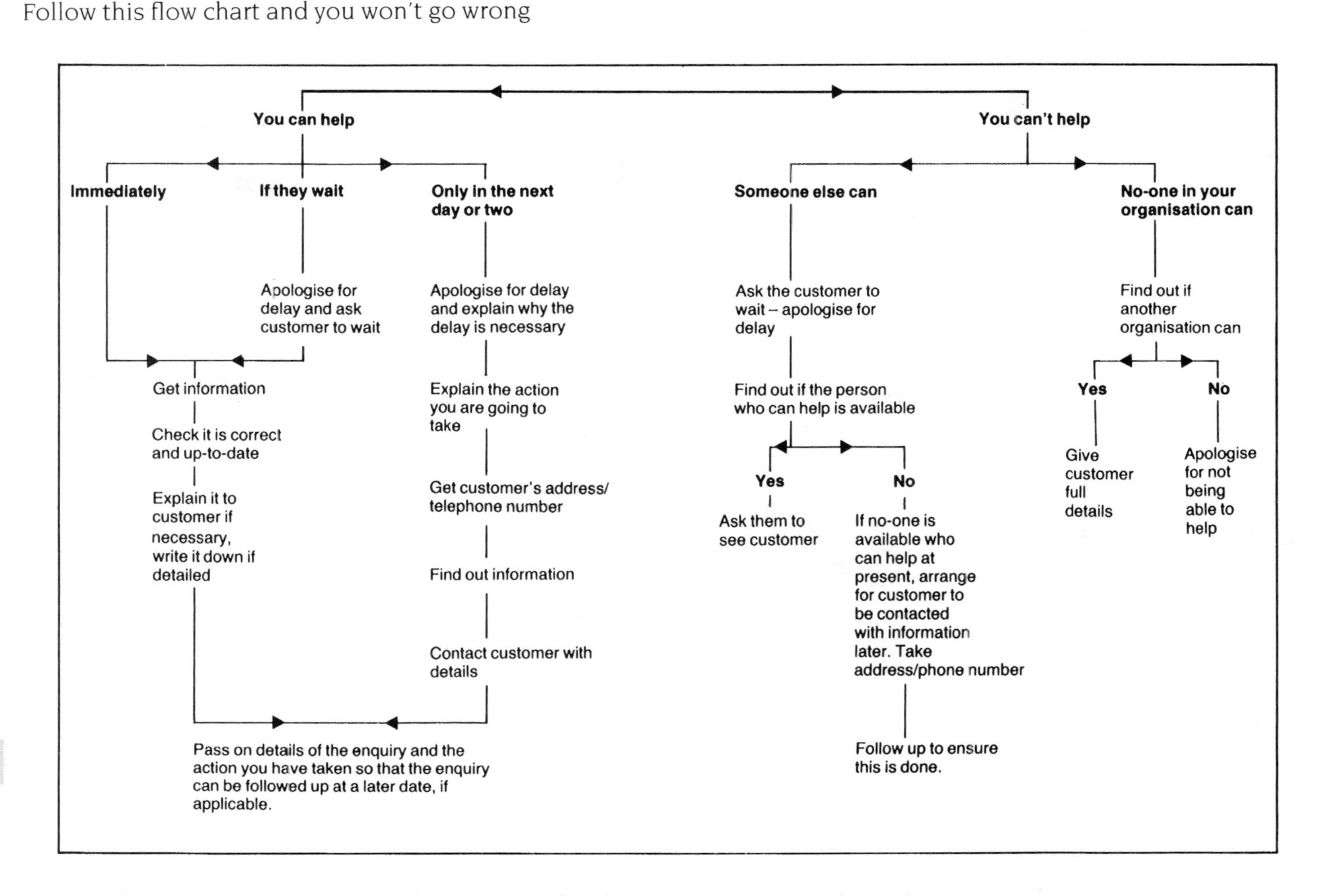

General calls and enquiries

- Greet the customer with a smile and a greeting, eg 'May I help you?'
- If you know their name, use it.
- Listen whilst you ascertain what their enquiry is about.
- If it is long or complicated, write down the details.
- Check anything you are not sure about.

Go back to the flow chart on page 265 and follow it through carefully.

CHECK IT YOURSELF

- Discuss as a group the occasions when
  - you have contacted a shop or other organisation and received very poor service
  - you have asked about products or services but the person you spoke to didn't know (or care!) enough to help you.

  What has been your opinion of these organisations afterwards?

- Have you ever worked for an organisation (full-time or part-time) where you have received specific training on customer service? If so, discuss the training you received with the rest of your group.

  Did your company have any type of merit system for service, eg the McDonald's 'star' badge system?

- If you are working at present (whether full-time or only at weekends) assess whether you feel you know enough about the products/services offered by your organisation to be able to help your customers.

  If not, how could you systematically go about finding out more information? Does your company issue advertising material or promotional literature – or even have a stock list – that would give you more details?

  Do you know who to contact for help and advice if you receive a difficult query?

General enquiries

Use the chart on page 265 to see how you should handle general enquiries. Make sure you know or find out:

- *where* to get the information you need and *what* type of information is available – leaflets, catalogues, printed pages. Don't forget people will always want to know about the price – and the ways in which they can pay (eg by cheque, credit card, instalments etc).
- *who* to ask for help or further information, if that is required. Don't 'overstep' your area of responsibility by promising anything to a customer which is outside your area of authority.
- *enough* about the customer to be able to recommend the right product or service for him (or her). You should not be so keen to recommend a product or service that you 'land' the customer with something that will not suit him as
  - he will probably come back to complain later, and/or
  - he will go elsewhere next time
  - in some service industries this is illegal! (see section on the Financial Services Act).
- *how* to follow up the enquiry. This means taking full details of the enquiry and making any special notes which will be useful or relevant to your colleagues who may have to follow it up. Most organisations have standard procedures for dealing with enquiries and standard forms to fill in. If there are any *additional* details which do not seem to 'fit' anywhere on the form then write these out neatly and clip your notes *securely* to the form. Make sure you process the enquiry on to its 'next stage' without undue delay.
- *how to keep the customer informed*! Tell the customer the procedure that is to be followed, how long it will take, what delays (if any) may be expected – and why. Promise to keep him/her informed if the situation changes in any way.
  This type of assurance would be essential of course if your company is out-of-stock of the product required and it has to be ordered. It is far more professional to tell the customer you will inform *him or her* when it is available – rather than asking him to ring you!

SPECIAL NOTE

If you are getting together literature to give to a customer *never* take the last copy without making sure that either

- you have ordered some more
- you get some more from stock to replace what you have taken.

There is nothing more infuriating for other staff to find that they have run out of essential information because someone keeps using the last copy without telling anyone!

CHECK IT YOURSELF

Discuss with your tutor

- the type of procedures which would be followed,
- the type of forms which would be completed,
- what could go wrong through staff inefficiency in the case of each of these enquiries:
  - an order for a book not in stock at a book shop
  - an application to open a bank account
  - an enquiry to replace existing window frames with plastic PVC frames
  - an application from a potential student to attend a college course.

Confidential enquiries and interviews

As you will know, part of the procedure for applying to attend a college course is that the potential student usually attends an interview with his or her prospective tutor. Normally this interview is confidential – because part of the enquiry will be relating to qualifications achieved, suitability for the course and so on and such details are only discussed in private.

There are a range of enquiries or queries where the content is such that it should not be discussed with the client in an open office area, eg

- **Financial** discussions on loans, income, expenditure, payment difficulties etc.
- **Medical** discussions about personal health or the health of close family, serious illnesses etc.
- **Personal** when information is relevant to past/future behaviour, criminal records, marital relations etc.

All organisations which have these type of discussions with clients will have private offices where interviews can be held. Every company will have a room where clients and customers can be taken if they need to pass on restricted information or discuss a particular problem.

You should always be sensitive to the type of information a customer will not want to discuss in public – think in terms of what *you* would not like other people to know if you were the customer.

The standard procedures and forms will still be completed with the relevant details – and often full, separate details of the interview are summarised for the benefit of other staff dealing with the case. Any such documents are usually kept in the customer file, marked confidential, and should *never* be the topic of open discussions with other staff *or* discussed outside the company.

TEST YOURSELF

Identify which of the following discussions should be held in private:

1. Travel agent – discussion with client regarding a holiday in Malta.
2. Building Society – discussion about extending a mortgage repayment period.
3. School – discussion with parent regarding child's absenteeism.
4. Estate agent – discussion with client about buying a property.
5. Insurance company – discussion with client regarding ineligibility for life assurance because of recent serious illness.
6. Accountant – discussion regarding tax payable on additional earnings.

In *each* of the cases you have identified note down *why* you think a record of the discussion must be kept in the relevant file.

SPECIAL NOTE

Do be aware that there will be facts and information about your company and other staff that you should not discuss with customers. Sometimes this can be difficult – especially if you are asked a question outright.

- Do make sure you are aware, in any organisation you work for, of the type of information which must not be given to customers.

- Look back at the notes on diplomacy on page 233 of Liaising with Callers and Colleagues and discuss with your tutor any other situations where you may have difficulty in deciding how much you should say, and how much you should not.

Eligibility

The word 'eligibility' refers to our right to be 'qualified' – or eligible for a certain item or service. For instance, you are not eligible to join a nightclub which is restricted to over 21s if you are only 18.

Just as you would be disappointed if you were refused membership of somewhere you wanted to join, so are clients if they find they are unable to have the benefit of a certain service because they are not eligible. For this reason, this type of interview, too, may be held in private.

Additionally, of course the client may be quite surprised or shocked. If a company has run a credit check on a customer and received a bad report, it has the task of telling the customer that credit will not be allowed. In a broad sense, we could say that the client is therefore not eligible for credit. In the same way, a bank will run a check, via computer, on a customer's account if he or she suddenly requests a large cash withdrawal.

It is important that you know, in any organisation you work for, what type of checks are required before a customer or client is eligible for the services or products you are offering – and make sure you follow any procedures laid down accurately and precisely.

Difficult clients

You may have problems dealing with people if

- they want a service you cannot provide
- they consider the service they have received to date is unsatisfactory
- they do not speak English very well
- you cannot seem to find out what it is they really want
- they have a query which no-one seems to be able to answer
- they are annoyed at something you have told them (ie they cannot have credit).

From the work you have already done in the chapters on Business Relationships and Liaising with Callers and Colleagues you should already be aware of

- how to recognise 'non-verbal' communication signals which indicate the way a client is reacting
- how to communicate with someone verbally
- how to deal with angry, aggressive or nervous people – or people who cannot speak English very well (see under Communicating Information – section 1).

If you have forgotten what you learned in these chapters, turn back to the relevant pages and refresh your memory. Then try the following exercise.

CHECK IT YOURSELF

Discuss with your tutor how you would deal with

- A customer complaining loudly that she has received a 'final demand' notice for payment when she paid her bill three weeks ago.
- A customer who insists that her friend bought the same item from you a week ago at two-thirds the price.
- An old lady who has trouble understanding you.
- A customer whose credit card, when processed, is rejected as he is already over his credit limit with the credit card company.
- A customer whose holiday is now subject to a £30 surcharge per person (assume you work for a travel agent).
- A customer who is extremely annoyed because, after calling your company four times for service, no-one has yet been to mend his machine.

SPECIAL NOTE

If you ever have to deal with an extremely aggressive customer – or one who threatens you in any way – do not hesitate to get help. If you are working in a small company on your own then you are within your rights to say you will call the police if you feel you are in any personal danger.

THE LAW AND THE PUBLIC

Anyone who works in an organisation where they deal with the general public should be aware of the legal framework which affects their business. In some organisations, eg those providing a financial service, this type of knowledge is essential as otherwise staff could find that they are unwittingly breaking the law – and ignorance has never been acceptable as a valid excuse!

Selling goods and services

The main Acts which affect the sale of goods and services include

- The Sale of Goods Act (1979)
- The Trades Descriptions Act (1968)
- The Consumer Protection Act (1987)

All these Acts are dealt with (in relation to buying goods) in the chapter on Stock control, on pages 252–255.

Other relevant Acts include

- The Supply of Goods and Services Act (1982)
- The Unfair Contract Terms Act (1977)
- The Consumer Credit Act (1974)
- The Financial Services Act (1986)

A brief resumé of each of these Acts is given below:

The Supply of Goods and Services Act 1982

This Act is in two parts, the first broadly concerned with goods and the second with services.

Part 1 Goods This extends the protection for consumers provided by the Sale of Goods Act to include goods supplied as part of a service, on hire or in part exchange. These, too, must be as described, of merchantable quality and fit for the purpose made known to the supplier. Therefore if a garage fits rear seat belts to a car, a woman hires a carpet cleaning machine (and specially asks if it can cope with long-pile rugs) and a couple trade in their old gas fire for a new one at the gas showrooms, these 'goods' are all covered under the Act.

Part 2 Services This part deals with the standard of services such as those provided by builders, plumbers, TV repairers, hairdressers, garages etc. It protects the buyer against shoddy workmanship, delays and exorbitant charges.

The Unfair Contract Terms Act 1977

Many organisations may try to evade their responsibility by using exclusion clauses or disclaimers on their premises, tickets, contract or booking forms, eg articles left at the owner's risk.

None of these disclaimers are valid unless the organisation can prove that their terms are fair and reasonable. Therefore, if they lose or damage an article through their own negligence then the owner is probably entitled to compensation. This will not be the case if the organisation can prove they took reasonable care of the goods and could not be held responsible for what occurred.

Notices and disclaimers can *never* absolve an organisation from its liability to either staff or customers if personal injury or death is caused through their negligence. (See under Public Liability).

Consumer Credit Act 1974

The Consumer Credit Act 1974 applies to a wide range of types of credit agreement and places strict controls upon persons who provide credit facilities in the course of their business.

The Act also lays down strict rules governing the form and content of agreements – the object of the rules is to protect the borrower by giving him the fullest possible information about his rights and obligations.

Three major provisions include the following.

1 A credit agreement must be issued to the buyer in a form which complies with regulations made under the Act. It must contain details such as:

- the names and addresses of the parties
- the **APR** (Annual Percentage Rate of charge)
- the cash price, deposit, total amount of credit

- the total amount payable
- the repayment dates and amount of each payment
- sums payable on default
- other rights and protections under the Act.

2 Customers who buy goods on credit may have the right to cancel the agreement if they change their minds, provided:

   - they have signed the agreement at home or anywhere else *except* on the trader's business premises
   - they have bought the goods 'face-to-face' with the dealer. (Therefore, if someone rings you up and persuades you to buy over the telephone then, under the law at present, you are not covered, although hopefully this will change soon.)

3 If a person signs a credit agreement at home they will get a copy immediately. Every copy of a cancellable agreement has a box labelled 'Your right to cancel' which tells the buyer what to do. About a week later a further copy or separate notice of the cancellation rights is sent to the buyer by post. Starting from the day after he receives this second copy he has 5 days in which to give the trader *written* notice that he wants to cancel.

SPECIAL NOTE

- **APR – Annual Percentage Rate** of charge *must* be calculated by all credit companies in a standard way set down by law. Basically all the interest and other charges for giving credit are added together and the total is expressed as an annual percentage rate.

  The lower the APR, the better!!

  Buyers should *always* 'shop around' and compare the APR of different companies. It is often given in adverts, can always be obtained by asking for a written quotation and *must* be clearly shown in all credit agreements.

- If you are working out any financial calculations for a customer *always* make sure they are accurate. Ask someone to check your figures *before* you give the information to the customer, if you have any doubts at all.

The Financial Services Act 1986

The aim of this Act is to protect people who wish to invest their money – whether in stocks and shares, life assurance or pension plans. The Act does *not* cover ordinary banking and building society deposits or other types of insurance.

The rules are complex but basically all investment businesses are now answerable to the Securities and Investments Board (SIB) and must be officially authorised to carry out their business by one of the five Self-Regulatory Organisations (SROs) set up for this purpose. Any investor losing money in one of the authorised businesses can claim full compensation from SIB.

Both SIB and the SROs have detailed rules about the conduct of the business. Some of these rules follow.

- Investment advisers must state whether they are giving independent advice or working as the agent or representative for one particular company.
- Advisers must find out enough information from the investor to give the best advice for *him* or *her* – not try to sell the best 'product' for their company.
- Any advertisements must avoid being misleading by exaggerating expected financial returns or missing out relevant information.
- Independent advisers must be prepared to reveal to the client the amount of commission they will be receiving.
- Any client who signs a contract in his/her own home has 14 days in which to cancel (28 days in some cases).
- High pressure selling is banned.

Anyone who has a complaint about an organisation should complain first to the company itself, then to the relevant SRO and then to SIB.

TEST YOURSELF

Below are given four problem situations. Can you state in each case *who* is right, why, and the Act which covers it. *Note* – you are advised to look back at pages

252–255 in the Stock Control chapter to review the other Acts relating to consumers if you have not already done so.

1 A customer has just taken delivery of a new photocopier from your company which you are advertising at £2700 + VAT. He has now telephoned you to point out that his invoice is for £3655 and he has no intention of paying any more than the advertised price.

When you investigate you find that the additional charges are for a variety of extras, including service, maintenance, paper not yet supplied by your company and so on. The customer says that had he known of these he wouldn't have bought the copier.

You insist that as he has taken delivery, and agreed to buy it, he must pay his bill. Are you right?

2 A customer left his personal computer with you for repair. Last night, despite the fact the premises have a burglar alarm fitted and security locks on the windows, your company had a break-in. The computer was one of the items stolen.

The customer has read the report of the burglary in the press and has now come in insisting that you have to reimburse him.

- Do you have to do this?
- Would the situation be different if you had a prominent notice saying that all the articles are left at the owner's own risk?

3 A gentleman telephones to tell you that he is going to report your company – an investment firm – as your latest advert is against the law. Your advertisement says '**No risk** – we can double your money in 14 days'.

Is he right?

4 Mr Thomas and his wife call in. They bought a car from your garage on credit two weeks ago and are now demanding their deposit back. They claim that the salesman said that the credit agreement with your garage would be at a reasonable interest rate and the repayments only small.

Mr Thomas has now calculated that the interest payable per annum is 25% and has discovered he could borrow the money cheaper from his bank. He says that if he had known this he would never have entered into the agreement.

- Can he insist on his deposit back?
- Would the situation be any different if the interest rate had been lower?

When you have completed this exercise discuss your conclusions with your tutor before referring to the answers at the end of this chapter.

Public liability

Any organisation which deals with or admits members of the public onto its premises can find it is liable to claims in law, eg

- If a visitor or workman is injured – through negligence on the part of an employee, unsafe premises or fittings etc.
- If a customer is injured because a product is faulty.
- If a customer suffers personal financial loss or distress through professional negligence, faulty workmanship etc.

For this reason most firms take out insurance to cover themselves against such claims. Typical policies include

- **Public liability insurance.** This is a legal requirement for some businesses such as hairdressers. It covers the business against claims because of personal injury caused by negligence, defects on the premises etc.
- **Product liability insurance.** This covers claims for injury caused by faulty goods.
- **Professional indemnity.** This covers claims for damages caused by professional negligence. This type of policy is usually taken out by architects, accountants, solicitors etc.

Most trade organisations offer policies for their members or insurance can be obtained through insurance brokers. Most policies have a condition attached that the insurance company will defend any claim on behalf of the insured and insist that the company shall not make any admission of liability to the person who has been injured.

SPECIAL NOTE

Trade associations are bodies associated with specific trades, eg the Building Employers Federation, the Association of British Travel Agents etc. They provide advice, assistance and information to their members and frequently have a voluntary code of practice to which their members subscribe. They will also deal with complaints from members of the public about companies in their industry, though they obviously have more influence over companies who are members, rather than those who are not.

CHECK IT YOURSELF

1 Discuss with your tutor the different types of public liability claims which might be received by

- a hairdresser
- a builder
- a hotel or restaurant
- a laundry

2 If you are working, find out if your organisation is a member of a trade association and, if so, which one.

3 How do you think you would be affected in your dealings with a customer who had been injured on your premises, on the condition made by your insurance company that your company must not make any admission of liability to the injured person? Discuss your answer with your tutor.

SPECIAL NOTE

All companies must *by law* insure their employees against accidents at work. This type of insurance is called Employer's Liability insurance and it covers employees against bodily injury or diseases contracted as a result of their work.

CHECK IT YOURSELF

How did you cope with the questions on pages 276–7? Check your suggested answers with the ones given below. Discuss with your tutor any areas where you went wrong and cannot work out why.

1 You cannot insist the buyer pays the additional £550 (£3655 less the amount of the copier plus VAT) as this price was not agreed with him beforehand. Any maintenance agreements and other extras must be agreed at the time of sale.

Your company has contravened the Consumer Protection Act 1987.

It is worth noting that customers also cannot be misled into believing they are being charged a price inclusive of VAT (eg the goods are advertised at £2500) and only when they get the bill then discover that the price is plus VAT, ie £2500 + 15%.

2 You are only liable to reimburse the customer for his stolen goods if you had not taken reasonable care of them whilst they were in your possession. The fact the company had an alarm fitted and security locks on the windows would make it seem likely they had done all they reasonably could to take care of his goods.

If the company has goods insured against theft it may be prepared to reimburse him from this money, but is not legally required to do so if it has not been negligent. The customer should be covered under his own insurance policy and can claim on this.

Having a notice disclaiming responsibility is irrelevant.

Supply of Goods and Services Act 1982, Unfair Contract Terms Act 1977.

3 Your advertisement is illegal under the terms of the Financial Services Act 1986. No investment can ever said to be without risk – and claims to double a person's money in two weeks are obviously grossly exaggerated.

The person involved has every right to complain to the SRO concerning that organisation.

4 Under the terms of the Consumer Credit Act 1974, Mr Thomas and his wife should have been issued with a credit agreement detailing all the terms of the sale, including the APR. As your company has not done this you have contravened the Consumer Credit Act 1974.

A customer cannot insist on cancelling a credit agreement just because he finds he could have borrowed the money cheaper elsewhere unless the amount of interest is exorbitant. The term 'exorbitant' would certainly not cover an APR of 25% (credit card companies charge between about 20% and 35% APR for borrowing on ordinary credit cards!) Exorbitant would be more likely to apply if the APR were somewhere in the region of 200%!

SECTION REVIEW

Having completed this section, you should now be able to:

1. Respond to customer or client enquiries promptly, politely and effectively.
2. Identify where to obtain the information you need to assist a customer or client.
3. Explain the importance of effective customer service.
4. Describe the correct procedure to be followed in dealing with general enquiries.
5. Identify the occasions when privacy is required and explain the importance of confidentiality.
6. Explain the term 'eligibility'.
7. Describe the most effective procedures for dealing with difficult customers or clients and identify the occasions on which help or assistance must be sought.
8. Explain the legal implications of dealing with the public and recognise how these constrain and affect the actions of staff.
9. Describe the importance of accurate and complete records.

REVIEW QUIZ

True or False?

1. Addressing a customer by name makes him/her feel important.
2. Selling an investment 'package' to a customer which suits the company but would not be sensible for the client is illegal.
3. Unless you have detailed knowledge about the products made by your company it is impossible to help a customer.
4. If a company hires an article, rather than buys it, he has no protection under the law.
5. All disclaimer notices are always invalid.

Complete the blanks . . .

6 APR stands for ....

7 Three types of enquiries which should be discussed in private involve ...., ... and .... matters.

8 Insurance taken out by companies to cover themselves against claims because of personal injury to customers is called .... insurance.

Work it out

9 A junior member of staff at your company has just started dealing with customer enquiries. Unfortunately she

- often asks customers embarrassing or personal questions in front of other staff and customers
- seems to have little appreciation of the type of information which is not usually disclosed to customers
- chats to other members of staff about the information she has found out about customers
- never seems to keep complete or accurate records – so that other staff have difficulty in following up the enquiries she receives.

Your boss has asked you to have a word with her in private. Prepare a checklist of the items you would discuss and how you would explain to her the importance of confidentiality, privacy and accurate record keeping.

10 A new salesman about to sell life assurance for your company, is bragging that he will make a fortune in commission in the first year

- by pestering people so much that they will have to buy
- by always recommending the policies which would give him the most commission
- by pretending that he is paid very little by your company, so that people feel sorry for him.

Your friend is very impressed, but you know better. You also know that when he attends the sales course run by your company he will have to change his ideas.

a which Act protects members of the public from these sort of activities?

b what will his sales course include that will make him realise that such tactics are illegal?

c what would you do if he persists with his ideas and a member of the public rings you to complain?

NUMERACY GUIDE 11

This section is in the form of a quiz – to see how much you have remembered and how good you have become at numeracy.

You can mark your answers yourself from the answers at the back of this book – but don't cheat!

See if you can get them all correct!

1 Write the number 1 million and two. (No crossings out!)
2 Add up the following numbers – 629, 487, 10 483, 10.382, 0.125, 65.
3 298.38 − 216.80 =
4 65.34 × 17.3 =
5 390.5 ÷ 14.2 =
6 16.28 + 3.12 − 15.4 − 3.01 =
7 Convert 50 lb to kg (to two decimal places)
8 How many kilogrammes in a metric tonne?
9 Estimate 25 kg in lb.
10 540 copies at 1.25 p each =
11 You depart from London at 1500 and arrive in New Zealand at 0600 two days later, glad to leave winter behind. If New Zealand is 12 hours ahead of GMT, how long have you been travelling?
12 Last year your friend visited the United States when the exchange rate was $1.54 to the £. This year you are visiting the US and are pleased to find that the rate is $1.92 to the £.

a if you both saved £500 for spending money, how many more dollars would you get this year, than she received last year?

b what is the percentage increase in the last twelve months? (Give your answer as a whole % number).

13 A rep for your company puts in an expense claim after travelling 625 miles at 34.2p a mile. How much is she owed?

14 If a VAT inclusive account is for £76.67 how much VAT can be reclaimed (to two decimal places)?

15 A company has a sale. All items previously marked £60 are now marked £48. What percentage is the reduction?

16 A courtyard is 243.5 m long and 168.5 metres in breadth. What is the length of the perimeter?

17 You have £800 invested in the bank. What is your interest if the rate is 12.5%?

18 Calculate the VAT (15%) on £284 *without a calculator*!

19 You return from holiday with 350 French francs. The exchange rate is 9.35 – how much is it worth in sterling?

20 How far is 3120 kilometres in miles?

Simple sum trick

Ask your friends to think of a small number, then ask them to

add 2, multiply the answer by 2, subtract the number they first thought of
add 2, subtract the number they first thought of, × 2,
then add 8.

The answer will *always* be 20!

As you should now be quite good at numeracy, you can try to work out yourself why this happens! If you manage this, you will also know how you can extend the riddle – to mystify everyone!

Processing petty cash and invoices

Section 1 – Processing petty cash transactions

WHAT IS PETTY CASH?

Petty cash is the term given for the money kept in an office to cover small day-to-day items of expenditure. The amount kept in petty cash is enough to cover expenditure for a week or a month.

Why petty cash is used

- To pay for small items which would not be paid for by cheque (eg magazines for reception, coffee, tea and sugar etc.)
- To reimburse (pay back) members of staff who have paid for an item out of their own pocket (eg a taxi fare)
- To pay service people who prefer their accounts settling immediately in cash (eg the milkman and the window cleaner)
- To pay for emergency requirements, where the goods are not normally kept in stock – eg letraset for a special display or a jiffy bag to protect a special parcel
- To pay for special items of postage, eg a registered fee.

Organisational differences

The type and size of organisation you work for will affect

- the total amount of the petty cash float (eg from £50 to £500). Each organisation will set its own fixed amount for petty cash – usually known as the **Imprest** amount

- the type of expenditure paid for out of petty cash. A large organisation, for example, may contract its window cleaner, have a canteen where staff purchase refreshments (so tea, coffee etc are not required) etc.

CHECK IT YOURSELF

If you are at work, or visit an organisation on work experience, try to find out

- The amount of petty cash float
- The type of expenditure paid for out of petty cash.

Compare your findings with other members of your group.

The petty cash system

There is usually a petty cashier in charge of petty cash. He or she is in charge of ensuring that

- all expenditure from petty cash is only for authorised payments.
- all expenditure is recorded accurately
- there are no discrepancies between recorded expenditure and the amount actually paid out
- security procedures for keeping petty cash are correctly followed
- the petty cash book balances at the end of the month.

If you are given the job of assisting the petty cashier then these objectives – with the exception of balancing the petty cash book – become *your* objectives. You are of no help at all if you pay out the wrong amounts, or pay people for unauthorised items of expenditure!

The voucher system

To make sure that only correct amounts are paid out, petty cash vouchers are used to record the money spent.

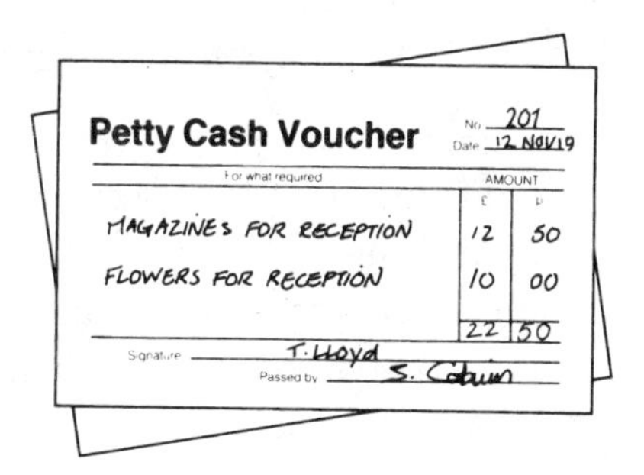

Petty Cash Voucher

No 201
Date 12 NOV 19

For what required	AMOUNT £	p
MAGAZINES FOR RECEPTION	12	50
FLOWERS FOR RECEPTION	10	00
	22	50

Signature T. Lloyd
Passed by S. Coburn

All vouchers are numbered and should be issued in *numerical* order.

- The vouchers are usually issued *before* the money is spent.
- Junior staff must obtain authorisation from a supervisor *before* spending any money on behalf of the company or claiming any money from petty cash. When authorisation is given the

supervisor countersigns the petty cash voucher (as shown above).

- Senior members of staff may spend money first and then present the petty cash voucher for reimbursement.
- An official receipt should be attached to the petty cash voucher as proof of the amount of money spent.
- Vouchers for multiple items must be checked to ensure the addition is correct.
- Completed vouchers must be filed safely, in numerical or date order.
- Any claims for unauthorised expenditure or discrepancies between official receipts and the amounts claimed should be referred to the petty cashier. N*o payment should be made* until the matter has been sorted out.

Balancing petty cash

At regular intervals you should add up the petty cash vouchers to find out the total amount paid out and *deduct* this from the amount of the petty cash float.

You should then check that this figure is the same amount as the money in the petty cash tin. If it is not, then tell the petty cashier immediately. (But do make sure you check your figures carefully first!)

At the end of the fixed period, eg a week or a month, the petty cashier will record the items in the petty cash book, balance this, and restore the imprest. This means that the amount held in petty cash will be brought back up to the full, fixed amount allocated for the petty cash float.

SPECIAL NOTE

Occasionally, because of a large amount withdrawn, or a few 'emergencies', the amount in petty cash may run low before the imprest is due to be restored. If this occurs, notify the petty cashier immediately.

TEST YOURSELF

In each of the following cases, work out how much money should be remaining in the petty cash tin on the date given. Identify any case(s) where the amount remaining is too low and should be reported to the petty cashier.

1. 16 November – imprest amount £100. Vouchers paid out to date: £16.50, £4.85, £2.00, 85p, £18.32.
2. 12 December – imprest amount £50. Vouchers paid out to date: £6.58, £3.20, 60p, 45p, £14.20, £3.48, 98p.
3. 16 December – imprest amount £500. Vouchers paid out to date: £64.20, £22, 75p, £23.20, £16.80, £85.43, £22.97, 56p, £40, £28.30.

SPECIAL NOTE

You obviously need small change in petty cash to be able to pay out small amounts. You will therefore need to note whether you are running out of small change at any point and ask the petty cashier to arrange for you to receive more when required.

For the petty cash tin to continue to balance you must obviously *pay* for any small change you receive – ie 20 × 10p and 6 × 50p means you owe £5 to the cashier.

Petty cash and security

Strict control must be kept over both the petty cash tin itself and the money paid out to prevent loss of money through mistakes, pilferage or deliberate fraud.

- The petty cash tin should be locked when not in use and kept in a secure place. You should not discuss where it is kept with other members of staff.
- The petty cash tin should never be left unattended on a desk.
- Unused vouchers should be kept safely – often inside the tin itself.
- Completed vouchers should be filed and kept in a secure place.
- Any missing vouchers should be reported immediately.
- Payments must *never* be made without an accompanying voucher. If you are ever requested for an 'advance' from petty cash by any member of staff, refer the matter to the petty cashier.

Petty cash analysis

When expenditure on petty cash is recorded, it is usually divided into different categories, so that a check can be kept on the amount being spent on such items as travel, stationery, postage etc. Usually there is a miscellaneous heading (eg Office Sundries) where expenditure can be recorded which doesn't 'fit' anywhere else.

These categories of expenditure will correspond with the analysis column headings in the petty cash book. Obviously the individual totals under each category, at the end of the period, will equal the total expenditure of petty cash.

SPECIAL NOTE

Be careful when recording items under Miscellaneous that they really can't be listed under any other main heading! Look back at *previous* records – or ask – rather than guess at where to put an unusual item.

SECTION REVIEW

Having completed this section, you should now be able to:

1. State what is meant by the term 'petty cash' and give examples of the type of expenditure paid out of petty cash.
2. Explain the responsibilities of a petty cashier and those of any person assisting the petty cashier.
3. Check petty cash vouchers carefully and identify discrepancies.
4. Identify the type of irregularities, problems and requests which should be reported or referred to higher authority.
5. Total and analyse voucher expenditure and balance this against actual petty cash held.
6. Describe the security procedures essential in maintaining a petty cash system.
7. Define the term 'imprest'.

REVIEW QUIZ

True or False?

1 Petty cash vouchers should be issued in numerical order.

2 Senior staff do not need to produce any receipts.

3 Special items of postage may be paid for out of petty cash.

4 The petty cash float must include small change.

5 The amount of the petty cash float varies from one organisation to another.

Complete the blanks ...

6 No voucher should be passed for payment without official .... by a senior member of staff.

7 At the end of a fixed period the petty cashier will restore the .... to the usual amount held.

8 Completed vouchers should be filed in .... or .... order.

Work it out

9 **a** Total the vouchers shown below and analyse these to identify how much has been spent on each of the following categories of expenditure: Travel, Stationery, Office Sundries. Calculate the total amount spent.

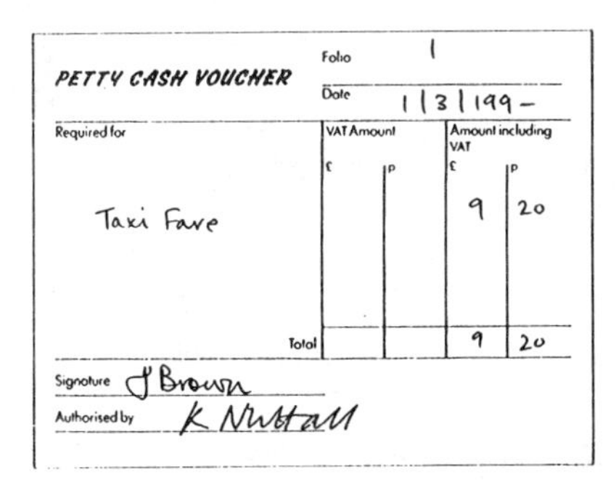

PETTY CASH VOUCHER

Folio 1

Date 1/3/199–

Required for	VAT Amount £	p	Amount including VAT £	p
Taxi Fare			9	20
Total			9	20

Signature J Brown

Authorised by K Nuttall

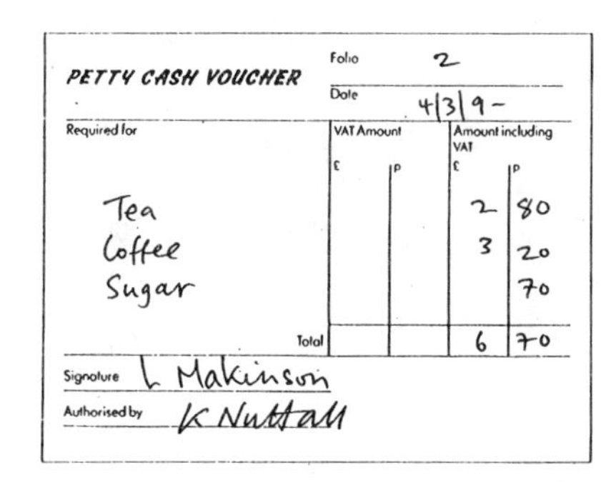

PETTY CASH VOUCHER

Folio 2

Date 4/3/9–

Required for	VAT Amount £	p	Amount including VAT £	p
Tea			2	80
Coffee			3	20
Sugar				70
Total			6	70

Signature L Makinson

Authorised by K Nuttall

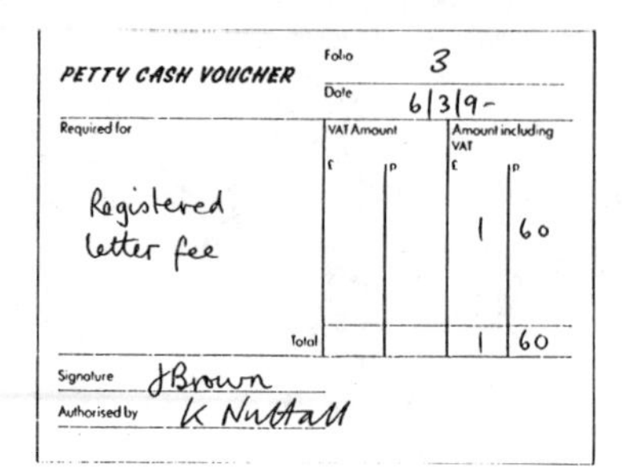

PETTY CASH VOUCHER Folio 3 Date 6/3/9-

Required for	VAT Amount £	p	Amount including VAT £	p
Registered letter fee			1	60
Total			1	60

Signature J Brown
Authorised by K Nuttall

PETTY CASH VOUCHER Folio 4 Date 10/3/9-

Required for	VAT Amount £	p	Amount including VAT £	p
Train fare			18	45
Taxi fare			3	30
Total			21	75

Signature L Quereshi
Authorised by K Nuttall

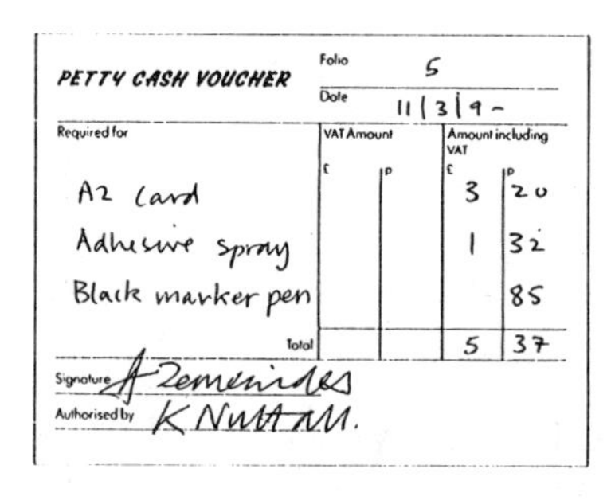

PETTY CASH VOUCHER Folio 5 Date 11/3/9-

Required for	VAT Amount £	p	Amount including VAT £	p
A2 card			3	20
Adhesive spray			1	32
Black marker pen				85
Total			5	37

Signature A Zemenides
Authorised by K Nuttall.

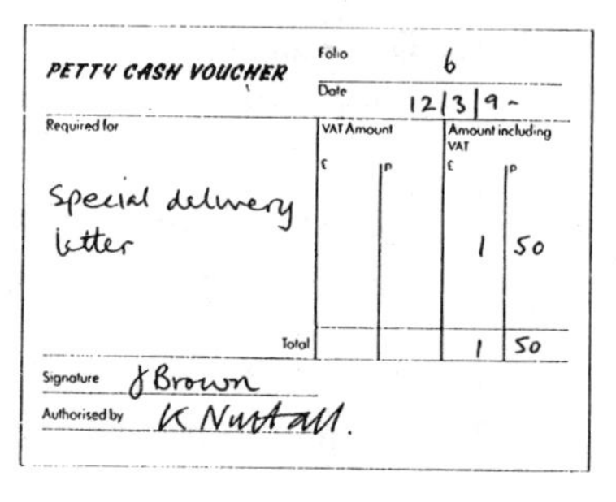

PETTY CASH VOUCHER Folio 6 Date 12/3/9-

Required for	VAT Amount £	p	Amount including VAT £	p
Special delivery letter			1	50
Total			1	50

Signature J Brown
Authorised by K Nuttall.

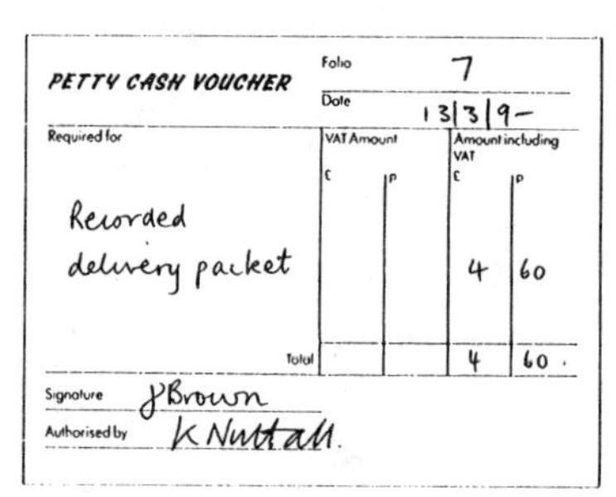

PETTY CASH VOUCHER Folio 7 Date 13/3/9-

Required for	VAT Amount £	p	Amount including VAT £	p
Recorded delivery packet			4	60
Total			4	60

Signature J Brown
Authorised by K Nuttall.

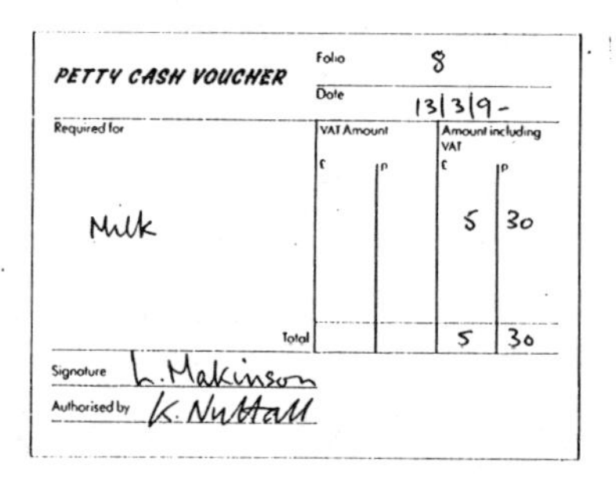

PETTY CASH VOUCHER Folio 8 Date 13/3/9-

Required for	VAT Amount £	p	Amount including VAT £	p
Milk			5	30
Total			5	30

Signature L. Makinson
Authorised by K. Nuttall

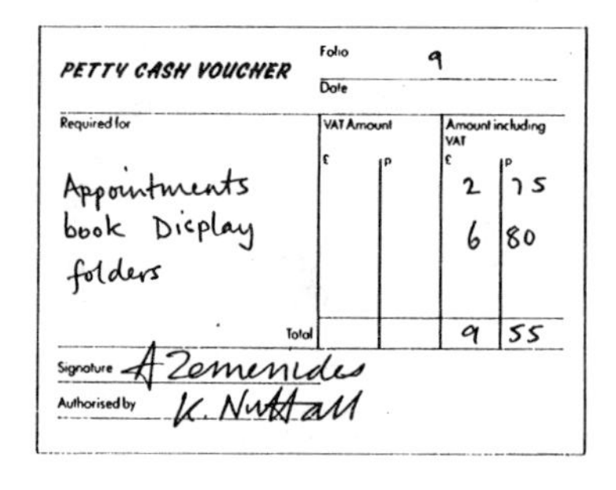

PETTY CASH VOUCHER Folio 9 Date

Required for	VAT Amount £	p	Amount including VAT £	p
Appointments book			2	75
Display folders			6	80
Total			9	55

Signature A Zemenides
Authorised by K. Nuttall

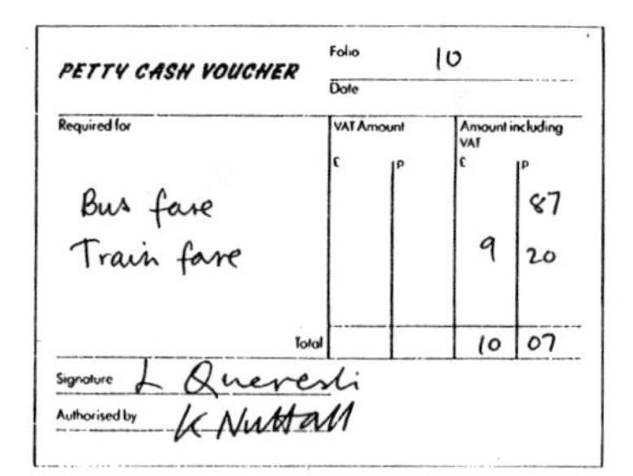

PETTY CASH VOUCHER Folio 10 Date

Required for	VAT Amount £	p	Amount including VAT £	p
Bus fare				87
Train fare			9	20
Total			10	07

Signature L Quereshi
Authorised by K Nuttall

b Your petty cash tin contains 1 × £5 note, 14 × £1 coins, 5 × 50p coins, 4 × 20p coins, 16 × 10p coins, 6 × 5p coins, 6 × 2p coins and 4 × 1p coins.

Your imprest amount is £100. Do you balance? If not, find out where you have gone wrong.

Section 2 – Processing invoices for payment

Invoices are one of the most commonly received documents in business – although not the most welcome! Every time an organisation buys any goods or service on credit, the supplier will send an invoice to the firm to claim payment. Before any payment is made the invoice **must** be checked to make sure it is correct.

Look at the invoice below and check the components on page 292.

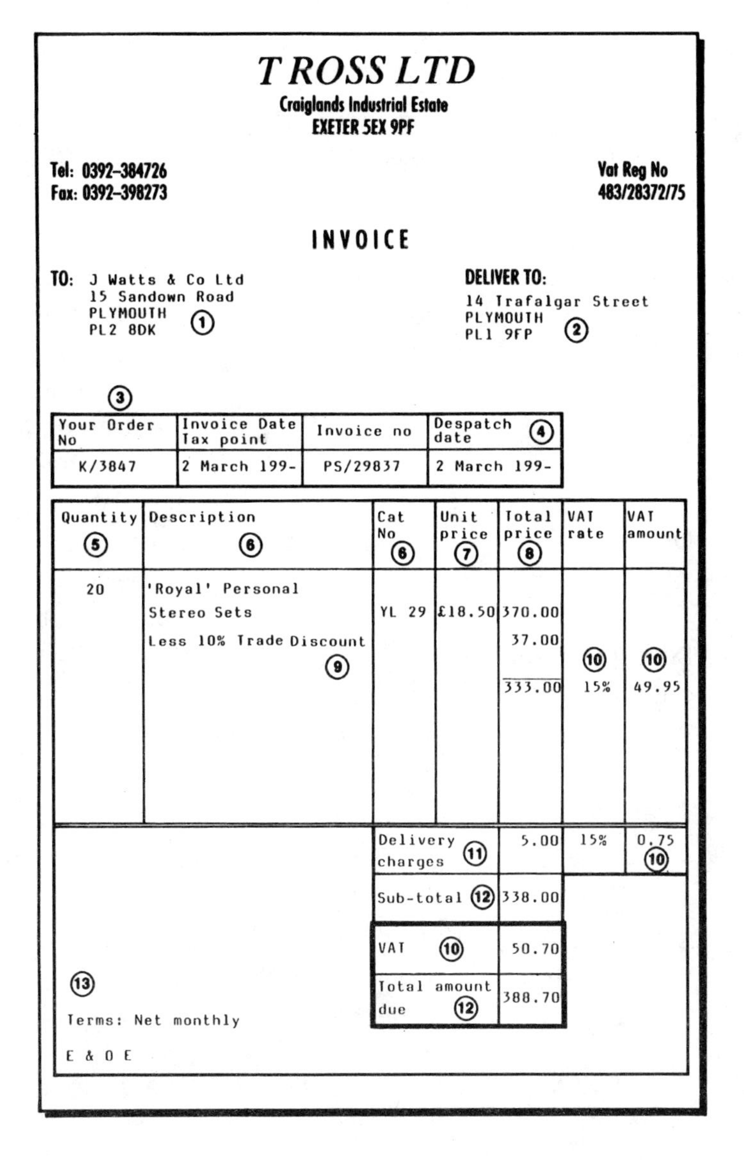

T ROSS LTD

Craiglands Industrial Estate
EXETER 5EX 9PF

Tel: 0392-384726
Fax: 0392-398273

Vat Reg No
483/28372/75

INVOICE

TO: J Watts & Co Ltd
15 Sandown Road
PLYMOUTH
PL2 8DK (1)

DELIVER TO:
14 Trafalgar Street
PLYMOUTH
PL1 9FP (2)

(3)

Your Order No	Invoice Date Tax point	Invoice no	Despatch date (4)
K/3847	2 March 199-	PS/29837	2 March 199-

Quantity (5)	Description (6)	Cat No (6)	Unit price (7)	Total price (8)	VAT rate	VAT amount
20	'Royal' Personal Stereo Sets	YL 29	£18.50	370.00		
	Less 10% Trade Discount (9)			37.00	(10)	(10)
				333.00	15%	49.95
		Delivery charges (11)		5.00	15%	0.75 (10)
		Sub-total (12)		338.00		
		VAT (10)		50.70		
		Total amount due (12)		388.70		

(13)

Terms: Net monthly

E & O E

The components of an invoice

Before you can start to check an invoice you must understand *all* the various parts or components of an invoice, which to check and how to check them.

Checking procedure

	Component	What to check	How to check it
1	Name of organisation/ address	Is this you?	–
2	Delivery address	Does this address relate to your organisation?	Ask or check the files
3	Order no	Does this match your order numbers?	Check against **order**
4	Despatch date	Whether the goods have been delivered	Check the **Goods Received Note** (made out by your organisation) or the **Delivery Note** (sent by the supplier).
5	Quantity	Has the right quantity been delivered?	Check Goods Received Note or Delivery Note
6	Description and catalogue no	Is this what you ordered?	Check order
7	Price	Is this as quoted?	Check **quotation** or order
8	Total price	Are calculations accurate?	Check them!
9	Trade discount	Is this the discount agreed?	Check quotation or order
10	VAT rate	Is this correct/is VAT calculation correct?	Work it out
11	Delivery charges	Are you liable to pay these?	Check quotation or order

12	Sub-total and totals	Are these correct?	Work them out
13	Terms	Are these as agreed?	Check quotation or order

SPECIAL NOTE

The letters E & O E are found on every invoice and stand for **Errors and Omissions Excepted**. This means that if there are any mistakes or items missed off, the supplier has the right to send a **supplementary invoice** to charge the extra amount still owing.

CHECK IT YOURSELF

Is there anything else you think should be checked, where no clues are given to you on the invoice itself?

Additional factors

Additional factors to check include the condition of the goods on arrival, whether any were returned as faulty or – if a service – whether the work was carried out to everyone's satisfaction.

The delivery note should tell you whether goods were received in good condition (if not the delivery note should be marked as 'goods received damaged'.) If you have any doubts at all *check with the person who received them*. It is certainly essential to check a service has been carried out properly with the person who arranged to have the work done.

SPECIAL NOTE

In many large organisations the Stores Section will send up a list of deliveries and the checks will be made from this – not the delivery notes themselves which are retained by stores. Only if there is a discrepancy will a delivery note itself be referred to.

Discounts and terms

- **Trade discount** is given as an allowance to people in the same type of business or if the buyer is placing a large order.
- **Cash discount** is a percentage off the price given for prompt payment. The terms are always stated on an invoice. The term

'net monthly' means that *no* cash discount is being allowed. The term 5% – one month would mean that the buyer can deduct 5% from the price if he pays within one month.

SPECIAL NOTE

In many organisations invoices with cash discount terms are processed more quickly to take advantage of the savings of paying promptly.

VAT and carriage

Value Added Tax (VAT) is added to the total cost of the goods (*after* any discounts have been subtracted). The current rate is 15%.

Whether your organisation is liable for carriage (delivery) charges or not will depend on the terms given on the quotation.

- **Carriage paid** means the *supplier* will pay for delivery
- **Carriage forward** means the *buyer* must pay for delivery.

TEST YOURSELF

1 In each of the following cases, calculate the final amount of the goods:

a 6 dozen @ 53p per dozen with 10% trade discount + VAT.

b 4 cartons @ £29.10 per carton with 6% trade discount + VAT.

c 48 @ £4.60 per dozen with 5% trade discount + VAT.

2 Examine the invoice shown on the next page. What is the difference between this and the one shown on page 291.

The difference is in the terms offered, and therefore the amount of VAT.

- VAT is levied on both the goods and any delivery charge.
- If the goods are supplied with cash discount available it is assumed that the buyer will want to take advantage of this. In the above example, if the buyer paid within 10 days he would

T ROSS LTD
Craiglands Industrial Estate
EXETER 5EX 9PF

Tel: 0392-384726
Fax: 0392-398273

Vat Reg No
483/28372/75

INVOICE

TO: J Watts & Co Ltd
15 Sandown Road
PLYMOUTH
PL2 8DK

DELIVER TO:
14 Trafalgar Street
PLYMOUTH
PL1 9FP

Your Order No	Invoice Date Tax point	Invoice no	Despatch date
K/3847	2 March 199-	PS/29837	2 March 199-

Quantity	Description	Cat No	Unit price	Total price	VAT rate	VAT amount
20	'Royal' Personal Stereo Sets	YL 29	£18.50	370.00		
	Less 10% Trade Discount			37.00		
				333.00	15%	47.45*
		Delivery charges		5.00	15%	0.75
		Sub-total		338.00		
		VAT		48.20		
		Total amount due		386.20		

Terms: 5%/10 days

E & O E

* Based on cash discounted price

pay £333 – £16.65 (5%) = £316.35 for the goods. The VAT is calculated on *this* figure – 15% of £316.35 = £47.45.

- The VAT for the delivery charge must then be added to the VAT for the goods to calculate the total amount of VAT.

SPECIAL NOTE

- Remember! If this invoice is settled within 10 days the amount owing is £316.35 (the discounted price) + £48.20 VAT = £364.55 *not* £386.20.
- If the invoice is settled *after* 10 days the full amount for the goods is due but the VAT figure *does not change*. The buyer therefore pays the total amount shown on the invoice of £386.20.

TEST YOURSELF

Goods are sold for £625 less 10% trade discount. 7½% cash discount is offered if the invoice is settled within 10 days. Delivery is £8 extra.

1 Which is the total VAT which should be shown on the invoice?

2 What is the total amount due if the company pays within 10 days?

3 How much is payable after this time?

Processing invoices for payment

- Ideally a variety of people should be involved in checking the invoice. It should *not* just be the responsibility of one person, especially if it is for a very large amount of money.
- Usually the document is stamped with a rubber stamp showing the stages it must pass through. As each person carries out their function they initial the appropriate box.

ACCOUNT VERIFICATION		
Item	Status	Verified By
Goods received		
Invoice details as Quote/Order		
Invoice correct		
Payment approved . . . . (Signed)		

SPECIAL NOTE

- In very large companies it may be uneconomic to employ someone to check every invoice, especially those for very small amounts. In this case invoices over a certain figure, eg £100, would be checked, and smaller totals would be *batch* checked, ie certain invoices would be checked at random.

CHECK IT YOURSELF

- Why do you think most organisations prefer several people to check accounts documents *as well* as the person making the payments?
- Check the invoice extract shown on page 298. Assuming the terms are correct and the goods were delivered, as ordered, in good condition, would you be prepared to authorise it for payment?
- If not, list all the errors you can find and then calculate the correct amounts.

Problem solving

If you find a mistake or discrepancy in any invoice you must know how to deal with it. The procedure may differ depending on whether you work for a large organisation, when it would be referred to the supervisor, or in a small one – when you may have to sort it out yourself.

If you are on your own, *first* calculate the amount the invoice should be and then double check you are still right!

- If the discrepancy is small and the organisation is one you deal with regularly then you could probably ring them up to point out the error. They may say they will issue a replacement invoice but they are more likely to issue a supplementary invoice or a credit note for the difference.
- If the discrepancy is large or if you do not know anyone personally at the organisation it is better to write to them. This means the correspondence will be on file and can be referred to if there is any dispute.
- If there are regular discrepancies from one particular organisation you may want to write a more formal letter of complaint to be signed by your manager.

INVOICE EXTRACT

Quantity	Description	Cat No	Unit price	Total price	VAT rate	VAT amount
22	Regency swivel chairs	283	£96.50	£2132.00		
2	Regency Executive chairs	286	£138.20	£276.40		
8	Visitors' chairs	288	£52.00	£418.00		
2	Reception Stools	296	58.00	£58.00		
				£2784.00		
	Less 10% Trade Discount			278.40		
				£3062.80	15%	£459.42
		Delivery charges		18.00	15%	£2.50
		Sub-total		£3080.80		
		VAT		461.29		
		Total amount due		£3542.72		

Terms: net monthly

E & O E

SPECIAL NOTE

A *reputable* company points out errors whether they are being overcharged or undercharged! Most companies would rather keep their reputation than save a few pounds by keeping quiet about a mistake which will probably be discovered by the supplier at a later date!

Supplementary invoices (debit notes)

If a mistake is made on an invoice and too *little* is charged then the supplier will issue a supplementary invoice for the additional amount. This may happen if:

- the goods were undercharged
- too many or better goods were sent and kept
- an item was omitted from the invoice.

A supplementary invoice used to be called a **debit note** but this term has gone out of use in most offices. A supplementary invoice is made out in exactly the same way as an ordinary one.

Credit notes

A credit note is sent if the supplier has charged too *much* on the invoice. This may happen if:

- the goods were overcharged
- some goods are returned to the supplier
- fewer were delivered than were stated on the invoice.

Credit notes used to be printed in red but as most are printed on computer today they are more likely to be printed in black. The trade discount and the cash discount on the credit note must be *identical* to that shown on the original invoice.

Paying the account

When the invoice has been passed for payment then the Accounts Department will pay the supplier, usually by cheque. However, in many cases the company waits until a **statement** has been received from the supplier, listing all the invoices, credit notes and payments made that month, and the balance owing to date. They are less likely to wait, however, if they can take advantage of cash discount terms by paying more promptly.

SECTION REVIEW

Having completed this section, you should now be able to:

1. Identify the main components of an invoice.
2. Explain where and how errors, omissions and discrepancies may occur on invoices.
3. Identify discrepancies between invoices and delivery notes.
4. Identify errors in invoice charges.
5. Explain the reporting procedures to follow should discrepancies occur.
6. Correct discrepancies on invoices.
7. Explain the terms **Supplementary Invoice**, **Credit Note** and **Statement**.
8. Describe how invoices are passed for payment after checking is completed.

REVIEW QUIZ

True or false?

1. VAT is calculated on an invoice after trade discount has been deducted.
2. A supplementary invoice is issued if the customer has been undercharged on the original invoice.
3. Trade discount is given to encourage prompt payment.
4. All invoices are paid after the statement has been received at the end of the month.
5. It isn't necessary to make a note if you have been undercharged – only when you have been overcharged.

Complete the blanks ...

6. The letters E & O E stand for ....
7. Carriage forward means the .... must pay for delivery.
8. The current VAT rate is ....

Work it out

9 Your organisation has received an invoice from Countryside Electrical Products for

18 Country Maid toasters @ £16.50 each
12 Country Maid jug kettles @ £18.75 each
6 Country Maid coffee percolators @ £26 each

Countryside Electrical allow your organisation 10% trade discount and terms are 2½%/10 days.

All the goods have been delivered in good condition and there are no delivery charges.

- **a** How much will your company owe Countryside if it pays immediately?
- **b** How much do you owe if you defer payment for 3 weeks?
- **c** What is the saving for your company if you pay promptly?

10 Draft the following letters:

- **a** a letter of complaint to an organisation who consistently overcharges you on its invoices.
- **b** a letter of apology to a firm where you have complained about an invoice being wrong (and made quite a fuss!) and then found out they were right after all!

You can add any details you need to make the letters more realistic.

Business Application Packages (Reference Section)

SPECIAL NOTE

This chapter provides reference material on a variety of business computer application packages. The subjects covered are:

Section 1 – Word processing

Hardware

Word processing is the only type of operation carried out by a computer where *specific* equipment can be bought which will only perform this function. This equipment is called a **dedicated word processor**.

Anyone who is going to be word processing therefore has a choice – either to buy a dedicated word processing machine or a micro computer with a word processing package.

Advantages and disadvantages of a dedicated word processor

Advantages:

- they have specific function keys which make the machine easier to use
- usually no system or program disk is required – immediately the machine is switched on it is ready to use as a word processor
- the program which controls the word processing function may be very user-friendly.

Disadvantages:

- they are often more expensive than micros

- they can only do word processing – nothing else
- many micro WP programs are now very sophisticated and much more user-friendly than they were in the past.

The decision will therefore probably depend on the type of work to be done on the machine and the cost of comparable machines.

What do word processors do?

Word processors (WP) have revolutionised the work of the typist and removed much of the drudgery and repetitive work which used to be necessary.

Imagine how you would feel in each of the following situations:

1. You have spent hours producing a ten page document for your boss perfectly. He now wants four paragraphs in the middle changed and an extra section inserted on page three.
2. You have stayed on an extra 20 minutes to type an emergency two-page memo for your boss. When you give it him he notices there are five uncorrected errors and you missed out two lines in the second paragraph.
3. Your boss wants twenty identical letters sent out to customers, only he wants them to look 'personal' and not as if they have been copied, with the names inserted later. This will mean typing the same letter twenty times.

If all you have is a typewriter then the only answer may be to grit your teeth and carry on (or cry!). If you have a word processor you have no problems at all.

- In situations **1** and **2** you bring the document back onto your screen from the disk where it is stored, make the necessary amendments, and print out the corrected version.
- In situation **3** you type the letter *once*, leaving gaps for the name and address and any other personal details you want to add. The names and addresses are typed separately and the WP is instructed to 'merge' the information correctly every time it prints a letter. This is known as **mail merge**.

The main uses, then, for word processors are:

- to produce standard, personalised letters with mail merge
- to produce standard paragraphs which can be 'put together' to create a document quickly and easily (eg a legal contract)
- to update documents as required (eg a customer address list)
- to edit documents whenever amendments are required.

Word processors can also be linked to communicate with each other. You can therefore type a memo and transmit it direct from your machine to another (eg from head office to branch office) without having to use the standard postal system.

Common features

There are a large number of word processing packages and systems on the market, though the vast majority have several features in common. It helps to be aware of these first, so you know what to expect on any system you use.

Wrap-around

You do not – and *must* not – press return at the end of each line when you are word processing. The text *automatically* continues on a new line.

If you press return by accident nothing will happen until you start to edit the text. If you take out words or letters no longer required, or typed in error, and try to close up the gaps you will find that the *returns* you have typed will get in your way and prevent the text from reflowing properly.

Hard returns

The only time you should press return is between paragraphs (press twice, just as if you were using a typewriter). A small sign will appear on the screen to show you where you pressed the return key (this will not show on the printed document).

This is called a *hard* return and means that your paragraphs will be protected when you reflow your text after editing. You can soon tell if you forget to press return – when the text is reflowed all your paragraphs will join together!

Scrolling

A standard VDU cannot show *all* of an A4 page at once, it therefore only shows the area you are working on. As you keep typing the *top* part of the document will disappear from your screen – **do not panic**! You can easily get it back again by 'scrolling' back up the screen with your cursor. The machine will think you want to work on the top portion again and this will come into view. To return to where you were, simply move the cursor down again.

SPECIAL NOTE

Most word processors have special commands or keys to enable you to move your cursor quickly around a page and from one page to another. It is well worth mastering these in the early stages to save yourself time later. Note that the cursor must always be at the position where you want the text to appear.

WYSIWYG

This strange word stands for 'What You See Is What You Get' and generally WP packages which use WYSIWYG are much easier to use than those which don't. Quite simply the document on your screen, as you edit and change it, looks exactly the same as it will when it is printed (except, possibly, for small signs such as hard returns).

Common functions

Functions are carried out by

- selecting an option from a menu or
- pressing a specific key or
- entering a special command.

The method used will depend on the package you are using and what you are trying to do. Virtually all word processing systems will:

- centre text (if the command says *center* you are using an American package!)
- move left and right hand margins and set a temporary left hand margin in the document if you want to inset text or use numbered paragraphs.
- allow you to use tabs, just as on a typewriter. All word processors enable you to draw horizontal lines, some do

vertical lines too, so you can produce a professional tabulation, fully ruled, quickly and easily.

- automatically underline and/or embolden (darken) text as required.
- justify the right hand margin.
- enable you to identify blocks of text (either by putting a mark at the beginning and end of the block or by highlighting the lines of text in the block) and then either delete the block or move or copy it to another part of the same document or to an entirely different document.
- let you completely reformat a document to cope with new text by
  - changing the margins (completely or just in certain parts of the document)
  - splitting or joining paragraphs
  - evening up the text throughout a document (so that the pages look 'even' throughout).
- save your document on disk and recall this later as required. Most systems allow you to resave the same document under a different name if required.
- search for a particular word or phrase and replace it automatically with another.
- print out the document in single or double line spacing and in either 10, 12 or 15 pitch. (This facility may depend on the printer you are using.)
- print selected pages only or multiple copies, as required.

TEST YOURSELF

From the information given on the functions and uses of word processors, list ten benefits of using a word processor for someone who has previously only used an electronic typewriter.

Proof-reading

All the functions in the world won't help you to produce perfect work if you aren't good at proof-reading! You must always bear in mind that

- proof-reading from a screen is a *skill* which must be developed.
- generally people find it harder to read 'word by word' from a screen than a piece of paper.

- proof-reading on a WP *may* mean having to scroll backwards and forwards, eg to check that you have spelled a word the same way every time.
- if you have problems then *always* take a trial copy of your work and proof-read the hard copy before you do your final print-out. (Proof reading is covered in more detail in Communicating information, pages 217–220.)

Spell checkers

Many of the latest WP programs have a spell checker incorporated into them. The word processor will compare your words with the dictionary in its memory and point out which words do not match. Before you think all your problems are solved *beware* – there are one or two snags.

- Most spell checkers will automatically stop at every word which cannot be matched – this will include all proper nouns (eg personal and place names). Although you may have the option to add these words to the dictionary, if you are not careful you will fill your dictionary 'space' with words you may never use again.
- A spell checker will *not* pick up typing mistakes if the 'word' typed is still recognisable, eg form instead of from, to instead of too, stationary instead of stationery.

So you still need to proof-read!

CHECK IT YOURSELF

- See if you can think of ten pairs of words which would be missed by a spell checker.
- Compare your list with that of everyone else in the group. See how many pairs you can think of between you.

Printing

When you are sure your document is perfect then print out your final version.

- Make sure your paper is straight and that the top of the paper is in the correct position for where you want the printing to start.

- Check you know how to *stop* the printer quickly if there is an emergency (there is usually a stop print command – it is not just a case of switching the printer off!)

On some word processors you can carry on with your next document whilst your first is printing out. This is obviously far less time consuming than having to wait until the document has printed before you can carry on work. Check with your tutor if this is possible with the system you are using.

Directory

All WP systems have a directory you can access which will show all the documents stored on a particular disk. Obviously you need to have the disk inserted into the disk drive before you can read its directory!

Systems vary in the way in which you can name documents for later identification. If your system will not allow you to mark each one very clearly it is sometimes a good idea to keep a notebook relating to the disk which gives more information on each document stored for easy access and reference later.

Typing confidential documents

Most word processing systems will allow you to:

- save a document under a security code which must be typed in every time the document is recalled
- allocate a 'save until' date so that important documents cannot be erased accidentally.

If you are called away from your machine when you are typing confidential work then *don't* leave your document showing on the screen for anyone to read! Save the work you are doing *first* and then make sure the screen is clear. If the document is not saved under a security code then remove the disk from the machine before leaving the room. In an emergency turn down the brightness control or scroll your work off screen.

SPECIAL NOTE

- If you are typing a long document (more than one or two pages) then you are very strongly advised to **save your work *frequently***. *Don't* wait until you have typed every page. If there is a power cut, you press a wrong key by mistake or anything goes wrong with your machine then all your work will be lost. By getting in the habit of saving often you will never be in the position of having to start all over again because of a minor disaster.

- If you allocate a security code to a document you *must* remember it! Without it there is no way you can recall your document on screen.

The limitations of word processors

Although, at first sight, word processors may seem the answer to everything, they do have their limitations.

- A word processor is only as good as its operator! Therefore excellent proof-reading skills, good spelling, grammar and accuracy are still important.
- Bad housekeeping on the part of the operator can result in mislaid disks, forgotten security codes and no back-up copies if a disk is corrupted.
- Word processors are usually not the quickest nor the most suitable system to use if you are
  - completing a form (spacing accurately can be impossible)
  - entering text in boxes (for the same reason)
  - making a minor amendment on a pre-prepared 'one-off' document
  - typing envelopes

  In all these cases it is easier to use a typewriter.
- It is impossible to squeeze text on a page with a word processor to avoid using two sheets of paper. Pre-set top and bottom margins can mean a new page is used for just one line.
- Some WP packages are more limited than others eg
  - no vertical ruling
  - no provision for landscape and/or A5 paper
  - limited line spacing/pitch settings
  - no spell checker
  - no decimal alignment
  - difficult mail merge commands
  - no facility to automatically calculate columns of figures if required
  - incompatible with many graphics and/or DTP packages.
- A machine breakdown or power cut usually spells disaster!

Integrated packages

It is possible to buy integrated packages, eg word processing, spreadsheet and database. With these packages you can:

- work out a table on the spreadsheet package and transfer it to a document you are creating on the word processing package.
- use a customer name and address list stored on the database package to link up with a standard letter created on the word processing package for a mail merge.

SECTION REVIEW

Having completed this section, you should now be able to:

1. Distinguish between a dedicated and a non-dedicated word processor.
2. Identify the benefits and limitations of using a word processor.
3. Explain the terms **wrap-around, hard returns, scrolling** and **WYSIWYG**.
4. List the common functions of word processors.
5. Explain the importance of proof-reading.
6. Describe the limitations of spell checkers.
7. State how confidential work should be undertaken on a word processor.

REVIEW QUIZ

True or false?

1. You should press return at the end of each line when word processing.
2. A dedicated word processor can only be used for word processing.

3 Spell checkers mean proof-reading is no longer necessary.

4 Confidential documents should be stored under a security code.

5 Work should be saved regularly, eg after every one or two pages.

Complete the blanks . . .

6 Moving up and down the screen to bring other parts of a document into view is called ....

7 Darkening text to make it stand out more is called ....

8 Word processing packages where the document you are working on looks the same on your screen as it will in print are known by the name of ....

Work it out

9 When you are familiar with your word processor carry out the following.
The office junior has handed you a notice she has typed on her typewriter. Your boss has asked if you will input it on your word processor, using the layout shown. However, he is horrified at the number of errors she has made in spelling, punctuation etc and has asked you to correct them.
Type a corrected version, print it out and save your work on disk. Check your printout with your tutor to make sure you have found and corrected *all* the errors.

Staff car park

The managment would like to remind staff and visiters that cars can be left in the staff car park. It must be pointed out, however, that cars are left at the owners' risk and no responsability can be excepted for damage or loss of any kind to cars or to valuables left in them. all visiters are asked to leave there car keys at the reception desk on the ground floor.

Thankyou

Geoffrey Knight
Personal Officer

BRYANT & BARNES LTD

Section 2 – Spreadsheets

What is a spreadsheet?

A spreadsheet is a document used by a company accountant or financial manager to assess how well the company is doing and/or how proposed changes will affect its performance. It is also used by Sales, Production and Personnel staff if they are involved in making calculations or predictions based on numerical information.

A large sheet of paper (which gives the spreadsheet its name) is ruled off into **columns** and **rows**. Figures can then be added for income, expenditure, sales, profit etc, perhaps on a week-by-week or month-by-month basis.

A simple example of a spreadsheet display might be like this:

eg

	January	February	March	Quarterly Total
Income	30000	32000	27000	89000
Expenditure	22000	23000	20500	65500
Profit	8000	9000	6500	23500

What if . . .

The problems with manual calculations start when:

- alterations have to be made to past figures
- we want to try to predict the results of possible changes in the future.

Alterations

Imagine we had to allow for the following changes:

- £2000 worth of goods sold in January were omitted
- expenditure for February later turned out to be £23500.

We would have to rub out the incorrect figures, write in the new ones and then *recalculate* all our profit and total figures which were affected by the changes.

Predictions

How much work would be involved if we wanted to:

- work out how our profit figure would be affected if we employed another member of staff at £5000, £6000 or £7000 a year?
- work out how our profit figure would be affected if we did this and also increased our sales by 10% over the next 12 months?

The idea of working this out may horrify you – and it would certainly mean a lot of work if you did it manually – constantly changing figures and recalculating your totals.

An electronic spreadsheet package will do any calculations like this *automatically* and adjust all the existing figures – again automatically – to take account of any changes or alterations.

Grid layout

An electronic spreadsheet is simply a grid of **cells** (boxes), arranged in rows and columns, with a numbering system so that any cell can be referred to instantly. The cell being worked on is always called the **active cell**.

A typical grid might consist of more than a hundred columns and more than two hundred rows. The top left-hand corner might look like this

eg

	A	B	C	D	E	F	etc
1							
2							
3							
4							
etc							

- **Columns** go *down* a spreadsheet and have an identifying letter.
- **Rows** go *across* a spreadsheet and have an identifying number.
- **Cells** are *always* referred to by using the column letter *first*, eg A1.

CHECK IT YOURSELF

Discuss with your tutor how you think columns are identified (remember there are usually more than 100) after the letter 'Z' has been reached!

Moving around

You can move the cursor around the spreadsheet, from one cell to another, by using the cursor arrow keys. Each cell is a 'slot' for information – a word, a label, a figure or the result of a calculation.

Most spreadsheets have a command to enable you to jump rapidly from one cell to another to save time.

SPECIAL NOTE

Because the spreadsheet is so large only a very small part of it can be shown on your screen at once. Therefore if you jump from cell A1 to, say, cell T85, you will be on a totally different part of the spreadsheet.

If you have problems visualising this, imagine a large sheet of squared paper spread all over your floor, and yourself jumping about from one part of it to another!

The entry line

Either underneath or above the spreadsheet layout you will have an entry line, where you enter text, figures, formulae or commands, depending on what you want to do. As you type text or commands they are displayed on the entry line (and can be corrected if you make a mistake). Nothing is entered on the spreadsheet until you press the return key after typing an entry.

No matter how much the spreadsheet scrolls from one part to another, the entry line always stays in the same place on the screen.

Entering figures

This is simple – just type the figure and press return. You may require the figures to be entered and calculated as *whole numbers* or to a specified number of decimal places (eg to two places if you are dealing with money). This is determined through a command sequence (see below) specifying either decimal places or **integers** (whole numbers).

Entering text

On some spreadsheet packages any text entries must be prefaced with a special sign, so that the computer knows you are entering text and not figures. Check this with your tutor for your particular package.

If a column is not wide enough to cope with the text you want to insert then it can easily be widened through a command sequence (see below).

Entering commands

How you do this will depend on the package you are using. However the type of command you are able to enter is given below:

- blank or erase a cell (to remove the information already in it)
- copy an entry from one cell to another
- delete rows or columns no longer required
- edit the content of a cell (often easier to blank it and start again!)
- change the format of a cell, eg to show integer (whole) numbers, adjust the column width, justify text to the left or right etc. You have the option whether to change the format of all the cells in the spreadsheet, specify one row or column or specify only one cell
- insert a row or column
- load an existing spreadsheet from a disk
- print out a spreadsheet
- protect specific cells and formulae against erasure
- save a spreadsheet to disk
- lock the title cells in place (eg January, February etc) so that they continue to show on screen as the spreadsheet scrolls
- zap the current spreadsheet you are working on (it is usual to save it first)
- quit the system.

Other commands – such as replicating formulae and graphic commands are dealt with later.

CHECK IT YOURSELF

Find out the essential commands you will need to use from the beginning on your particular package. These include blank, edit, load, save, print, zap, quit and format commands.

Understanding formulae

It is only any use being able to enter figures in a spreadsheet if we can then tell the computer what to do with them – whether to add, subtract, multiply or divide! We do this by entering a formula into a cell, rather than text or figures.

To understand how formulae work try this exercise – it doesn't matter which spreadsheet package you are using. (R= return.)

CHECK IT YOURSELF

Formulae – Stage 1

1 Start with your cursor in cell A1 and enter the figure 2. In cell B1 enter the figure 4, in C1 enter 6 and in D1 enter 8.
Now move your cursor to cell A2.

2 This time, instead of entering a figure you are going to instruct the spreadsheet to put a *total* in A2. On the entry line type 2+6 (no spaces) and then R (return). Instead of the sum itself being put into A2, the machine calculates it and puts the answer into A2.

3 Now move to cell B2. This time type 4–1 (four subtract one) and R. Obviously the answer should be 3 in B2!

4 In C2 you are going to put a multiplication. Type Type 5*32 (the symbol * means multiply on a computer) and then R.

5 Finally, in D2, put 24/4 (the symbol / means divide on a computer) then R and look at your answer – it should be 6!

6 You have now seen that you can enter simple sums in a cell instead of just figures. Now take this a stage further. Move your cursor to cell A3. This time type 22+A1. You are now telling the spreadsheet that in cell A3 you want entered the total in A1 plus the number 22. Press R and watch the answer. Then enter these
– Cell B3 27–B2
– Cell C3 28×C1
– Cell D3 36/D2

Formulae – Stage 2

1 Let's assume you now need to add all the figures and enter the totals. Before you do this it is worth noting that your **worksheet** (the usual term for the current spreadsheet you are working on) will look much better if you use the next row to underline your sum so that the answer is clear.

The usual method on a spreadsheet is to enter a command which will enter a row of hyphens across the columns you have used. Check how to do this with your tutor.

When you have entered the hyphens along row 4, move your cursor to cell A5 to continue.

2 You have seen in Stage 1 that if we want to add we merely type the cell names with a plus sign. It would therefore seem logical to assume that to add cells A1 to A3 we do the same thing with all three cell names, eg A1+A2+A3.

Whilst this would work it would obviously be useless if we had 50 columns to add – the entry would be enormous! To add a row of columns we therefore need to use a **sum** formula and specify the cells in the range to be added.

Check the exact formula you need with your tutor and type this on your entry line.

3 Rather than keep entering the sum command for all the other columns (there could be dozens!) it is usual to use a **replicate** formula. This instructs the spreadsheet to do exactly the same calculation in all the other specified columns.

Check with your tutor the exact formula you need to enter and watch the totals appear across your worksheet.

4 Now finish off your total by drawing another row of hyphens across row 6.

!

SPECIAL NOTE

A professional tip – when specifying the *range* of cells for a sum command always add one on. Therefore if your sum is in cells B2 to B6, specify your range as B2 to B7. Then if you need to insert an extra figure later on this can be entered in cell B7 and your formula won't need altering!

Developing your skills

It is a good idea to:

- note down the type of formulae you use often for easy reference
- check if you have a **help** screen which will prompt you with commands
- practise entering a variety of figures (including decimals) in different cells and then adding them up
- practise using the replicate formula.

SPECIAL NOTE

You should notice, as you change previously entered figures from one number to another, that the spreadsheet *automatically* recalculates the answer in every affected column and/or row.

In addition to the type of formulae you have entered so far you can also:

- ask the spreadsheet to calculate an average of the figures across a row
- use the integer command to change decimals to whole numbers and back again. (On many packages you have a choice whether to use the command for integer or whether to specify integer in the formula you enter – check this with your tutor.)

SPECIAL NOTE

If you are producing a worksheet where the total of the figures of a column going down have to equal the total of a row of figures going across then it is possible to enter a special formula which will check the two sums are identical and, if not, print an error message in the cell.

As this is quite an advanced technique your tutor may add this formula for you if you need to use it.

Recalculating

Whilst automatic recalculating is one of the major benefits of using a spreadsheet package it can be time-consuming on a very large spreadsheet having to wait, after each entry, for the whole worksheet to be recalculated.

On most packages you therefore have the option to turn the recalculating function *off* whilst you enter all the changes you need to make. You then simply turn it back on again when you are ready, and the computer will recalculate the whole worksheet in one operation. Obviously you mustn't forget to put recalculate back on again – or all your work will have been pointless!

Printing out with formulae

As an option to printing out your spreadsheet with the figures and the answers showing, you can use a command to print out your spreadsheet with any formula you have entered showing on the printout.

This is useful if you want to save a spreadsheet showing the formulae so that you can easily repeat the operation on another set of figures later, without working out which formula to use all over again.

Practise this by asking your tutor for the command for your package and printing out a copy of your work showing the formulae instead of the answers.

Spreadsheet graphics

Most spreadsheet packages give you the option to create a variety of graphs and charts to illustrate graphically the figures you have entered. For instance

- sales figures for January to June could be shown as a line graph

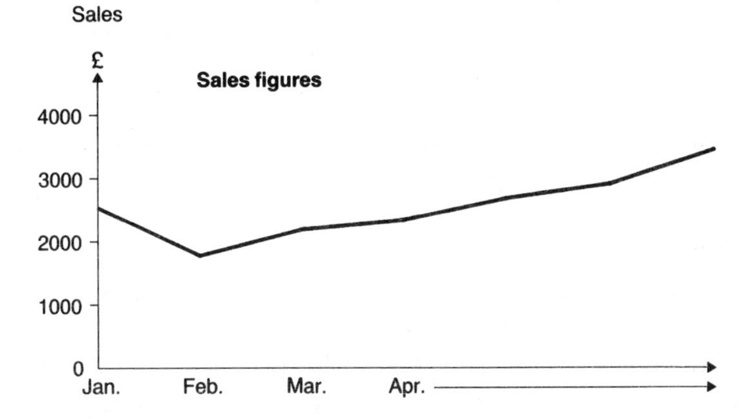

- sales figures for different products could be shown as a bar chart

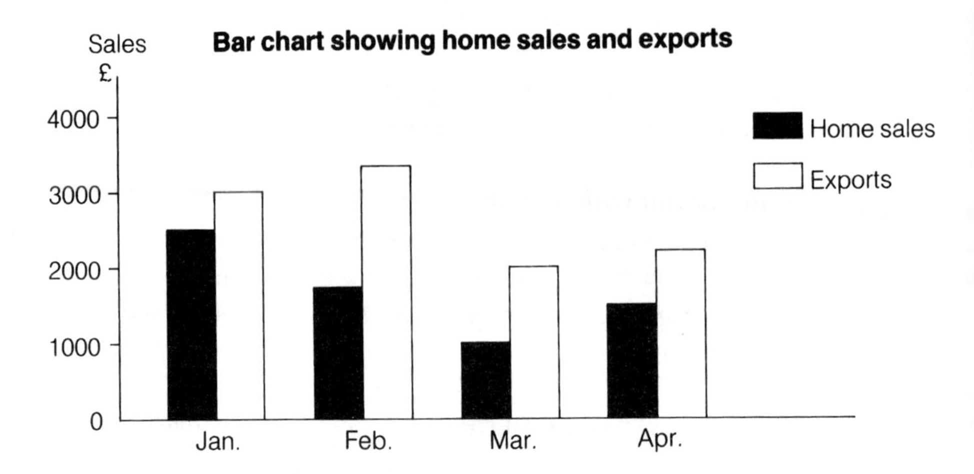

- expenditure for a particular month could be shown as a pie chart.

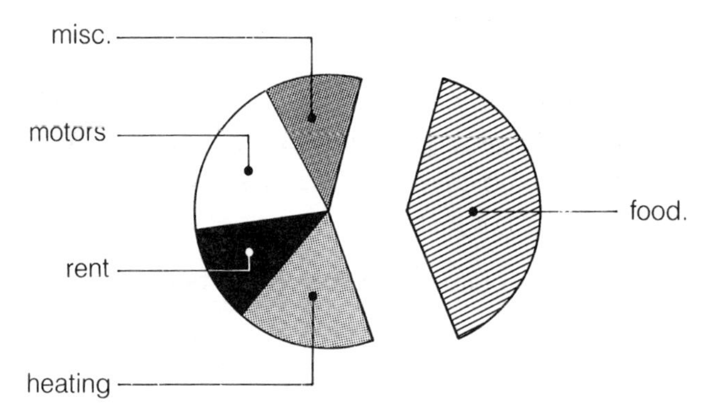

Creating graphics

The commands to do this will vary from one package to another. However, tips to help you include:

- decide on the type of graph or chart you want to produce.
- work out:
  - the **headings** and **labels** which must be included. Each heading which has to appear on your graph or chart,

and which is not already in your spreadsheet, will have to be inserted in a blank cell. (Choose one away from your main working area.)
  - identify the cells which will be illustrated on your graphic.
- if you are creating a line graph or bar chart you need to know that the **vertical** axis is the ***y*-axis** and the **horizontal** axis is the ***x*-axis**, so that you can label each axis correctly.
- **variables** is the term used for the sets of information which will be shown on the graph or chart. For instance a bar chart for savings and expenditure has *two* variables, a bar chart for income, expenditure and profit has *three* variables and so on. Obviously a pie chart can only have one variable or you would end up with more than one circle! You will need to know the range of cells in which each variable (set of information) is shown.
- **time labels** are only used on line graphs and bar charts and refer to the time period the graph or chart is covering.
- **point labels** is the term given to the labels on a pie chart.
- **variable labels** are used to give a bar chart or line graph its *key* – otherwise no-one will understand what the lines or bars represent.

SECTION REVIEW

Having completed this section, you should now be able to:

1. Describe the main components of a spreadsheet.
2. Identify the benefits to be gained by using a spreadsheet.
3. Explain how to enter figures and text.
4. List the most commonly used commands.
5. Compose simple formulae, including **sum** and **replicate** formulae.
6. Explain the terms **integer** and **recalculate**.
7. Create bar charts, pie charts and line graphs using a spreadsheet package.

REVIEW QUIZ

True or false?

1 Columns go across a spreadsheet and have an identifying number.

2 Columns go down a spreadsheet and have an identifying letter.

3 Cells are always referred to by using the letter first.

4 The entry line always stays in the same place on the screen.

5 The symbol * in a calculation means divide.

Complete the blanks . . .

6 The cell you are working on is called the ....

7 The command used for the answer to appear as a whole number is the .... command.

8 The *x*-axis is the name given to the .... axis of a graph.

Work it out

9 Start with a clean worksheet. Assume the company you work for has branches in the south, Midlands and north of England. You have been asked to enter the monthly sales figures for January to May, and find the totals for each region and each month.

Adjust column widths as necessary and rule off appropriately.

SALES BY REGION

	Jan.	Feb.	March	April	May	Total
South	7600	5900	6200	8209	7928	
Midlands	6840	3498	5698	6309	5609	
North	2309	2098	3980	3284	3890	
Total Sales						

Note – ask your tutor to help you enter a formula which will check that the total of the Total Sales (horizontally) agrees with the total for each region when added together.

10 If you have the ability to produce graphs and charts on your package, use the data in question **9** to produce:

- a line graph showing the performance of each region
- a bar chart showing the sales per region per month
- a pie chart just for one month, showing the percentage of sales per region.

Section 3 – Databases

What is a computer database?

A database is an **electronic filing system** which not only stores and recalls information quickly and easily but can also sort it in various ways to suit the needs of the user.

You can keep a database on *anything* which you might record on ordinary paper records eg:

- a list of customers – names, addresses, telephone numbers, credit allowed etc
- a list of cars in a fleet (eg for a hire car company) with model, year, registration number, date last serviced etc
- a list of books in a library with title, author, publisher, index number, year of publication etc
- a list of students in a college or school with name, address, course attended, work experience placements etc.

We shall use the last one as an example.

Manual filing – and its limitations

Your college or school will keep a record of each student. This is important for a variety of reasons – ex-students may request references some time after they have left, organisations may also request references. Various forms will also have to be filled in by the college or school on numbers of students and so on.

This information may be kept on a manual system and may involve the completion of cards which are then filed in a card index system.

CHECK IT YOURSELF

Discuss with your tutor:

- the *headings* you would use on a card index for the various types of information you need to include
- the way in which you would file the cards.

A simplified card index system is shown below. Your headings do not have to agree with ours – hopefully you should have more headings than we do.

Example record card

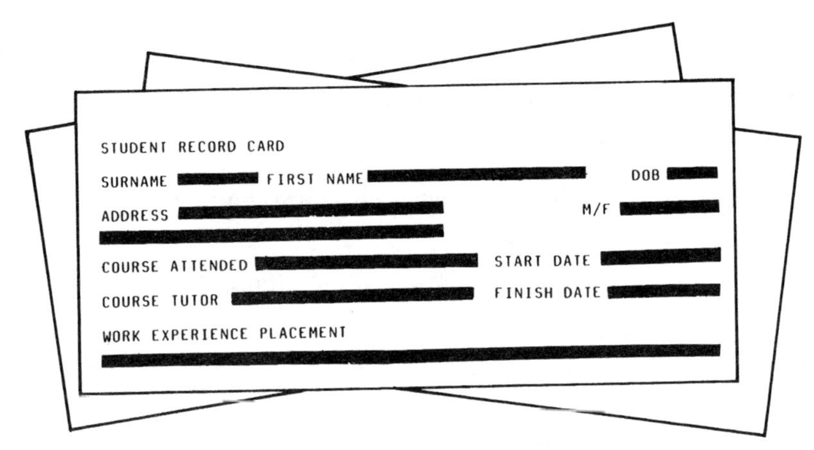

What method did you choose to file the cards? Probably one of the following:

- alphabetically under the student's last name
- alphabetically by course but each course kept separate.

Now what would you do if you were responsible for operating the system and:

- on Monday you are asked for a full list of all students but separated into male and female and in alphabetical order
- on Tuesday you are asked for a list of all students under 17
- on Wednesday you are asked for a list of all students who live within 5 miles of the college (or school)

- on Thursday you are asked for a list of all students who have left during the year
- on Friday you are asked for a list of all students who have already been on work experience and the organisations they have visited.

Cry? Give in your notice? In each case you would have to sort through all your cards *looking for something different*! And it would probably take you hours.

Database filing

With a computer database all the listings above would bc done quickly and automatically – at the press of a button.

Database terms

On a database the 'card index' appears on screen, with headings and gaps for information just as in a manual system. However the terms used are slightly different.

form • is the 'card' (display on screen) in which the information is placed

blank form • a form that has not yet been filled in

data • the specific information entered on a form

field • the area available to hold specific information (the black areas on the card above)

record • a filled-in form (the card shown above when completed)

editing • making changes to the fields of a record

file • the name of that specific system – in the case above our file name would be 'students'. When finished the file will hold a number of filled-in forms.

Creating a database

To create a database the same type of procedures are followed regardless of the specific database package you use.

- Decide on the file you are going to create. This might be given to you by your boss. In our example we are creating a file on students. Other files could be on customers, cars or books (as shown on page 323).
- Plan out the blank form on paper, decide on the field names you want to use.
- Think about the maximum length of information which will have to be inserted after each field name. This will determine the length of your fields.
- You can now create a record card on your screen. Any database system will give you the option to change and rearrange the field names and fields until you are happy with your design. It is then a good idea to print out a copy of your blank form for reference.

Reports

You now need to consider what type of information you may be asked for. In our example on pages 324–325 you were asked for the information to be:

- sorted into male and female
- sorted by age
- sorted by district or town
- sorted into 'early leavers'
- sorted by work experience.

To ask the computer to do this, and print out a **report** according to the type of *sort* you want, the computer has to be instructed what to look for. This is quite complicated on some packages and will be done by a computer technician. What he or she does is to:

- tell the computer to look at certain fields (eg town, course etc)
- *only* list those students who 'qualify' under those criteria.

The technician will then give you a list of *all* the reports you can run, just by giving a command to the computer.

SPECIAL NOTE

- Straightforward reports are set up purely to look up and repeat the information from a field on to the report, ie:

PRIVATE SECRETARIAL COURSE		*(Report Heading)*
Name of Student (taken from field)	Address (from field)	DOB (from field)

- In other cases, a calculation may be required. If, say, all students could reclaim their bus fares for every day they attended College then two fields may be:

  Amount of bus fares Numbers of days attended

  The computer technician would enter a **formula** into the report to multiply the figures entered in each of these fields to calculate the total amount which could be reclaimed, and the report would only show the result, ie:

REPORT ON BUS FARES		*(Report Heading)*
Name of Student (taken from field)	Course (from field)	Amount reclaimed (calculated ie formula is amount of bus fares × days attended)

Entering the data

Once the system has been 'set up', eg in terms of the blank forms and the reports which can be generated, then the hard work begins! Information on every student in the college would now need to be entered by

- bringing on screen a blank record card
- completing each field with the relevant information for that student
- checking the record was correct
- saving the completed records on disk.

Often it is a good idea to take a hard copy of each record, especially when you are first setting up a file.

SPECIAL NOTE

- On many systems, at the setting up stage, you can specify for each field whether data *must* be entered or not. Obviously in our example the name of the student would be classified as essential data but work experience would not be – many students may not yet have been on a work experience placement.
- A large file can take up a lot of storage space and use several floppy disks.

For this reason databases are always better operated on computers with a hard disk because of their greater storage capacity.

- The computer technician will design the report so that the layout or order of information is as you want it. For instance, if students had to be listed under course then it would be better if the report listed them in alphabetical order and, perhaps, included their address.

Database maintenance

For the system to remain valuable it *must* be kept up-to-date, therefore regular checks have to be made to ensure that:

- all the data is still correct for each student
- all the students are still attending.

A system would have to be set up so that the database operator was informed of any changes, eg students moving house, leaving a course, going out on work placement etc.

Searching for a record

The operator can, of course, search for any specific record he or she wants to view either:

- for information on a particular student
- to update existing data.

This is done by:

- bringing up a blank record card on screen and completing one or two fields with known data (eg name of student)
- asking the computer to search for a 'match' to the data you have just typed
- the matching record is then shown on screen (at this point you should check it is the one you want)
- the data is then edited as appropriate
- the updated record is then *resaved* on disk – in place of the old one.

Safety and security

Many database records are subject to the provisions of the Data Protection Act and it would therefore be usual to have a password system in operation so that the records could not be accessed by unauthorised personnel. Refer back to page 108 if you have forgotten the main provisions of this Act.

It is also essential that the whole database is backed up regularly so that if the original system is damaged in any way the *copy* disks can be loaded into the machine. Otherwise the whole database would have to be set up all over again and all the data input again from scratch!

Commercial databases

There are many commercial databases on the market, which organisations can subscribe to, eg to access information on other companies to check their credit rating.

SECTION REVIEW

Having completed this section, you should now be able to:

1 Explain the main uses of a database.

2 Identify the benefits to be gained from using a database.

3 Describe the terms **form**, **field**, **record** and **report** as they apply to a database.

4 Explain how to search for a record, enter and edit data on a database.

5 Explain how reports may be accessed to display specified information.

6 Describe the importance of security and the relevance of the Data Protection Act to a database.

REVIEW QUIZ

True or false?

1 Records in a computer database are always subject to the provisions of the Data Protection Act.

2 Every field *must* be filled before the computer will accept the record.

3 All fields must be the same length.

4 Database records must be backed up regularly.

5 A large database is always better set up on a computer with a hard disk.

Complete the blanks . . .

6 The specific information entered on a form is called the ......
....

7 A filled-in form is called a ....

8 Selected information from the file is presented visually in a specified format on a ....

Work it out

9 Your organisation has many visitors from other parts of the UK and from abroad who are frequently entertained by your executives. It has been decided to create a database file on restaurants in your area.

   a) Plan a suitable record card with field names and fields for information you think would be useful.

   b) Decide on what criteria you would want to sort the cards to produce different reports. Produce a list for your computer technician.

   c) Use your local Yellow Pages to make a list of twelve restaurants you think should be included.

10 If possible

   a) create the record card you have designed in the exercise above on a database and print out a blank form.

   b) enter six of the restaurants you have chosen and print out a hard copy of each record.

Section 4 – Stock Control

Computerised stock control packages are simply a database where the records are designed as stock cards and the reports which can be generated are those which would be helpful to a stock control clerk.

Stock record cards

These will contain the same type of headings as you would find in a manual system, eg

- item name
- cost of one unit
- description of unit, eg kg, dozen
- quantity in stock
- minimum stock (before needing re-order)
- re-order quantity
- quantity on order (to stop the computer reminding you to re-order something when you are still waiting for it to be delivered)
- supplier's name.

In addition you may find included

- sales for this month and/or this year.

You may also find included a brief **code** field. This is so you can enter a short code for each item which can be used to find a specific record very quickly – the computer merely looks for a code 'match' when searching for a particular record.

CHECK IT YOURSELF

From the information given above, design a suitable record for a stock control system. Clearly show the length of the fields you would require against each field name.

Booking stock in and out

Once the system has been set up, and a record completed for each item kept in stock, the system must be kept up-to-date by recording all stock issued and all stock received.

On most systems this is done by searching for the appropriate record and then instructing the computer whether you want to book stock *in* or *out*. The program will then usually prompt you to state the quantity received or issued.

The computer then automatically recalculates the 'Quantity in stock' field to show the up-to-date amount.

Stock control reports

The type of reports you can run will be determined by the package you are using. Your options normally include:

- a print-out of all the stock at cost price, therefore giving an instant stock valuation
- a list of all stock needing re-order
- a price list
- a list of all items and the number currently in stock with a blank column to one side. This column is completed during a stock inventory and compared with the number recorded by the computer.
- a sales analysis. More sophisticated stock control packages will include a breakdown here to show you not only the quantity of each sold (your most popular lines) but also the amount of money you should have received from sales for that week (or month).

Adjustments

After a physical stock inventory it may be necessary to make adjustments to your computer records to allow for damaged goods, loss and so on. You will normally find you have an 'adjustments' option which will not only ask for the number to be altered but also ask you why!

Audit list

This is another report which can be taken by the accountants or auditors to check the movement of stock. An audit list gives details of all computer entries which have been made throughout each month.

Explanations are also given against unusual entries – which is the reason you had to state why you were making adjustments to your stock in the previous section!

Integrated stock control packages

Stock control packages may be purchased as separate programs but are also often found as one option on integrated accounts packages. In this case the value of the stock each month, and the amount spent on stock, has also to be transferred to the accounts section of the package so that all the figures agree. On more sophisticated packages this transfer of information may be carried out automatically.

SECTION REVIEW

Having completed this section, you should now be able to:

1 Identify the benefits of operating a computerised stock control package.

2 Explain the main components of a computerised stock record card.

3 Describe how to enter new stock and record stock sold.

4 Explain the term **adjustments**.

5 Identify the type of lists and reports which can be produced by a computerised stock control package.

Keys to the numeracy guides

NUMERACY GUIDE 1 (PAGES 9–12)

Test yourself 1

1 91 409 **2** 1 777 280 **3** 15 137 918 **4** 6 503 138

No key possible for reading exercise

Test yourself 2

1 162 953.16 **2** 87 999.296 **3** 1 131 134.0735

Test yourself 3

Descending order:

30 487	928 382	8 875 938	6 004 903
30 003	666 391	4 587 398	247 950
19 827	109 382	1 309 290	209 385
7 092	56 091	309 291	40 509
4 000	17 034	56 001	391

Ascending order:

6 008.42	6.5	6.9735
6 092.92	14.65	110.40
15 758.82	402.983	10 002.94
17 874.002	4 389.09	20 005.72
45 709.3	19 093.98	101 005.00
71 509.709	64 092.093	1 000 003.04

NUMERACY GUIDE 2 (PAGES 20–25)

Test yourself 1

Addition **1** 4442 **2** 22 991 **3** 2650.62 **4** 1106 **5** 5928.96

Subtraction **1** 434 471 **2** 46 **3** 8364 **4** 184.52 **4** 26 787.93

Test yourself 2

Multiplication **1** 4361 **2** 53 694 **3** 600 **4** 36 134 **5** 58 910 **6** 742.9

Division **1** 129 **2** 84 **3** 159 **4** 125 **5** 5624 **6** 92.489

Test yourself 3

1 45 230 **2** 47 873 **3** 9 872 800 **4** 2389 **5** 67 400
6 978 **7** 69.738 **8** 55.7 **9** 23.428 **10** 426.2813

Test yourself 4

Addition **1** £263.72 **2** £1376.70 **3** £26.67
4 £226.97 **5** £238.02

Subtraction **6** £11.15 **7** £412.53 **8** 28p
9 £186.48 **10** £1482.78

Multiplication **11** £747 **12** £1742.40 **13** £1600.55
14 £2187 **15** £15745.52

Division **16** £12 **17** £23.35 **18** £84.28
19 £156 **20** 88p

Test yourself 5

1 74.89 **2** 18.98 **3** 16.66 **4** 4.28 **5** 6.32
6 15.24 **7** £9.51 **8** £15.93 **9** £6.86 **10** £1.91
11 £12.15 **12** £112.05

NUMERACY GUIDE 3 (PAGES 68–70)

Check it Yourself

112 lb = 1 cwt 2240 lb = 1 ton

Test yourself 1

1 7 kg **2** 38 kg **3** 28 kg **4** 73 kg **5** 24 kg
6 8 kg 182 g **7** 41 kg 818 g **8** 66 kg 363 g
9 10 kg **10** 17 kg 727 g

Test yourself 2

1 26 lb **2** 59 lb **3** 403 lb **4** 35 lb **5** 202 lb
6 70.4 lb **7** 41.8 lb **8** 301.4 lb **9** 136.4 lb **10** 41.8 lb

Test yourself 3

(Exact answers only given)

1 4.091 kg **2** 50 kg **3** 26.364 kg **4** 10 kg **5** 43.182 kg
6 11 lb **7** 44 lb **8** 237.6 lb **9** 180.4 lb **10** 27.5 lb

NUMERACY GUIDE 4 (PAGES 85–89)

Test yourself 1

1 36.134 **2** 48.535 **3** 226.1655 **4** 288.894
5 53.65224 **6** 3.0135

Test yourself 2

1 36.13 **2** 48.54 **3** 226.17 **4** 288.89 **5** 53.65
6 3.01

Test yourself 3

1 14 **2** 18 **3** 116 **4** 136 **5** 15 **6** 120

Test yourself 4

1 0600 **2** 2000 **3** 1715 **4** 2230 **5** 0815
6 1545 **7** 2345 **8** 0520 **9** 1940
10 4 pm **11** 2.30 am **12** 9.20 pm **13** 5.45 pm
14 9.50 am **15** 7.16 pm **16** 2.10 pm **17** 8.20 pm
18 6.02 pm

Test yourself 5

1 5 hrs 37 mins **2** 2 hrs 52 mins **3** 6 hrs 34 mins
4 5 hrs 14 mins **5** 39 hrs 21 mins **6** 6 hrs 35 mins
7 7 hrs 50 mins **8** 10 hrs 15 mins **9** 4 hrs 15 mins
10 29 hrs 40 mins

NUMERACY GUIDE 5 (PAGES 112–115)

Test yourself 1

1 £19.45 **2** £51.68 **3** £52.27 **4** £70.31 **5** £26.65
6 £122.90 **7** £78.75 **8** £50.20 **9** £32.49
10 £139.83 **11** £113.56 **12** £290.50

Test yourself 2

1 5083 schillings **2** 7464 francs **3** 1256 marks
4 87 750 pesetas **5** $853 **6** 156 325 escudos

Test yourself 3

1 £88.40 **2** £45.30 **3** £40.82 **4** £25.71 **5** £74.64
6 £75.12

Test yourself 4

1 38 **2** 106 **3** 1.79 **4** £17.15 **5** 2 hrs 34 mins
6 309 kg **7** 66°F **8** 3024 **9** 9 stone **10** 3423

NUMERACY GUIDE 6 (PAGES 136–141)

Test yourself 1

1 4 **2** 402.6 **3** £54 **4** £61.07 **5** 13.75 kg
6 89.6 **7** £715.68 **8** £14.92 **9** 1741.96 kg

10 £9.96

11 42 – purchasing, 84 – office admin., 70 – sales, 49 – personnel, 63 – accounts, 7 – transport, 35 – production

12 A = £6.30, B = £18.41, C = £51.81

Test yourself 2

1 30% **2** 12.5% **3** 2.68% **4** 33.75% **5** 3.6%
6 170% **7** 190% **8** 98.15 **9** 61.73% **10** 33.64%
11 (Rounded answers) coffee – 41%, tea – 26%, orange – 14%, chocolate – 10%, don't mind – 6%, wouldn't use – 3%

Test yourself 3

1 £52 **2** £74.75 **3** £82.88 **4** £89.38

Test yourself 4

A – £103.75 B – £87.50 C – £74.50 D – £61.63
(Monthly rates included as distractors)

Test yourself 5

1 £1.50 **2** £27 **3** £3.30 **4** £3.75

Test yourself 6

1 £63.06 **2** £2.79 **3** £17.52 **4** £3.84 **5** £91.50
6 £12.79

Test yourself 7

1 £483.46 **2** £21.39 **3** £134.32 **4** £29.42
5 £701.50 **6** £98.04

Test yourself 8

1 £8.55, £57 **2** £12.75, £85 **3** £4.65, £31
4 £2.30, £15.33 **5** £8.41, £56.09 **6** £2.95, £19.65

Test yourself 9

1 VAT 5% = $\frac{1}{21}$. $\frac{20}{21}$ **2** VAT 10% = $\frac{1}{11}$, $\frac{10}{11}$

NUMERACY GUIDE 7 (PAGES 159–163)

Test yourself 1

(Down) £385.99, £222.98, £316.71 = £925.68
(Across) £279.70, £356.11, £289.87 = £925.68

Practice memory test

(Columns) 1 – 152, 2 – 95, 3 – 131, = 378
(Rows) A – 92, B – 117, C – 169 = 378

Test yourself 2

(Down) £2054.27, £1292.20, £2629.58 = £5976.05

(Across) £1353.98, £397.72, £834.34, £204.45
£1956.52, £776.07, £452.97 = £5976.05

Test yourself 3

£940 + £2232 + £1470 = £4642 – £464.20 = £4177.80

Test yourself 4

(Down) 21 726 – 13 957 = 7769

(Across) 2009 + 2020 + 121 + 2158 + 1461 = 7769

NUMERACY GUIDE 8 (PAGES 221–223)

Test yourself 1

1 £72 **2** £33.12 **3** £977.50 **4** £920.20 **5** £225.25

Test yourself 2

1 6 people **2** 25 workers

Test yourself 3

1 58% **2** Media chart – 17.46%, 6.12%, 13.89%, 5.71%, 14.29%, Total % = 11.68%

Test yourself 4

12.5%, 10%, 8%, 4.5%, 14% – average = 9.8%

NUMERACY GUIDE 9 (PAGES 237–240)

Test yourself 1

1 45 cm **2** 75 cm **3** 500 m **4** 1008 km **5** 2960 km
6 8 in **7** 2 yards **8** 3 yards 2 feet **9** 525 miles
10 1460 miles **11** wood – 190 cm and 140 cm
12 45 strips

Test yourself 2

1 Fence is 640 m × 460 m – perimeter = 2,200 metres
2 walking distance per night = 6.6 km

Test yourself 3

A = 3300 m^2 B = 1225 m^2 C = 2400 m^2

Test yourself 4

Main area = 19.5 m × 26.5 m = 516.75 m^2
office 1 = 11.5 m × 12.5 m = 143.75 m^2,
office 2 = 12.5 m × 8.5 m = 106.25 m^2,

office 3 = 7.5 m × 8 m = 60 m^2,
typing pool = 19.5 m × 8.5 m = 165.75 m^2,
office 4 = 8.5 m × 10 m = 85 m^2,
office 5 = 10 m × 15 m = 150 m^2,
office 6 = 11.5 m × 10 m = 115 m^2.
Total area = 1342.5 m^2.
Cost of tiles = £10 068.75

NUMERACY GUIDE 10 (PAGES 258–262)

Test yourself 1

1 10 pints **2** 14 litres **3** 24 gallons **4** 1000 litres

Test yourself 2

1 18 gallons **2** 34 gallons **3** 6 gallons **4** 15 gallons
5 48 gallons **6** 250 litres **7** 136.36 litres
8 618.18 litres **9** 359.09 litres **10** 950 litres

Test yourself 3

1 10 hrs 10 mins **2** 13 hours **3** 6 hrs 20 mins
4 7 hours **5** 25 hours

Test yourself 4
Estimated answers

1 430 to 500 **2** £1800 to £1990 **3** £2.78 to £3
4 540 **5** £15 200 **6** £156 or £160

NUMERACY GUIDE 11 – REVIEW QUIZ (PAGES 282–283)

1 1 000 002 **2** 11 674.507 **3** 81.58 **4** 1130.382
5 27.5 **6** 0.99 **7** 22.72 kg **8** 1000 **9** exact answer = 55 lb **10** £67.50 **11** 27 hours **12** a) $190 b) 25%
13 £213.75 **14** £10 **15** 20% **16** 824 m **17** £100
18 £42.60 **19** £37.43 **20** 1950 miles

Index